The Black Hole of Auschwitz

The Black Hole of Auschwitz

PRIMO LEVI

Edited by Marco Belpoliti

Translated by Sharon Wood

polity

First published in Italian as *L'asimmetria e la vita* © Giulio Einaudi editore s.p.a., Torino 2002

This translation first published in 2005 © Polity Press

The right of Primo Levi to be identified as Author of this Work has been asserted in accordance with the UK Copyright, Designs and Patents Act 1988.

First published in 2005 by Polity Press

Published with the financial assistance of the Italian Ministry of Foreign Affairs

Polity Press
65 Bridge Street
Cambridge CB2 1UR, UK.

Polity Press
350 Main Street
Malden, MA 02148, USA

ISBN: 0-7456-3240-8
ISBN: 0-7456-3241-6 (pb)

A catalogue record for this book is available from the British Library.

Typeset in 11 on 13 pt Scala
by Servis Filmsetting Ltd, Manchester
Printed and bound in the United States by
the Maple-Vail Book Manufacturing Group

The publisher has used its best endeavours to ensure that the URLs for external websites referred to in this book are correct and active at the time of going to press. However, the publisher has no responsibility for the websites and can make no guarantee that a site will remain live or that the content is or will remain appropriate.

Every effort has been made to trace all copyright holders, but if any have been inadvertently overlooked the publishers will be pleased to include any necessary credits in any subsequent reprint or edition.

For further information on Polity, visit our website: www.polity.co.uk

Contents

PART II: OTHER PEOPLE'S TRADES

Through the Looking Glass: Preface to the Italian Edition

In 1955, ten years after the end of the Second World War, Primo Levi wrote a brief piece for a Turin paper on the memory of the concentration camps, called 'Deportees. Anniversary'. His argument was disheartening: the subject of the extermination camps, far from entering into historical memory, was in the process of becoming completely forgotten. It is a bitter article, but written in Levi's habitual tone, measured, precise, and always to the point. He never surrenders to rhetoric, to wailing or cursing. The article also includes ideas which anticipate by thirty years parts of his most important, yet still little known, book, one of the most significant works of the twentieth century, *The Drowned and the Saved*. He speaks here of shame, of the common humanity of victims and torturers, and the contamination which was the lot of both groups in the camps, of European culture, the responsibility it bears, its science; he speaks of 'a defenceless and naked death, ignominious and vile', of the 'unsuspected reserves of viciousness and madness that lie latent in man'.

The writer here is the author of *If This is a Man*, a book that is much more than an act of witness. A work of clearly literary inspiration, whose models are to be found in the Italian literary tradition and in the great European writers of the nineteenth century, this first book by the young Turinese chemist who survived the extermination camp of Monowitz, is also a treatise on human ethology. The camp, as he writes in the chapter of *If This is a Man* entitled 'The Drowned and the Saved', was 'a gigantic biological and social experiment'. In the texts on Auschwitz published at intervals by Levi over the next two decades, whether in ex-deportee journals or in the columns of the most important national newspapers, he returns insistently to this experimental aspect, and to the fate that would have befallen the whole of Europe had Hitler's armies won the war.

Levi feels himself to be, more deeply even than being a Jew, a combatant for liberty, a resistance fighter, and the accent falls not only on the destiny of his people, but on that of all men and women deported to Germany, including the thousands of Italian soldiers who refused to swear an oath of loyalty to the fledgling Republic of Salò, over which the post-war period has cast a veil of silence. But across the rest of Europe too, and even in the State of Israel, there was silence on the subject of the death camps. Until the beginning of the sixties, and the trial of Eichmann, people preferred to forget. In these articles, the gaze Levi casts over the entire phenomenon is, as far as is possible, distanced, analytical, scientific almost. The ethologist of Auschwitz sought first of all to call on reason to describe what had happened, although the problem of understanding these dreadful events is from the outset beset with difficulty. Understanding means getting inside the head of the people who planned and carried out these crimes that are beyond all human measure; it means, as the ex-deportee points out several times, justifying something that is beyond human reason itself.

There is clearly no way out: stupidity and lack of reason, he writes, are forces that operate historically, and yet the perpetrators of Auschwitz, as he states in his preface to a book published in 1968 ('Preface to L. Poliakov: *Auschwitz*'), are prey neither to delirium nor to anger: 'they are diligent, calm, vulgar and one-dimensional.' He goes so far as to hope that no man will appear in the near future who is able to elucidate, to explain why, at the centre of our Europe and of our century, 'the commandment "Thou shalt not kill" has been turned upside down'. The work of banal and ordinary men, Auschwitz is something that plainly belongs to an asymmetry, to something that is human – for they are still men, those who planned and carried out the monstrous extermination – but at the same time, it is no longer human. Men who appear to be measured, grey, colourless – 'empty, idiotic, placid and diligent', as he defines them in a 1959 text – have been capable of carrying out acts that go beyond human understanding ('The Monument at Auschwitz').

There is something inexplicable, as well as unacceptable. The rational root of man, postulated by the Greek thought that lies behind the anthropological reflections of the ex-Turinese schoolboy, is denied at root; and yet these men, the murderers of Auschwitz, remain nonetheless part of the human species. Incomprehensibility is invoked at various points throughout these writings. There are questions that in a low-key but subtly anguished tone find no answer: why Auschwitz? Will it happen again?

Faced with the collective suicide of the 'Temple of the People' in 1978, and the solitary suicide of the philosopher Jean Améry, himself an Auschwitz deportee, Levi writes: 'Each and every human action contains a kernel of incomprehensibility. If this were not the case, we would be in a position to foresee what our neighbour will do. Clearly we cannot do this, and perhaps it is just as well that we cannot.' This is the same problem as the camps. There are questions which recur insistently over the course of these pages, which span three decades, some dedicated to the black hole of Auschwitz, others, more curious and extravagant, on science, Judaism and literature; they return insistently and concern themselves precisely with the kernel of 'incomprehensibility'.

For a man of scientific training, dedicated to a technical trade both practical and theoretical – the chemist works with his hands but also with his brain, he is a detective of matter – it is no minor thing to state that there exists a hard nucleus which, in a moral sense also, can be neither explained nor understood. Besides, it is plain to the ex-deportee there is both method and rationality in the madness and abnormal design of Auschwitz. Madness does not preclude this. Indeed, the very appearance of modesty and banality of the slaughterers fits perfectly with the anonymous and blind rationality of large modern institutions. Höss himself, the petit-bourgeois commandant of Auschwitz, is an inventor in his own way: it was he who solved the problem of extermination by inventing the gas chambers, Levi notes ironically.

Rationality and irrationality are opposed and symmetrical; between the two of them there is a relationship of equality, even in opposition. Auschwitz is asymmetrical with regard to reason, and is its absolute opposite, but at the same time, at Auschwitz, in the *anus mundi* as Levi defines it in 'The Drowned and the Saved', reason dominates: in the organization of the camp, in the management of the prisoners, in the systematic elimination of the 'Muselmänner', the 'drowned'. It is a coherent system, however upside down it may be with regard to normal life.

As an acute observer of human behaviour, of relations and systems of exchange and barter in the extermination camps, the young Turinese chemist never tires of repeating in the pages of *If This is a Man* that the inverted hierarchy of the camps, as well as its logic, are perfectly clear to him. From what he has seen he draws a lesson on human nature, as a moralist in the manner of Montaigne, on the uncertain boundary that separates not only reason and unreason, but also good and evil. He sees with absolute clarity, as evidenced by the pages in this book, the double root of human behaviour. In human rationality, in civilization itself, we already see the germ that can generate its opposite, the unleashing of irrational and destructive forces. Not only as an act of anger, of which war, as he has learnt from Homer, is an extension, but as an act of cold detachment. It is the very lack of symmetry in reason itself that is incalculable and unpredictable.

In a long conversation, held in the course of a series of lectures in Turin and later transcribed, Levi deals with the question of racism ('Racial Intolerance'). We are in 1979, right in the middle of a social and political crisis in Italy, just one year after the murder of Aldo Moro by the Red Brigades, about which he also wrote. After humbly confessing his lack of expertise, the writer radically differentiates the ethological and even biological problems of racism from the historical and cultural ones. An attentive reader of Konrad Lorenz, he lingers over the problem of aggression within the species, 'so-called evil', whose existence he has seen for himself, and whose biological root cannot be eliminated. However shot through with determinism this may be, Levi has no doubts about the matter: there is a pre-human, prehistoric racial intolerance which precedes and justifies (only in part) the historic form of which his people – the Jews – have had dreadful and recurrent experience over the centuries.

Once again, at the heart of the question, why evil and not good, why racism, why the hell of Auschwitz, there is a question of dissymmetry: the root of evil is in human behaviour, in its animality.

The key figure of If This is a Man is the animal-man, Buck, the character created by Jack London, first a peaceful domestic animal and later an innocent victim, then Kapo of the dog pack, 'primitive dominant beast'. The analogy between the protagonist of The Call of the Wild, translated by Gianni Celati and reviewed by Levi, and the life of the deportee, torn from his tranquil bourgeois home and flung into the inferno of the camps, is very close: in extreme conditions, in concentration camps, at Auschwitz, man is dramatically faced with having to confront his own irrationality, which he cannot shed, neither yesterday nor today. In describing a whole range of questions about racial intolerance, as a self-declared non-expert, the writer and ex-deportee follows the thread of an argument based on a rationalist matrix, on a pessimism of reason which, if it does not succeed in easing the wounds inflicted by man on man, nonetheless appears as a lucid and pitiless description of evil. But the thread of his argument has once more to come to terms with the dissymmetry between reason and non-reason, between explanation and comprehension. And since

Primo Levi is fundamentally a Stoic, on both the philosophical and the moral plane, the contradiction does not frighten him; in all probability it causes him suffering, and yet in no way does he abdicate his own rationality which offers itself, despite everything, as a solid bastion against the irruption of the irrational. The problem lies, if anything, elsewhere.

In a text of a scientific flavour, published in 1984 in a popular science and culture journal, the ex-chemist Primo Levi – he retired ten years before in order to dedicate himself to writing – considers the relationship between asymmetry and life. Here he picks up once more the problem he had tackled in his degree thesis, 'Walden's inversion', which the racial laws had forced him to finish in a hurried and incomplete manner. Although it takes the form of an extract and summary, and although the experimental section is missing, this essay is his real thesis, the one drawn up by the writer after passing through the asymmetrical experience of the camps, on which he has reflected over the years both alone and with others. In 'Asymmetry and Life', Levi discusses the problem that has long interested him: why all 'major players in the living world, such as proteins, cellulose, sugars and DNA, are all asymmetrical'. As a scientist he cannot but notice that 'right–left asymmetry is intrinsic to life; indeed it coincides with life. It is invariably present in all organisms, from viruses to lichen to oak trees, fish and man.'

This is not a negligible fact, but one that has aroused the curiosity of many generations of scientists. The subject, he writes, is that of the 'final cause' (Aristotle), or, 'in modern terms, that of the adaptive utility of asymmetry'. Levi reviews much of his own reading, and revisits the problem addressed for his thesis in the light of developments in physics and chemistry over the past twenty to thirty years. He sketches out five hypotheses to explain the asymmetry he is dealing with, he even hypothesizes the existence of anti-matter, the presence of a symmetry for earthly right- or left-handed lactic acid in 'the distant world of anti-matter' (has Levi, like Alice, perhaps passed, however briefly, through the looking glass, into the asymmetrical realm of death?). In the final lines he speaks of the 'chirality' of the universe, or just of our galaxy, as a deeply disturbing phenomenon that is both dramatic and enigmatic.

Chirality, scientists tell us, is the condition whereby a molecule cannot be superimposed on its specular image. In other words, it points to a symmetry that is enantiomorphic, like that of the right hand and left hand which are indeed symmetrical, but as a reflection, so that they can be superimposed not by translation but by rotation, in a higher dimension. The theme of symmetry and dissymmetry apparently fascinated Levi, for he returns to it on various occasions, particularly in *The Wrench*. Why? We can hypothesize that it is not just a matter of science, but a question which recalls the experience in the camps and the relationship between rationality and irrationality so sorely tested in Auschwitz.

Is it not true, perhaps, that in the extermination camp reason and non-reason are enantiomorphic? That the rationality of everyday life is undone by the logic of the camp which, in its turn, contains a clear principle of intrinsic rationality? In the same way, it seemed plain to Levi the scientist from this experience that Western science contained a principle of irrationality, the ever-looming possibility that its potential could be utilized for destructive rather than constructive purposes. There is a chiasmus, a crossroads, a crossed symmetry between rational and irrational. And this, as his fantasy and science fiction stories make clear, regards not only the extreme, extra-territorial place, the concentration camp, but also the daily life of men. The 'format defect' (*vizio di forma*), as one collection of his stories is entitled, is exactly this. This is how we should interpret the adjectives with which, at the end of 'Asymmetry and Life', Levi defines the announcement of the non-symmetrical symmetry of the universe. Disturbing, dramatic, enigmatic: these are terms that are perfectly adapted to the description of the incomprehensible event of Auschwitz. Nonetheless asymmetry is also a vital fact, a fundamental part of life itself.

Although there also exist asymmetrical substances that do not belong to the world of the living – quartz crystals, for example – asymmetry, writes Levi, is 'intrinsic to life; indeed it coincides with life'. Can we hypothesize that for the writer Auschwitz, a world turned upside down, enantiomorphic with regard to civil life, is part of life? Yes. The unresolvable contradiction, eternal source of pain and remembering, is just this. And for more than one reason. Because the experience of Auschwitz is an integral part of his personality, from which, as he repeats in these pages, he received the gift of writing; and this is a source of both joy and torment. Furthermore, the camp at Monowitz has led him to understand the irrational root of the rational behaviour of man, and this is underlined and clarified by his voyage of return to the world of the living, his *Odyssey*, narrated in *The Truce*, which is by turns light-hearted and easy-going, and dark and gloomy. The chemistry exam of Dr Pannwitz and the experience of the chemical laboratory of Buna may have saved his life but they have, on the other hand, clarified the evil power implicit in science, in the use to which it is put. More deeply, in this tormented but highly lucid consciousness, which we have come to know through his books, we sense that the asymmetrical symmetry of the concentration camp rests on the asymmetrical coupling of the 'drowned' and the 'saved'. Primo Levi belongs to the second group, and is a witness precisely because he is 'saved'. The chiasmus is dreadful to bear.

In his last book, *The Drowned and the Saved*, he writes: 'The thought that my bearing witness might have granted me alone the privilege of surviving, and living for many years without serious problems, disturbs me, because I see no proportion between the privilege and the result'. It is not a question of a sense of guilt. Levi, as we understand from reading the pieces in this book dedicated to Auschwitz and to the camps in general, has not attempted to forget, to live in the shelter of a more or less successful repression. Rather, he has exposed himself in the role of witness, he has faced the problem of not wishing to forget. He continues to write: 'But We Were There'. For this reason he has continued to collide with the asymmetrical root of his talent as a writer. Levi is not by mental habit an extremist. Instead, he poses himself problems, he continually interrogates himself, and this does not prevent him from taking up firm, hard, unshakeable positions on Fascism, on Nazism, on the negationism of Robert Faurisson, on historical revisionism (the article, 'Black Hole of Auschwitz', is still highly relevant today) and on the Soviet Union.

In *If This is a Man* there is a precise point at which this aspect of his human and intellectual personality emerges. It is in the chapter called 'Initiation', which the writer added in 1958, ten years after the book's publication, when the second revised and updated edition came out with Einaudi. Here the figure of Steinlauf appears, a former sergeant in the Austro-Hungarian army, decorated with the Iron Cross in the 1914–18 war. A soldier who has fallen into the bottomless pit of the concentration camp, Steinlauf teaches the Jewish Italian prisoner the harsh law of the camp: 'precisely because the Lager was a great machine to reduce us to beasts, we must not become beasts; that even in this place one can survive, and therefore one must want to survive, to tell the story, to bear witness; and that to survive we must force ourselves to save at least the skeleton, the scaffolding, the form of civilization.' This is followed by a series of practical lessons handed on by the Austrian sergeant to his pupil: wash your face without soap, polish your shoes, walk with your head held high. It is a paradox, one of the many imposed by the camp: to oppose the formlessness of the camp with the form of civilized life. The formality of behaviour is as important as the merciless struggle to get bread, like the character in *Lilìt* who maintains his dignity by refusing to scratch in public the scab that torments him. The strategies of survival undo the habitual relationship between what it is logical and what it is illogical to do, between the rational and the irrational. But this is not to say that this is how the Italian Jew, Primo Levi, thinks.

Once more he has a surprise in store for us. The words of Steinlauf are not enough for him, and not only because of the Italian custom of mitigating everything, of rendering every doctrine bland and malleable, as he writes, but because the wisdom and virtue of the ex-soldier are not enough for the young chemist: 'In the face of this complicated world of damnation my ideas are confused; is it really necessary to elaborate a system and put it into practice? Or would it not be better to acknowledge one's lack of a system?'

These short pieces show that the greatness of Primo Levi lies not so much in the act of denunciation or of witness, although it is also, of course in this. Rather it is his persistence in asking himself questions that have no certain answers or which, if they have them, undermine received opinion, whether of individuals or groups of people. We glimpse the white-hot anger beneath his marble prose, beneath the reasonable and calm tone with which he enunciates his accusations against all professional liars, hypocrites, falsifiers ('Seekers of Lies to Deny the Holocaust'), against those who use the terrible event of Auschwitz to pass off facile truths or cheap sordidness ('Film and Swastikas'). We see the same attitude when he examines the media event of *Holocaust* ('Images of *Holocaust*'), or when he shows an excessive optimism in modern science ('Let's See How Much has Come True' and 'What was it that Burned Up in Space?'), or when he touches on the problem of the end of ideologies: 'Many tears are shed these days over the end of ideologies, but this book seems to me to show in exemplary fashion where an ideology can lead when it is accepted as radically as it was by Hitler's Germans, and by extremists in general. Ideologies can be good or bad; it is good to know them, to compare them and attempt to evaluate them; it is always bad to take one on completely, even when it is decked out with respectable words such as Fatherland and Duty' (Preface to R. Höss: *Commandant of Auschwitz*).

All of Primo Levi's work, whether as witness or as writer, whether as chemist or narrator, exists under the sign of an asymmetrical symmetry, which seeks, with difficulty but with great intelligence and honesty, to give a reasoned account of the disturbing, dramatic and enigmatic event that was Auschwitz. The impossibility of forgetting follows not so much, or not only, from the incalculable scale of the tragedy, but from the fact that tangled within it are questions that are difficult to unravel and which right up to the present day have repeated themselves in the grievous history of humanity, in Cambodia as in Bosnia, in Uganda as in Afghanistan. And that is why we still need the writing of Primo Levi.

Marco Belpoliti

Note to the Texts

This collection of newspaper articles and essays by Primo Levi is drawn from the edition of the *Opere* (Collected Works), published in two volumes in the Nuova Universale Einaudi series, 1997, edited by Marco Belpoliti. It amounts overall to 450 pages from various parts of the two volumes, which had been gathered from daily newspapers, journals, news sheets and annuals. Another recently discovered text was added to these writings, 'The Community of Venice and its Ancient Cemetery', drafted in 1985 as a preface and unpublished until 2000. The choice of pieces to be included has followed two main lines: the theme of the concentration camp on the one hand, and on the other a range of writings displaying Levi's interest in scientific, historical or literary matters, including the history of Italian and European Jews. The first group of writings was given the title of the well-known article, 'The Black Hole of Auschwitz' and the second, echoing the title of a volume put together by Levi himself, 'Other People's Trades'. Arranged in chronological order, the two sections shed light on Levi's double trade, that of witness and writer, as well as that of chemist and assiduous contributor to newspapers. The article which in 1959 marked the beginning of his collaboration with the newspaper *La Stampa*, 'The Monument at Auschwitz', is included here. For further information about the different texts, about their publication or editorial history, the reader should consult the notes in the Appendix to the volume of the *Opere* previously cited, pp. 1458–69 of Volume I and pp. 1571–75 of Volume II.

The aim of this book is to make accessible to the non-specialist reader the journalistic and essayistic writings of Primo Levi that have remained largely unknown (for nothing is more unpublished than what has already been published!), writings which help us reconstruct his journey as witness and intellectual from the 1950s until his death, in 1987. The ideal readers of this new collection are the young, and the book is dedicated to them.

Warm thanks are offered to Primo Levi's family for giving their consent to this project.

Part I   The Black Hole
of Auschwitz

1 Deportees. Anniversary

Ten years on from the liberation of the concentration camps, it is both distressing and deeply indicative to note that in Italy at least, far from being an important part of our history, the subject of the extermination camps is in the process of being completely forgotten.

It is unnecessary to remind readers of the statistics, to remember that this was a massacre on a scale the world had never before seen, practically wiping out the Jewish population of whole nations of Eastern Europe. Nor should we need to remind ourselves that had Nazi Germany been in a position to carry out its plans, the techniques tried and tested in Auschwitz and elsewhere would, with the famed thoroughness of the Germans, have been applied to whole continents.

Nowadays it is bad taste to speak of the concentration camps. We risk being accused of victimism: at best of a gratuitous fascination with the macabre, at worst, of pure and simple mendacity, of an outrage to decency.

Is this silence justified? Should it be tolerated by those of us who are survivors? Should it be tolerated by those who were rigid with fear and disgust as they witnessed the departure of the sealed trains amidst beatings, curses and inhuman screams, and who were there years later when just a handful of survivors returned, broken in body and spirit? Is it right that the task of bearing witness, which we felt then as a necessary and pressing obligation, should be considered over and done with?

There is just one answer to this. It is not permissible to forget, nor is it permissible to keep silent. If we fall silent, who then will speak? Certainly not the perpetrators and their accomplices. If we fail to bear witness, in a not too distant future we could well see the deeds of Nazi bestiality relegated by their very enormity to the status of legend. It is vital, therefore, to speak out.

Yet silence prevails. There is a silence which is the fruit of an uneasy conscience, or even of bad conscience; it is the silence of those who, when pressed or compelled to pass judgement, try their hardest to steer the debate in a different direction altogether, conjuring up nuclear weapons, carpet bombing, the Nuremberg trials as well as the problematic Soviet work camps. These arguments are not in themselves worthless, but they carry little weight in the attempt to provide a moral justification for Fascist crimes whose manner and scale together constitute a monument of viciousness never before seen in the whole history of humanity.

But perhaps it is fitting to focus on another aspect of this silence, this reticence and evasiveness. It is hardly surprising that it is not spoken of in Germany, or by the Fascists, nor need this bother us. Their words are of no use to us, and we need not expect any laughable attempts at justification from them. But what should we say about the silence of the civilized world, the silence of culture, our own silence towards our children, towards our friends who return after long years of exile in far-off places? This silence cannot be put down simply to weariness, the attrition of the years, our habitual human stance of *primum vivere*. It cannot be put down to cowardice. There is in us a deeper, worthier instinct that in many circumstances urges us to remain silent about the camps, or at least to tone down or censor the images which are still vivid in our memories.

It is shameful. We are men; we are part of the same human family to which our murderers belonged. Faced with the enormity of their crime, we feel ourselves citizens still of Sodom and Gomorrah, and we cannot feel ourselves exempt from the indictment which our act of witness would prompt an extraterrestrial judge to lay at the door of the whole of humanity.

We are children of the Europe where Auschwitz lies. We have inhabited the century in which science has become warped, giving birth to racial laws and the gas chambers. Who can say that he is immune from infection?

There is more yet to say: painful, hard things which will not be new to those who have read *Les armes et la nuit*. It is absurd to proclaim as glorious the deaths of countless victims in the extermination camps. It was not glorious: it was a defenceless and naked death, ignominious and vile. There is nothing honourable about slavery. There were those who managed to bear it unharmed, and these are exceptions to be contemplated with reverent amazement. But slavery is a condition that is essentially ignoble, the fount of almost irresistible degradation and moral shipwreck.

It is good that these things be said, because they are true. But let us be clear that this does not mean lumping victims and assassins together. The guilt of the Fascists and the Nazis, far from being alleviated, is aggravated a hundredfold. They have demonstrated for all centuries to come what unsuspected reserves of viciousness and madness lie latent in man even after millennia of civilized life, and this is the work of the devil. They worked with astonishing tenacity to create their gigantic death-dealing and corrupting machine, and no greater crime can be imagined. They insolently constructed their kingdom with the tools of hatred, violence and lies: their failure is a warning.

In *Torino*, XXX1, no. 4, April 1955, a special issue dedicated to the ten-year anniversary of the Liberation, pp. 53–54. A shorter version of this article appeared in *L'eco dell'educazione ebraica* in a special issue marking the decade since Liberation.

2   The Monument at Auschwitz

Within what is a relatively short time, if we consider the scale of the undertaking, within two years or maybe even less, a monument will rise in Auschwitz, on the very site which saw the greatest massacre in human history. The second stage of the competition recently held to select the project was won jointly by a group of Polish artists and two groups of Italian architects and sculptors. Collaboration between these groups resulted in the executive project which has been on public view in Rome since 1 July [1959] in the National Gallery of Modern Art. We should be more exact here: the monument will not 'rise' literally, in that for the most part it will be at ground level or below. Nor will it be a monument in the usual sense of the word, since it will take up no less than 30 hectares of ground. Furthermore it will not be in the centre of Auschwitz, in other words not in the Polish town of Oswiecim, but at Birkenau.

There are few to whom the name Auschwitz can be new. Around 400,000 prisoners were registered in this camp, of whom just a few thousand survived. Almost four million other innocents were swallowed up by the extermination plants erected by the Nazis at Birkenau, two kilometres from Auschwitz. They were not political enemies; for the most part they were whole families of Jews, with children, old people and women rounded up in the ghettoes or taken from their own homes. Usually they had just a few hours' notice, and were ordered to carry with them 'everything they would need for a long journey'. Unofficial advice was not to forget their gold, currency and any valuables they owned. Everything they carried with them (everything: including shoes, linen, glasses) was taken from them when the convoy entered the camp. Out of every transport, a tenth on average were sent straight into the forced labour camps. Nine-tenths of them (including all the children, the elderly and infirm, and the majority of the women) were killed immediately with a toxic gas originally intended to free ships' holds of rats. Their bodies were cremated in colossal plants, built for the purpose by the honest firm Topf and Sons of Erfurt, who had been commissioned to supply ovens capable of incinerating 24,000 bodies each day. When Auschwitz was liberated, seven tons of female hair were found.

These are the facts: tragic, vile, largely incomprehensible. Why, how did this happen? Will it ever happen again?

I do not believe it is possible fully to answer these questions, either now or in the future; and perhaps it is just as well. If there were to be an answer to these questions, it would mean that the facts of Auschwitz form part of the tissue of human endeavour; that they have a cause and hence a seed of justification. To some extent we can put ourselves in the shoes of the thief, of the assassin. But it is not possible to put ourselves in the shoes of the madman. It is equally impossible to retrace the steps of the main people responsible: their actions, their words, remain encircled by shadows, we cannot reconstruct how it came about, we cannot say 'from their point of view . . .'. Fundamental to human action is a goal: the massacre at Auschwitz, which destroyed a tradition and a civilization, benefited nobody.

In this sense (and only this sense!) it is highly instructive to read the diary of Höss, former Commandant of Auschwitz. This book, translated into Italian, is a chilling document. The author is not a bloody sadist or a hate-filled fanatic, but an empty man, a tranquil and diligent idiot, whose purpose it is to carry out with the utmost care the bestial initiatives entrusted to him, and in this obedience he appears to succeed in appeasing every niggling doubt and anxiety.

The truth about Auschwitz can only be understood, it seems to me, through the folly of the few, and the cowardly, foolish consensus of the many. Indeed, aside from any moral judgement and keeping to the level of *realpolitik*, we are inevitably led to conclude that attempts such as Hitler's, carried through in Auschwitz and meticulously planned for the whole of the New Europe, were errors on a colossal scale. Everywhere, in every single country, there is a capacity for indignation and harmony of judgement in the face of similar atrocities, which Nazism had not bargained for, and which explains the state of quarantine in which the German people still finds itself. Reason suggests that we are not threatened by a restoration of the concentration camp.

But it would not be wise to make predictions on the basis of reason. As Jemolo observed not so very long ago in this same column, it is pointless to credit our enemies with far-sighted plans and diabolical cunning, for stupidity and unreason are powerful historical forces. Experience has sadly demonstrated this point, and continues to demonstrate it. A second Hitler could be born, has perhaps already been born, and we should always be on our guard. Auschwitz can, then, be repeated. Once they have been discovered, techniques take on a life of their own, in a state of potentiality, waiting for the moment to be put into practice. Over fifteen years the techniques of destruction and propaganda have progressed to the point where the destruction of a million human lives at the press of a button is easier today than ever before, while distorting the memory, conscience and judgement of 200 million people becomes simpler with each passing year.

Nor does it stop there. The Nazi massacre bears the mark of folly, but another mark also. It is the sign of the inhuman, of human solidarity denied, forbidden, broken; of slave-driving exploitation; of the shameless assertion that might is right, smuggled in under the banner of order. It is the sign of oppression, the sign of Fascism. It is the coming to pass of a demented dream in which there is but one commander; nobody thinks any more, everybody marches in line, everybody obeys to the death, everybody always says yes.

It is, therefore, both right and important that in our age of facile enthusiasms and deep weariness a monument should rise in Auschwitz, and it should be a work that is both new and perennial, which can speak with the utmost clarity to whoever visits it both today, tomorrow and in centuries to come. It does not have to be 'beautiful', it doesn't matter if it verges on the rhetorical, or even if it succumbs to it. It must not be used by any one side. It must be a warning dedicated by humanity to itself, which can bear witness and repeat a message not new to history but all too often forgotten: that man is, must be, sacred to man, everywhere and for ever.

La Stampa, 18 July 1959

3   'Arbeit Macht Frei'

These are the well-known words written over the entrance gate of the Auschwitz concentration camp. Their literal meaning is 'work makes free', but their real meaning is somewhat less clear; it inevitably leaves us puzzled, and is worth some consideration.

The concentration camp at Auschwitz was created relatively late, and was conceived from the start not as a work camp but as an extermination camp. It became a work camp later, in 1943, and then only in partial and subsidiary fashion. I think we can therefore exclude the hypothesis that in the intention of the person who coined it, this phrase was to be understood in its straightforward sense and for its obvious proverbial and moral value.

It is more likely that the meaning is ironic, springing from the heavy, arrogant, funereal wit to which only Germans are privy, and which only in German has a name. Translated into explicit language it should, it seems, have gone something like this: 'Work is humiliation and suffering, and is fit not for us, the *Herrenvolk*, the people of masters and heroes, but for you, enemies of the Third Reich. The only freedom which awaits you is death.'

In reality, and despite appearances to the contrary, denial of and contempt for the moral value of work is fundamental to the Fascist myth in all its forms. Under each form of militarism, colonialism and corporatism lies the precise desire of one class to exploit the work of others, and at the same time to deny that class any human value. This desire was already clear in the anti-worker position adopted by Italian Fascism right from its early years, and became increasingly refined in the evolution of the German version of Fascism, reaching the point of the wide-scale deportations to Germany of workers from all the occupied countries. But it is in the universe of the camps that it finds both its crowning glory and its *reductio ad absurdum*.

The exaltation of violence has a similar goal in mind and this, too, is essential to Fascism; the club, which quickly assumes a symbolic value, is the instrument used to stimulate beasts of burden and haulage to work harder.

The experimental character of the camps is clear to us today and arouses an intense retrospective horror. We know now that the German camps, whether intended for work or for extermination, were not, so to speak, a by-product of conditions of national emergency (the Nazi revolution first, then the war). They were not an unfortunate transitory necessity, but the early seedlings of the New Order. In the New Order, some human races (Jews, Gypsies) would be wiped out while others, for example the Slavs in general and the Russians in particular, would be enslaved and subject to a carefully controlled regime of biological degradation, transforming individuals into good labouring animals, illiterate, devoid of all initiative, incapable of either rebellion or criticism.

The camps were thus largely 'pilot plants', an anticipation of the future assigned to Europe in Nazi planning. In the light of these considerations, phrases such as the one at Auschwitz, 'Work makes free', or the one at Buchenwald, 'To each his own', take on a precise and sinister meaning. They are, in their turn, an anticipation of the new tablets of the Law, dictated by master to slave, and valid only for the slave.

If Fascism had prevailed, the whole of Europe would have been transformed into a complex system of forced labour and extermination camps, and those cynically edifying words would have been read on the entrance to every workshop and every worksite.

In *Triangolo Rosso*, Aned, November 1959

4   The Time of Swastikas

The Deportation Exhibition, which opened in Turin in a seemingly minor key, has been an unexpected success. Each and every day a close-packed crowd stood, deeply moved, before those terrible images; the closing date had to be postponed not once, but twice. Equally surprising was the welcome given by the Turin public to two talks aimed at young people, given in the Cultural Union in Palazzo Carignano to an attentive, thoughtful and packed public. These two results, in themselves positive and worthy of more than superficial comment, nonetheless contain the seed of a reproach: maybe it took us too long, and we wasted too many years; maybe we were silent when we should have spoken out, maybe we did not measure up to what was expected of us.

But there is also a lesson to be learnt here, and not a new one, to tell the truth, for the history of customs is a series of rediscoveries: in these noisy and paper-thin times of ours, full of bare-faced propaganda and hidden attempts to persuade, of mechanical rhetoric, compromises, scandals and world-weariness, the voice of truth is far from lost and indeed acquires a new resonance, a clearer and more distinctive tone. It seems too good to be true, but that's the way it is: the widespread devaluation of the word, whether written or spoken, is neither definitive nor final: something has survived. Strange as it may seem, whoever speaks the truth today finds a listener and is believed.

We should be heartened by this. But such a display of trust compels all of us to examine our consciences. For in this thorny question of how to communicate to our children a moral and emotional patrimony that we hold to be of the utmost importance, have we not also been in error? Probably yes, we have been wrong. We have sinned both by omission and commission. By remaining silent we have been guilty of laziness and of mistrust in the value of the word; and when we have spoken, we have frequently been guilty of adopting and accepting a language that was not ours. We know very well that the Resistance had, and still has, enemies; of course their manoeuvres are attempts to muffle any mention of the Resistance. But I have the suspicion that, whether consciously or not, more subtle methods are also used to suffocate the Resistance, embalm it before its time, and despatch it with a good deal of lip service to the noble castle of our national history. My fear is that we, too, have contributed to this process of embalming. In order to describe the facts of yesterday, we have too often adopted a rhetorical, hagiographic and hence vague language. There are excellent arguments both for and against labelling the Resistance with the term 'Second Risorgimento', but I wonder if it is wise to underline this aspect rather than insist on the fact that the Resistance goes on, or at least should go on, because its objectives have been achieved only in part. Indeed, this way we can affirm an ideal continuity between the events of 1848, 1860, 1918 and 1945, to the detriment of the rather more scorching and self-evident continuity between 1945 and today: the caesura of the two decades of Fascism thus loses some of its prominence.

To conclude, I believe that if we want our children to feel these things, and thus feel themselves to be our children, we need to talk to them a little less about glory and victory, of heroism and sacred soil, and a little more about the days of hope and despair of our companions who died accepting their duty in silence, their harsh, risky and unrewarding life, their daily struggle. We should talk to them about the participation of the people (but not all the people), errors committed and errors avoided, about the hard-won experience of fighting and common struggle, gained through errors whose price was paid in human blood, of the laborious, not spontaneous, and not always perfect concord between different political groups.

Only in this way will young people be able to feel our most recent history as a web of real human events, and not as a 'pensum' to be added to all the others decreed by ministerial programmes.

In *Il giornale dei genitori*. II, n.1, 15 January 1960

5   Preface to the German Edition of *If This is a Man*

[. . .] And so we have come to the end. I am happy about this and satisfied with the result, and I am grateful to you, yet at the same time rather sad. You see, it is the only book I have written, and now that we have finished transplanting it into German I feel like a father whose son has reached adulthood, and leaves, and I can no longer take care of him.

But that is not all. You will perhaps have realized that for me the concentration camp, and writing about the concentration camp, was a matter of great importance. It changed me radically, and gave me maturity and a reason for living. Perhaps I am presumptuous but here today, I, number 174517, can speak through you to the German people, remind them of what they have done, and say to them 'I am alive, and I would like to understand you in order to judge you.'

I do not believe that a man's life necessarily has a particular goal, but if I think of my own life and the goals I have set myself up until now, I recognize only one of them precisely and consciously, and it is this: to bear witness, to make my voice heard by the German people, to respond to the SS man with the truss, to the Kapo who wiped his hand on my shoulder, to Dr Pannwitz, to those who hanged Ultimo, and make myself heard also by their descendants.

I am sure that you have not misunderstood me. I have never harboured a sense of hatred towards the German people, and had this been the case I would certainly be cured of it by now, after meeting you. I don't understand and I can't bear how a man can be judged not for what he is but because of the group to which he happens to belong. Indeed I realize, since I learnt to understand Thomas Mann, since I learnt a little German (and I learnt it in the camps!) that in Germany there is something worthwhile, and that Germany, now asleep, is pregnant, a breeding ground, at the same time a danger and a hope for the rest of Europe.

But I can't say I understand the Germans, and something which cannot be understood constitutes an aching emptiness, a painful stinging, a permanent stimulus that demands to be satisfied. I hope that this book will find some echo in Germany, not just out of ambition but also because the nature of this echo will perhaps allow me to understand Germans better, and to soothe this pain.

Preface to the German edition of *If This is a Man*, published by Fischer in 1961

6   Preface to the School Edition of *The Truce*

I was born in Turin, in 1919, in a reasonably well-off family of Piedmontese Jews. There are many different ways of being Jewish, ranging from the full observance of religious rules and traditions, through to total indifference, or the acceptance of the majority way of thinking and living. Being a Jew meant something rather vague to me, not a problem as such. It meant an untroubled awareness of my people's ancient history, a sort of benevolent disbelief as far as religion was concerned, a marked tendency towards books and abstract discussions. As for everything else, I did not feel myself to be different from my Christian friends and fellow students, and I felt perfectly comfortable in their company.

When I was a boy I wanted to follow several different paths. Between the ages of twelve and fourteen I wanted to become a linguist; from fourteen to seventeen I wanted to be an astronomer. When I was eighteen I enrolled at the University for a degree in chemistry. I would certainly never have thought of becoming a writer if it had not been for a long chain of events. As it is easy to work out from my date of birth, I grew up and completed my studies in the time of Fascism. I didn't fully understand the oppressive sense of Fascism, but I nurtured an undefined irritation and dislike for the most vulgar and illogical aspects of so-called Fascist culture. In 1938 the Racial Laws were proclaimed in Italy. These measures were not as severe as those in Germany, which were tightening a deadly net around the Jewish minority, together with other 'enemies of the State'. Nonetheless, the laws separated the Jews from the rest of the populace and re-ignited in our minds painful memories of the ghettoes which had disappeared ninety years before. Other absurd laws followed, iniquitous and harassing, and every day the newspapers were full of lies and insults. Everything was back to front in a ridiculous, and cruel, overturning of the truth: the Jews had 'always' been not only the enemies of the people and the State, but were those who repudiated justice and morality, who destroyed science and art, the woodworm whose hidden labour gnaws away at the base of the social edifice; and the Jews were guiltily responsible for the now imminent conflict. This persistent campaign of calumny had at least the merit of acting on the conscience of the Italians, dormant after fifteen years of Fascism, and it served to draw a clear line between those who believed and obeyed, and those who refused faith and obedience. It also opened everybody's eyes (and not only the Jews) as to the true nature of Fascism and Nazism.

When Fascism fell, in the summer of 1943, I felt joy and enthusiasm for what seemed to me a spontaneous act of justice by history, but I was not in the least prepared for the hard period of struggle which followed, and which could not but follow. I felt indecisive, inexperienced, and the prospect of fighting terrified me. All the same, I set off for the mountains and joined a partisan band of the 'Justice and Liberty' movement, a group still being formed, still without arms and extremely poor. Just a few weeks later we ran into a large search party of the Fascist militia. Many managed to escape, while I and a few others were captured. When I was interrogated I admitted I was a Jew, hoping that the Fascists would do no more than send me to a concentration camp in Italy, or to prison. Instead, in February 1944 I was handed over to the Germans.

Finding yourself in German hands, during those years, meant a terrible fate for any Jew. The hatred for the Jews that had lain dormant for centuries in Germany and in the whole of Eastern Europe found in Hitler its prophet and town crier, and Hitler had found, in millions of Germans, an army of obedient and willing collaborators. For years now, Jews had been thrown out of the life of the country and forced into hunger, into new ghettoes and into forced labour for the war industries. But around 1943, in great secret, they had begun to put into action an unheard-of programme, so horrific that even in official documents it was indicated only by sinister allusions, such as 'appropriate treatment' and 'final solution of the Jewish problem'. This programme was simple and appalling: all Jews were to be destroyed. All, without exception, even the old, the sick, the children, all the millions of Jews who after a succession of invasions across Europe now found themselves in the hands of the Germans: Jews from Germany, Poland, France, Holland, Russia, Italy, Hungary, Greece and Yugoslavia. But silently killing millions of people, even when they are unarmed, is no easy undertaking, and so the celebrated German technical and organizational skills sprang into action. Special installations were built, new machines never before conceived, true factories of death, capable of exterminating thousands of human beings in an hour of toxic gas, as happens to rats in the hold of a ship, and capable then of incinerating their bodies. The biggest of these centres of destruction was called Auschwitz. Every day three, five, ten trains arrived at Auschwitz, full of prisoners from every corner of Europe. In just a few hours after their arrival the work of extermination was already complete. Very few were spared an immediate end: only the youngest and strongest men and women, who were sent by the Germans to work camps. But even in these camps death was always lying in wait: death from hunger, or cold, or from the diseases which accompany hunger, cold, and overwork. Any of these people who were judged to be no longer capable of work were sent immediately to the extermination centres.

The Germans deported me to Auschwitz itself. I was judged capable of heavy labour and sent to the Buna-Monowitz work camp. All the prisoners in this camp worked in an enormous factory of chemical products. I lived in Buna for a year, during which three-quarters of my companions died and were immediately replaced by masses of new prisoners, destined for death in their turn. I survived, thanks to a combination of rare pieces of luck: I never fell ill, I was given food by a 'free' Italian workman, and over the final months I could put my skill as a chemist to good use, working in a laboratory of the immense factory rather than in the mud and the snow. Besides this I knew a little German, and I made an effort to learn the language as well and as quickly as I could, because I had realized how necessary this was in order to find your way through the complex and lethal world of the concentration camp.

The Auschwitz camp was liberated by Soviet troops in January 1945, but our hopes for a swift return to Italy were to be disappointed. For reasons which were unclear, perhaps simply as a consequence of the extreme, disordered confusion which the war had left behind in Europe, and in Russia in particular, our repatriation took place only in October, following a long and roundabout route which was both absurd and unlikely, through Poland, the Ukraine, White Russia, Romania, Hungary and Austria.

Back in Italy, I had to quickly find work in order to keep myself and my family. But the uncommon experience which had been my lot, the infernal world of Auschwitz, my miraculous salvation, the words and faces of my companions who had disappeared or survived, my rediscovered liberty, the extraordinary and exhausting journey home, all of these things were pressing inside me with great urgency. I needed to tell these things, and it seemed to me important not to let them just lie inside me, like a nightmare; they should be known, not only by my friends but by everybody, by the widest possible public. As soon as I could I began to write furiously, but also methodically, almost obsessed by the fear that a single one of my memories might be forgotten. And so my first book was born, *If This is a Man*, which describes my year of imprisonment at Auschwitz. I wrote it without great effort or difficulty, with profound satisfaction and relief, and with the impression that it 'wrote itself', somehow finding a direct path from my memory onto the paper.

If This is a Man was a success, but not to the point of making me feel I could describe myself as a 'writer'. I had said what I had to say, I had picked up my profession as chemist once more; I no longer felt the need, the urgent necessity to tell my story, which had compelled me to pick up a pen. Nonetheless this new experience, so far removed from the world of my daily work, the experience of writing, of creating something from nothing, of searching for and finding the right word, of crafting a balanced and expressive sentence, had been too pleasurable and intense for me not to try and attempt it again. I still had many things to tell: no longer fearsome things, inevitable and necessary, but cheerful or sad adventures, strange and immense lands, the roguish endeavours of my innumerable travelling companions, the multicoloured and fascinating vortex of post-war Europe, drunk with freedom and yet uneasy in the terror of a new war.

These are the themes of *The Truce*, the book of the long journey home. I think it is easy to spot that it was written by a different man, not only fifteen years older but calmer and more at peace, more attentive to the texture of the phrase, more aware: in other words more of a writer in all senses of the word, both good and bad. And yet, even today, I still cannot consider myself a writer. I am satisfied with this double condition of mine and conscious of its advantages. It allows me to write only when I wish to, and does not compel me to write in order to live. From another point of view my daily work has taught me, and continues to teach me, many things which every writer needs. It has instilled in me the value of concreteness and precision and the habit of 'weighing' every word with the same care as when carrying out quantitative analysis. Above all it has accustomed me to the state of mind that normally goes by the name of objectivity, which is to say the recognition of the intrinsic dignity not only of people but also of things, of their own truth, which we should recognize and not distort if we do not wish to fall into the generic, into falseness and emptiness.

From *La Tregua*, in the series 'Letture per la scuola media', Einaudi, Turin 1965, pp. 5–10

7   Resistance in the Camps

It is difficult to grasp the import and significance of a historic event as it is unfolding, or just a few short years after it has come to an end. While the tracks are still at their freshest, the wounds at their most painful, the voices of the survivors and witnesses at their most numerous and pressing, it is particularly hard, if not impossible, to maintain the necessary objectivity in proceeding with the patient, in-depth work of historical reconstruction. It takes time for the picture to emerge clearly, for distortions and errors to be cancelled out, even in this age of ours where the march of history seems to step up its rhythm from year to year.

Only over the last few years has the terrible phenomenon of massacre and slavery in its modern, restored form in the concentration

camps, begun to find a historical perspective in the collective conscience of Europe and the world. Only now is it possible to evaluate its
significance and measure its threat, and understand what the destiny
of our civilization would have been had Hitler prevailed. If this
far from absurd hypothesis had come about, we would be living in a
monstrous world, a bipartite world of masters and slaves, of masters
above all law, of slaves deprived of the most basic of rights and subject
to the will of their owners, condemned to an existence of shattering
work, ignorance, imprisonment and hunger.

Indeed, the condition of imprisonment in the modern concentration camp reproduces (should we write 'reproduced'?) the condition
of the slave in degraded and aggravated form. It is the master's
purpose to turn the slave into an abject person, who is known and who
feels himself to be abject, a person who has not only lost his liberty but
has forgotten it, no longer feels the need for it, barely even the desire.
Generally he succeeds, and the material oppression of the individual
is followed by a more painful victory, the victory of total oppression, in
flesh and spirit, the demolition of man as man.

It is of the utmost importance that the seed of European resistance
against Fascism nonetheless took root within this inhuman situation,
amidst a discordant and disconnected human heap worn down by
exhaustion and periodic massacres. This phenomenon calls for a new
and careful study in order to bring into focus its parameters and its
significance. Resistance in the concentration camps, like the resistance which developed in the Polish ghettoes, should be numbered
amongst the greatest victories of the spirit over the flesh, alongside the
most heroic deeds of human history, the most desperate, fought with
no covering fire and with no hope of victory to sustain the fighters and
renew their strength.

Not only perpetual hunger and the consequent state of physical
exhaustion served to make the organization of resistance in the
concentration camps deeply problematic; other equally serious obstacles had to be overcome.

It was impossible, or at least highly dangerous, to communicate
with the outside world, not only to maintain contact with the centres
of resistance which had sprung up everywhere in the countries occupied by the Germans, but even simply to send and receive news from
outside. Weapons, of course, were totally lacking, as was the money or
the means to acquire them. In every camp there was a section of the
dreaded Gestapo, disguised under the name of 'Political Section' or
'Work Office', which employed the services of a large number of spies,

chosen amongst the prisoners themselves; each and every word, the slightest hint of a defence organization, could lead to denunciations and collective reprisals of the utmost severity. This atmosphere of suspicion, of mutual mistrust, poisoned every effort at human relationships, and served to undermine every attempt at opposition. And finally, the population of the camps was extraordinarily diverse, and not by chance, for the SS commanders seconded to the concentration camps made a constant effort to maintain there a permanent Babel of languages and nationalities. Nor should we forget that the camps consisted of prisoners belonging to three main categories (as well as many smaller ones which I will not mention here). These categories were the political prisoners, Jews and common criminals.

The last of these, the so-called 'greens', from the colour of their badge, were largely hardened German criminals, generally habitual offenders, who had been taken out of prisons and offered privileged positions in the concentration camps. Despite their unruly behaviour and lack of discipline, they showed themselves to be very useful instruments of oppression, corruption and espionage in the hands of the SS, and were the most immediate enemies of the political prisoners and the Jews. It is worth recalling that after the rout of Stalingrad a large number of 'greens' were released *en masse* from the camps and enrolled in the fighting units of the SS. Since internal organization was left to the prisoners themselves, in many camps there was a secret struggle for power between the 'greens' and the 'reds' (the political prisoners). The 'reds' had in their favour their experience of conspiracy and their determined anti-Nazi stance, while the 'greens' had the advantage of better physical conditions and the support of the SS. Only in those camps where the 'greens' came off worst was it possible for the other two categories to set up structures of self-defence or opposition.

And yet, despite all these adverse circumstances, almost all the larger camps managed some form of resistance. The undertaking was easier in the camps in which political prisoners were more numerous and better organized, typically at Mauthausen and Buchenwald where powerful clandestine defence committees were set up, with all the main parties and nationalities of the camp represented.

It would not have been realistic to attempt the impossible or the premature, such as armed resistance or liberation of the camp from within; the committees were focused on achieving more immediate and concrete aims. Men who could be trusted were placed in key positions in the administration of the camp: the infirmary, the work office, the secretariat, supplies. In this way it became possible to contain, or at least to control, the decimation of those most useful from a political point of view, to save Allied parachutists and eliminate on the other hand many spies and collaborators. Cautious acts of sabotage were carried out in the workshops and building sites, and especially in the armaments factories. They heard and broadcast news about the war fronts using radio sets constructed in secret, and kept contact with other camps. Finally, and this was perhaps the action of most immediate service and benefit to their prison comrades, it was possible to eliminate or at least assuage the serious injustices and theft all too common in the distribution of food rations, and this was a fundamental factor in survival.

Nor should we undervalue the moral factor: the intuition, the whisper that inside the barbed wire something friendly survived yet, a power mysterious and undefined but different and hostile to National Socialism, was an extraordinary boost to all prisoners, helping them hold on to the will to live.

In many cases they began to prepare a real and active resistance, which would come into place as the front approached and block any future German efforts to wipe out the camps together with the prisoners, or to deport the prisoners deeper into the countryside. In Buchenwald and Mauthausen they fashioned rudimentary weapons, with explosives purloined from the workshops; in the general collapse which everywhere accompanied the German retreat, however, these emergency squads rarely had occasion to intervene.

Things were different in the camps which fulfilled the purpose indicated by their name, *Vernichtungslager*, annihilation camps: Auschwitz-Birkenau, Treblinka, Maidanek, Sobibor. People went into these places of utter horror only to die, and the average survival rate did not exceed three months. Their constantly renewed population consisted largely of Jews who arrived already exhausted by months or years of ghetto, hunger, desperate flight, and a precarious existence at the margins of human consort. These were generally whole families, with women, children, the elderly, the sick: a few hours after their arrival, after a summary selection process, four-fifths of every convoy ended up *en masse* in the extermination blocks. Only the younger men and women, those judged fit for work, were sent into the camps but after just a few weeks the hard labour, hunger, disease and blows wore down even the strongest constitution, the strongest will to resist.

Amongst this wretched humanity, the will to resist understandably took only the form of individual and occasional attempts, principally on the part of young men who adhered to Zionist organizations. But, even in the death camps, the internal structure set up by the Germans and based on the corruption and collaboration of 'chosen' functionaries-prisoners, became a paradoxical vehicle and matrix of resistance. Melting in with the oppressed and the many docile and abject instruments of oppression, men of superhuman courage acted in the shadows. While sometimes they managed to put a spoke in the wheel of the German death machine, their main achievement was in preserving a vestige of human dignity in the camps. They gathered and hid documentary material, sometimes even photographs boldly taken under the noses of the SS, diaries, lists of names, copies of archival documents which would serve, as indeed they did serve, to transmit to posterity an authentic image of the world of concentration camps.

The most important episode of active rebellion against Nazi power in the extermination camps was the uprising of the Auschwitz-Birkenau *Sonderkommando* in October 1944. It was a tragic and sinister episode whose exact details we will never fully learn because all the protagonists were exterminated. Under the reticent name of *Sonderkommando* ('Special Squad') was concealed a monstrous institution: the complex of prisoners who serviced the gas chambers and cremation ovens. It was made up of 900–1000 strong, young men of different nationalities, who were offered the alternative of work in the death blocks or death itself. Their horrific work was recompensed by exceptional treatment, including abundant food, cigarettes, alcohol, good clothes and shoes, but everybody knew, and they knew themselves, that within two or three months they would be massacred in their turn and replaced with new men.

When the deportation of 100,000 Hungarian Jews had reached its conclusion, the news spread throughout the camp that the systematic slaughter would be suspended. The men of the *Sonderkommando* realized that this meant their immediate end: the Germans would certainly not let witnesses such as themselves continue to live. The revolt, which was supposed to be coordinated with the Polish partisans from the surrounding forests, flared up prematurely, however, under the pressure of necessity, when under some pretext the Germans took away the first 160 men of the *Kommando* and killed them. The others then attacked the SS headquarters with desperate boldness, armed with just one single sub-machine gun, a few pistols and rudimentary hand bombs made with glass bottles. One of the four crematoria was set alight and exploded. A section of the heavily electrified barbed wire fence was thrown down. Only a few dozen of the rebels were able to get out of the camp alive, finding refuge on a Polish farm. Later they were betrayed, captured once more and murdered.

In this desperate struggle at the gates of the cremation ovens, only a dozen or so SS lost their lives, but news of the insurrection swiftly spread to all the camps in the district of Auschwitz. It was an event of huge importance, and had shown up a gap, a crack in the iron edifice of the concentration camp; it had demonstrated that the Germans were not invincible. For the Germans themselves it must have sounded an alarm bell, for a few days later the camp command began to dismantle and blow up the death buildings of Auschwitz, which alone had swallowed up more lives than all the other camps put together: perhaps in the absurd hope of destroying all evidence of the worst crime ever to have been committed in the already bloody history of the human race.

In *Il telefono della Resistenza*, a special issue edited by the Committee for the Celebrations of the Twentieth Anniversary of the Resistance in Stipel (1945–1965), Ilte, Turin 1965 (and *Quaderni del Centro Studi sulla deportazione e l'internamento* no. 3, Associazione Nazionale Ex Internati, Rome 1966)

8   Preface to Y. Katzenelson's *The Song of the Murdered Jewish People*

On hearing the 'singing' of Yitzhak Katzenelson, each and every reader can only catch his breath, deeply troubled and reverent. It is not comparable to any other work in the history of any literature. His is the voice of a man about to die, one man amongst hundreds of thousands who are about to die, atrociously aware of his own destiny and that of his people. His is not a distant destiny, but imminent: Katzenelson writes and sings from the midst of massacre; German death is prowling around him, it has carried out more than half the massacre but the measure is not yet full, there is no truce, no breath to be drawn; it is about to strike again, and again, to the last old man and the last child, to the end of everything.

The fact that in such conditions and in such a state of mind a condemned man should sing, and reveal himself a poet, leaves us quivering with both abhorrence and exaltation. These are essential poems, if ever there were poems of any other kind. By this I mean that while sometimes we are assailed by doubt before a page, wondering whether those things should or should not have been written, whether they might or might not have been written in another way, here all doubt is silenced.

Over and above the horror which grips us in the face of these testimonies, even those familiar to us, we cannot fail to experience a sense of astonishment at the purity and power of the voice.

This is the voice of a cultural universe that has never been heard in Italy, which today has disappeared: the voice of a people weeping for itself. The lines in which Katzenelson's anguish is most poignant and most concrete are precisely those in which he relives the cultural world of Eastern Judaism. 'The sun, rising over the *shtetlekh* of Lithuania and Poland, will never more meet / an ancient radiant Jew busy reciting a psalm at a window . . . / the market is dead . . . / Never more will a Jew bring there his joy, his life, his spirit.' This culture, whose instrument down the ages has been the Yiddish language, is unreservedly of the people. Its spoken form has always been more alive than its written form, and it is the spoken form that has nourished the written form. An extraordinary musical sensibility flowed through it, rooted in the village festivals described by Babel and painted by Chagall, and gave rise to the most illustrious modern schools of musicians and players; through it flowed an overwhelmingly vital theatrical tradition that was then destroyed, blow by blow, in Hitler's massacres. A literature both vast and vital, rich in spirituality, with its own sad sense of the comic, and with a humble and powerful thirst for life, depicted once and for all by Shalom Aleichem's small masterpiece, *The Story of Tevye the Milkman*.

Katzenelson, too, like the majority of Yiddish writers, musicians and performers, is a poet of the people. But he comes out of, and draws nourishment from, a people unique in Europe and in the world, a people for whom culture (their own particular culture) is not the privilege of a class or a caste, but belongs to everybody, and in which the Book has substituted Nature as a fount of excellence for each and every mystic, philosophical or poetic insight. It comes as no surprise, then, to discover in the desperate and sometimes raw lament of Katzenelson the echo of eternal words, the legitimate continuity and inheritance of Ezechiel, Isaiah, Jeremiah and Job; nor does it surprise us that he is both conscious and proud of this: '. . . in every Jew cries out a despairing Jeremiah, a Job'.

Precisely because of this accepted and proclaimed biblical inheritance, the best of the poems collected here seems to me to be the one entitled 'To the Skies'. Here Job speaks, a modern Job, both truer and more complete than the ancient one, wounded to the quick in the things he holds most dear, in his family and his faith, now bereft (why? why?) of both. Voices were raised in reply to the eternal questions of ancient Job, the prudent and fearful voices of the 'annoying consolers', the sovereign voice of the Lord. But nobody replies to the questions of the modern Job, no voice comes out of the whirlwind. There is no longer a God in the 'void and empty' skies, which watch impassively as a senseless massacre is brought to a close, as the people who created God are brought to their end.

From Y. Katzenelson, *Il canto del popolo ebraico massacrato* edited by F. Beltrami Segré and M. Novitich, Beit Lohamei Haghetaot, Turin 1966 (and Cdec, Milan 1977, pp. 5–6)

9 Note to the Theatre Version of *If This is a Man*

Whoever wrote that 'books, too, have their own destiny' was absolutely right. We only need to concentrate our thoughts for a moment and suddenly strange and unexpected paths jostle before us. There are books of illustrious birth, loved for decades, reduced now to the exclusive interest of a few specialists; books so heavy with prophecy, or satire or threat, that they were rejected by their first readers and then denigrated, for centuries in some cases, to the status of stories for children; others which flowered before their time, incomprehensible to contemporary critics, yet today both popular and famous; others still full of an immeasurable explosive charge, still hermetically sealed, but from inside of which we can hear a sinister ticking, like a time bomb.

I don't know – no writer can ever know – what my *If This is a Man* is worth, and which of the destinies I have just outlined it can expect in the near or distant future. But I can state that up to now it has had a curious and instructive history.

The book is about the camp at Auschwitz, and it was born in Auschwitz. The concentration camp was not a place in which it was easy to elaborate one's own experience, and even less to fix it into written form. Any form of personal possession was prohibited, unthinkable even. To own a pencil or a piece of paper was therefore impossible, and would in any case have represented extreme danger, an act of daring that was absurd as well as useless. And yet for many of us the hope of survival was identified with another, more precise, hope: we hoped not to live *and* tell our story, but to live *in order to* tell our story. It is the dream of survivors over the ages, of the strong man and the coward, the poet and the simpleton, of Ulysses and of Ruzante.

But it was at the same time a more profound and reflective need, the more urgently felt the harder the experience to be communicated: the same need which prompted the fighters in the Warsaw ghetto to dedicate a part of their last desperate energies to writing the drama they were living out and entrust it to a safe hiding place so that it might become history. Indeed, it has become history, and would not have done so without their superhuman diligence. It was clear to each and every one of us that the things we had seen needed to be told, and should not be forgotten. If it was impossible in the concentration camps, it became possible for those few whom fortune permitted to survive to write, indeed communicate, with the world. Each of us survivors, as soon as we returned home, transformed himself into a tireless narrator, imperious and maniacal. We did not all say the same things, because each of us had lived imprisonment in his own way, but nobody could speak of anything else or permit others to speak of anything else. I, too, began to tell my story even before my physical hunger was satiated, and I have not finished even now. I had become similar to the ancient mariner in Coleridge's ballad, who goes into the street and buttonholes guests on their way to a party in order to inflict on them his sinister story of evil doings and ghosts. I repeated my stories dozens of times in just a few days, to friends, enemies and strangers. Then I realized that my tale was crystallizing into a definitive and unchanging form. All I needed in order to write it all down was paper, pen and time. Time, which now is so scarce, grew up around me as if by enchantment: I wrote at night, in the train, in the factory canteen, in the factory itself, in the middle of the din of machinery. I wrote quickly, with no hesitation and no order. I was not conscious of writing a book, I was not conscious of intervening in some way, I was a million miles away from any literary scruples, and everything seemed to write itself. In just a few months the work was finished. Prompted by the urgency of my memories, I had written the seventeen chapters almost exactly in reverse order, starting, that is, with the last one. Then I wrote the preface, and finally I added an epigraph, a poem which had been dancing around my head even while I was in Auschwitz, and which I had written down a few days after my return.

I presented the manuscript to two publishers, who rejected it with the usual vague pretexts. Possibly they were right, at least from a business point of view: the times were not ripe, the public was not yet ready to understand and measure the phenomenon of the concentration camp. In fact a third publisher, De Silva in Turin, directed at the time by Antonicelli, accepted and published the book, but it ran aground after a couple of thousand copies, together with the publishing house and my tenuous hopes of a literary future.

The critics had given the book a warm reception, but after a year *If This is a Man* was forgotten. People carried on talking about it in Turin, within a limited circle of readers either of particular sensibility or who were personally touched by it. Ten years went by, and the public read *Les Armes de la nuit* by Vercors, *The Scourge of the Swastika* by Russell, Rousset's two books, *Si fa presto a dire fame* ('Hunger is Swiftly Said') by Caleffi, *The Human Race* by Antelme, *The Forest of the Dead: An Account of the Author's Experiences in Buchenwald* by Wiechert. The concentration camps began to be discussed again, with greater distance and from a broader perspective, as a historical object, and no longer as feverish news. In 1957 Einaudi agreed to reprint the book, and from then on it started to live a life of its own, as it were. In 1959 the English and American editions appeared, in 1961 the French and German editions, in 1962 the translation into Finnish and in 1963 into Dutch. In the meantime, in 1962 I had begun writing *The Truce*, the sequel to *If This is a Man*, the diary of my complicated journey back to my homeland. *The Truce* was barely off the press when I received a letter. Radio Canada informed me that they had made a radio version of *If This is a Man*, and they sought my advice on some details: soon after, the script and a recorded tape arrived. Never, perhaps, had I received such a welcome gift. Not only had they done an excellent job, but for me it was a real revelation. The authors of the script, far off in time and space, and whose experience was very different from my own, had brought out of the book everything I had enclosed within it, and something more. It was a spoken 'meditation', of high technical and dramatic quality and at the same time punctiliously faithful to the reality that had been. They had understood full well the importance in the camp of a lack of communication, exacerbated by the lack of a common language, and they had bravely set their work within the framework of the theme of the Tower of Babel and the confusion of languages:

> We believe that even for the listener who understands only English, this use of other languages will not present any obstacle to understanding . . .. But even when [the sense] is not immediately evident, when we find ourselves groping for a moment in puzzlement at a foreign and incomprehensible line, that is when we penetrate most deeply into the experience of the author, because this isolation is a fundamental part of his suffering. His suffering, and that of all the prisoners, sprang from the deliberate attempt to expel them from the human community, to wipe out their identity, to reduce them from men to things.

The enterprise, its result and the medium of the radio, which was new to me, all filled me with enthusiasm, and a few months later I offered Rai an Italian adaptation of the play, which I had written not just retranslating the Canadian version but developing the episodes which seemed to me most appropriate and keeping, as far as possible, the technique of multilingual dialogue which seemed to me of the utmost importance.

The idea that the book could give birth to a theatre version came from my friend, Pieralberto Marché. At first I resisted his suggestion, for it seemed to me that *If This is a Man* had already shed its skin too many times and been cooked in too many different sauces, and I was afraid I would weary the public. I was also afraid of the theatre itself, for I knew too little about it, either as spectator or as reader, to feel comfortable with the enterprise. The reading public, even the public which listens to the radio, is far off, hidden, anonymous, while the theatre audience is right there looking at you, lying in wait for you, judging you.

But on the other hand it meant telling the story once more, and telling it in the most immediate way, bringing back to life, inflicting our experience, ours and that of our lost comrades, on a different and much wider audience. I could see them, judge their response, put it to the test. And so, despite my doubts and the obvious dangers, and a certain sense of overcome reluctance, I agreed to put the concentration camp on the stage, and Marché and I set to work.

We tried to say everything, and at the same time not to overload it. The material we were dealing with was already burning hot, and our job was to decant it, channel it, to bring out its civil and universal significance, to guide the spectator to a conclusion and a verdict without shouting it in his ears, without handing it to him on a plate. This is why, for example, the SS from the camp never appear on stage, and for the same reason we focused on the marginal episodes and aspects of life in the camps, moments of relief, of reflection, of dream and refuge, and for each and every character we tried to keep his original human essence, even where it was worn down by the permanent conflict with the savage and inhuman environment of the camps.

Note to the theatre version of *If This is a Man*, Einaudi, Turin 1966, pp. 5–8

10   Preface to L. Poliakov's *Auschwitz*

Almost a quarter of a century after the liberation of the camps, we still cannot read their history today with a dispassionate spirit. Each year that passes serves to define and broaden the historical proportions of the phenomenon; it is now clear to the conscience of the great majority of people that together with nuclear arms, the extermination camps of the Third Reich, which laid waste a civilization and gave rise to an incalculable amount of pain and death, constitute the dark centre of contemporary history.

Everything, or almost everything, is now known about the 'what', even the most obscure details of camp organization, because even the diligence of the defeated Nazis in destroying all traces was not enough. But little is still known about the 'why'; the recent or distant causes and motives that spawned a gigantic death factory in this civilized continent of ours, acting with atrocious efficiency right up to the German collapse, remain an enigma. The surprise of the Allied troops who first penetrated, into that subhuman world, shaken and disbelieving, has not abated. The explanations put forward by historians, sociologists and psychologists can be acute and ingenious, but none of them is fully satisfactory.

It is no reproach to the diligence and documentary skill of Poliakov, both of which are beyond doubt, to observe that the work of his we present here does not resolve this enigma. In the chapter 'Auschwitz and Germany', the author himself indicates as much, and besides no essay, no treatise, could resolve the problem, because what happened at Auschwitz cannot be understood – indeed perhaps it should *not* be understood. Let me explain what I mean: to 'understand' (*comprendere*) a human proposition or action means, etymologically as well, to contain it, contain the subject of the action, put ourselves in his place, identify with him. But here we will never succeed, and no normal man will ever succeed, in identifying ourselves, even for a moment, with the disgusting specimens of the human race (Himmler, Goering, Goebbels, Eichmann, Höss and many others) here so abundantly quoted, and this is another reason why these pages are so disturbing. They disturb us, and at the same time bring us relief, because it is right and desirable that the words of these people, and unfortunately their works too, should no longer be comprehensible to us. They must not be comprehensible, for they are words and works outside of humanity, indeed against humanity, without historical precedent, barely comparable to the worst cruelties of the biological struggle for survival. War can be seen as part of this struggle, but Auschwitz has nothing to do with war, it is not an episode of war, nor is it war in its extreme form. War is a sad fact that has always existed. It is despicable, but it is in us, an archetype, its seed present in Cain's crime, in every conflict between individuals. It is an extension of anger, and who does not know anger, who has not felt it in himself, sometimes repressed, sometimes mature and pleasurable?

But in Auschwitz there is no anger. Auschwitz is not in us, it is not an archetype; it is outside of man. The authors of Auschwitz, who are introduced to us here, are not in the grip of anger or delirium: they are diligent, calm, vulgar and flat; their discussions, declarations and observations, even when they are posthumous, are empty and cold. We cannot understand them, and the effort to understand them, to go back to their source, appears to us vain and sterile. We should not hope for the early appearance of a man capable of commenting on them, of showing us how, at the heart of our Europe and our century, the commandment 'Thou shalt not kill' has been turned upside down.

And yet every civilized man needs to know that Auschwitz existed, and what was done there. If it is impossible to understand, it is necessary to know. In this sense Poliakov's vast work of history is necessary, especially this collection of documents, which is its compendium. Auschwitz is outside of us, but it is all around us, in the air. The plague has died away, but the infection still lingers and it would be foolish to deny it. In this book the signs of the infection are described: rejection of human solidarity, obtuse and cynical indifference to the suffering of others, abdication of the intellect and of moral sense to the principle of authority, and above all, at the root of everything, a sweeping tide of cowardice, a colossal cowardice which masks itself as warring virtue, love of country and faith in an idea. It is impossible to read without despondent surprise the abject and servile voices cited here: Stark, physicist and Nobel laureate; Heidegger, philosopher and Sartre's teacher; Cardinal Faulhaber, supreme Catholic authority in Germany.

The plague has died away, but Bormann and Dr Mengele live undisturbed in South America; Austro-German courts pile up scandalous absolutions and semi-absolutions; Globke enjoys a dignified retirement after long years as secretary to Adenauer; and deportations and torture have reappeared in Algeria, in Stalin's Russia and elsewhere; in Vietnam an entire people is threatened with destruction.

For as long as all this happens around us, the reading of these bitter pages is a duty for all. They arouse in us a sense of bewilderment, despair and retrospective fury, but they are vital nourishment for anyone who sets out to watch over his own conscience and the conscience of his country.

From L. Poliakov, *Auschwitz*, Ventro, Rome 1968, pp. 9–11

11   To the Young: Preface to *If This is a Man*

When this book was written, in 1946, there was much that was not yet known about the concentration camps. We did not know that in Auschwitz alone millions of men, women and children were exterminated with scientific meticulousness. Not only their belongings and their clothes were 'utilized', but also their bones, their teeth, even their hair (seven tonnes of it were found when the camps were liberated). Nor was it known that the number of victims of the entire concentration camp system ran to nine or ten million. Above all, it was not known that Nazi Germany, and alongside her all the occupied countries, including Italy, were a single monstrous web of slave camps. A geographical map of Europe at that time is enough to make your head spin. In Germany alone, the real extermination camps (in other words the antechambers of death, as described in this book) numbered in the hundreds, and to these we should add the thousands of camps belonging to other categories. We should remember, for example, that six hundred thousand Italian soldiers were interned. According to an estimate by Shirer in *The Story of the Third Reich* in 1944, the number of forced labourers in Germany was at least as high as nine million.

This same book shows the close and binding relationship between German heavy industry and the camp administration. It was certainly no accident that the area around Auschwitz came to be chosen to set up the main sites of the enormous Buna plants. It was a matter of a return to a Pharaonic economy and simultaneously a sensible planning decision; it made self-evident good sense to place the great factories and the slave camps side by side.

The camps were not, then, a marginal or additional phenomenon. German industry was founded on the camps, which were fundamental institutions of Fascist Europe, and indeed the Nazi authorities made no secret of the fact that in the event of an Axis victory the system would be not only maintained, but perfected and extended. A New Order was being planned, on an 'aristocratic' basis: on the one hand a dominant class made up of the People of the Masters (in other words the Germans themselves), and on the other an endless horde of slaves, from the Atlantic to the Urals, who would work and obey. It would have been the full realization of Fascism: the consecration of privilege, the definitive establishment of non-equality and non-liberty.

Now, Fascism did not win, but was swept away, in Italy and in Germany, by the war which it had itself brought about. The two countries rose up renewed out of the ruins, and began a painful reconstruction. The world learnt with disbelieving horror of the existence of 'death factories' in Auschwitz, Dachau, Mauthausen, Buchenwald, and at the same time was relieved by the thought that the concentration camp was dead, that the whole thing was a monster belonging to the past, a tragic but unique convulsion, the fault of a single man, Hitler, and Hitler was dead, and his bloody empire had collapsed with him.

Almost a quarter of a century has gone by. Now we look around us, and uneasily we note that perhaps our relief was premature. No, there are no gas chambers now, no cremation ovens, but there are concentration camps in Greece, in the Soviet Union, in Vietnam, in Brazil. There are, in almost every country, prisons, young offenders' institutions, psychiatric hospitals in which, as in Auschwitz, man loses his name and his face, all dignity and all hope. Above all, Fascism has not died. In some countries it has consolidated, in others it cautiously awaits its chance: it has never ceased promising the world a New Order. It has never repudiated the Nazi concentration camps, even if it frequently dares to cast doubt on their reality. Books like this one can no longer be read today with the same serenity with which we study testimony of past history. As Brecht wrote, 'the matrix which gave birth to this monster is still fertile'.

Precisely for that reason, and because I do not believe that the reverence we owe young people should lead us to be silent on the errors of our generation, I willingly agreed to edit a school edition of *If This is a Man*. I will be happy to know that just one of its new readers will understand the risks along a path that begins with nationalist fanaticism and the renunciation of reason.

From *Se questo è un uomo*, series 'Letture per la scuola media', Einaudi, Turin 1973, pp. 5–7

12 A Past We Thought Would Never Return

It is now twenty-nine years since the concentration camps were liberated. If somebody had predicted at that moment that the free world, into which we were about to be absorbed once more, would be less than perfect, we would not have believed him. It would have seemed an absurdity, a hypothesis so foolish as to not be worth taking into consideration.

It was a naive dream, but a dream we all shared. Our experience would have seemed to us completely pointless, and hence all the more cruel, while the deaths of our comrades would have seemed even more unjust, had we been able to foresee that the Fascism we fought against, which stripped us of everything as slaves and marked us as beasts of burden, was defeated but not dead, and was to transplant itself from country to country. Our condition as lifelong prisoners, condemned without trial to an existence of hunger, beatings, cold and hard labour, then finally to death by gas like so many rats, was in itself so unjust that, we thought, it would easily discredit Nazism and Fascism once and for all, demonstrating its horrors just as theorems demonstrate geometrical truths: indeed, it would sweep it away for generations to come, perhaps for ever.

Only those who did not wish to see, would not see. Testimonies were so abundant and eloquent that every thinking person should realize that what was called the universe of the camps, in Nazi Germany and across occupied and allied countries, was hardly just a marginal or additional phenomenon, but the very essence of Fascism, its crowning glory, its ultimate and definitive realization. At the cost of repeating things already widely written about, and to which an impressive bulk of documentation bears witness, I believe we need to remind ourselves as to the nature and the scope of the phenomenon of the concentration camp.

The first concentration camps, about fifty of them, were set up as early as 1933, as soon as the Nazis came to power. These were abandoned barracks and factories where political opponents to Nazism were hurriedly imprisoned. They were subjected to a regime of inhuman torture, at the whim of individual commandants. For the moment the aim was simply to spread terror and decapitate any party or movement which tried to oppose the new regime. But soon order prevailed. Of the first 'primitive' camps only Dachau and Oranienburg survived, and by 1934 they were already institutions destined to last, housing several thousand prisoners. Acts of individual bestiality were overtaken by a coldly organized regime of repression and collective suppression.

By 1936–37 the camps had begun to proliferate. The commandants, all from the SS, were specially trained, and groups of prisoners were deported to various regions of Germany and then to Austria where, following a precise plan, they were made to erect the new barbed wire that surrounded them: and thus Buchenwald, Ravensbrück, Mauthausen and many other camps came into being.

By 1939, at the start of the war, there were about one hundred camps. But with the lightning occupation of Poland, the Third Reich suddenly found that it had in its hands, to use Eichmann's expression, 'the biological wellsprings of Judaism', and a second purpose emerged for the camps. Maidanek, Treblinka and then Auschwitz were rapidly constructed, and these were something new, something never seen in the history of humanity. They were no longer a cruel version of jail in which political opponents are made to suffer and die, but inverted factories; trains heavily laden with human beings went in each day, and all that came out was the ashes of their bodies, their hair, the gold of their teeth.

After various experiments, the most 'profitable' method was found, and Commandant Höss boasts of it in his memoirs: the gas chambers, in which upwards of a thousand human beings at a time did not even need to be absorbed into the camp, but were killed using cyanide; and the crematorium ovens, in which their bodies were then turned to ash. Auschwitz alone could destroy ten thousand lives in a single day, and could cope with more than thirty thousand when necessary.

But the war showed no sign of ending; it devoured men on every front, and the workforce necessary for the German war effort was becoming ever more scarce. A conflict emerged between the SS, who insisted on prosecuting the massacre with blind fanaticism, and industry, which needed workers. A compromise was reached: the fittest people from each convoy, men and women, would work to the point of exhaustion, while others (the less strong, the old, children) would go 'through the chimney'. This was the third purpose to which the camps could be put, and at the same time it was a model for the New Order which Nazis and Fascists wanted to impose in Europe. It was a New Order with an 'aristocratic' basis: on one side the People of the Masters, in other words the ruling class, who organize and command, and on the other side endless hordes of slaves, from the Atlantic to the Urals, whose role is to work and obey.

This would have been the full and complete realization of Fascism, of its order and its hierarchy: the consecration of privilege, of non-equality, of non-liberty. I do not believe that in any part of the world today there are gas chambers or crematorium ovens, but we can only be alarmed when we read that the first goal of the Colonels in Greece and of the Generals in Chile was to set up enormous concentration camps, at Yaros and at Dawson. And in almost every country today there are prisons, correctional institutions and hospitals where all too frequently, as in Auschwitz, man loses his name and his face, his dignity and hope.

The very brutality of our experience in the camps turned us into accusers rather than judges, but it both disgusts us and gives us much to think about when we see the seeds of Fascism taking hold in those same countries (not their peoples) who are owed the world's gratitude for the defeat of Nazifascism. In the Soviet Union, there are still work camps from which people emerge humiliated and broken. Indiscriminate bombing has returned in Vietnam. Torture is practised in all the countries of South America where useful governments are propped up by the United States.

Every age has its own Fascism, and we see the warning signs wherever the concentration of power denies citizens the possibility and the means of expressing and acting on their own will. There are many ways of reaching this point, not just through the terror of police intimidation, but by denying and distorting information, by undermining systems of justice, by paralysing the education system, and by spreading in a myriad subtle ways nostalgia for a world where order reigned, and where the security of the privileged few depended on the forced labour and the forced silence of the many.

In *Corriere della Sera*, 8 May 1974

13   Preface to J. Presser's *The Night of the Girondins*

I came across this tale completely by chance, a few years ago. I read it, reread it a number of times, and it has stayed in my mind ever since. Perhaps it would be worth considering why: the reasons we become attached to a particular book can be many, some of them decipherable and rational, others deep and obscure.

I do not think it has to be with how the story is narrated. It is narrated in uneven fashion: some pages are skilfully done, while others display a certain intellectualism, the business of literature a little overburdened by clever cunning and artfulness. Nonetheless, it is plainly a true account, point by point, episode by episode (and this is confirmed by a number of other sources, and whoever was at Auschwitz encounters here the 'passenger' survivors of the Westerbork train), such that despite its novelistic style it has the character of a historical document. But this is not its only importance.

This brief work is one of the few to portray Western European Judaism with literary dignity. While there is an abundant and glorious

literature on Eastern, Ashkenazi Judaism, its Western branch, profoundly integrated into the bourgeois cultures of Germany, France,
Holland and Italy, has made a great and generous contribution
to these cultures but has rarely portrayed itself. It is a Judaism
conditioned by dispersal and therefore unified only to a small degree,
and it is so intertwined with the culture of the host country that, as
we know, it no longer even has its own language. It favoured
Enlightenment in the age of Enlightenment, it was romantic with
Romanticism, liberal, socialist, bourgeois, nationalist: through all the
metamorphoses wrought by time and place, it nonetheless kept some
features of its own, reproduced in this book.

The Western Jew, caught between and fought over by the two poles
of loyalty and assimilation, is in a perennial identity crisis, and this is
the source of his equally perennial neurosis, his adaptability and his
sharpness. The figure of the Jew content with his Jewishness, whose
Judaism is enough for him (Shalom Aleichem's immortal Tevye the
milkman), is rare if not absent in the West.

This is a tale about an identity crisis, which is so intense that the
protagonist finds himself split into two. Within him live 'I', Jacques,
assimilated, tied to the land of Holland but not to the Dutch people, a
versatile and decadent intellectual, emotionally immature, politically
suspect, morally a nonentity; and 'I', Jacob, brought back from the past
through the work and the example of Rabbi Hirsch, who draws
strength from the Jewish roots he has ignored and denied until now,
and who sacrifices himself to save from nothingness the Book in
which Jacques no longer believes. How many European Jews have not
been through something similar? How many have not discovered, in
time of need, a support and moral framework precisely in the Jewish
culture which during years of peace seemed outmoded and outdated?
Hirsch says as much to Jacques: barbed wire is a wire that binds, and
binds tightly. I do not mean by this that a return to one's origins is the
only path to health, but it is certainly one of them.

Another aspect that lends weight to this tale is its irreverent free-
thinking. On some chilling pages the author seems indeed to participate in the 'Jews' self-hatred' which his father Henriques attributes to
his son and wife, and which has sprouted many anti-Semitic Jews in
Western Europe, such as Weininger, here quoted and admired by
Georg Cohn. To be reminded that at Westerbork a man such as Cohn
lived and acted burns like cauterized skin and is worthy of comment.
Such individuals did exist, and certainly still exist among us in a
virtual state: under normal conditions they are unrecognizable (Cohn

wanted to be a banker) but a pitiless persecution causes them to develop, bringing them to light and to power. It is naive, absurd and historically false to claim that a devilish system such as National Socialism sanctifies its victims: on the contrary, it degrades and defiles them, assimilates them to itself, all the more so when they are willing, white and devoid of political and moral backbone. Cohn is hateful, monstrous and deserving of punishment, but his crime is the reflection of another much more serious and widespread crime.

It is no accident that in the last few years, in Italy and abroad, books have been published such as *Menschen in Auschwitz* by H. Langbein (not yet translated into Italian) and Gitta Sereny's *Into That Darkness*. There are a number of signs to suggest that the time has come to explore the space that separates the victims from the executioner, and to do it with a lighter touch and a less troubled spirit than has been done, for example, in some well-known recent films. Only a Manichean rhetoric can maintain that this space is empty: it is not; it is sprinkled with sordid, wretched and pathetic figures (sometimes they possess all three qualities simultaneously), whom we are obliged to get to know if we wish to know the human species, if we wish to defend our souls were a similar trial to return amongst us.

Evil is contagious. The man who is a non-man dehumanizes others, every crime radiates outwards and takes root all around, corrupting consciences and surrounding itself with accomplices won over by fear or seduction (like Suasso) to the opposite camp. It is typical of a criminal regime such as Nazism to undermine and confuse our capacity for judgement. Is somebody who talks under torture guilty? Someone who kills in order not to be killed? Or the soldier on the Russian front who cannot desert? Where should we draw the line that cuts into two the empty space I was speaking of, and what separates the weak from the wicked? Can Cohn be judged?

Well, the sense of the book is that Cohn can be judged. His speech about the 'leaking ship' is fraudulent, as is his claim (how many times have we heard it!) that 'If I didn't do it someone else would, and worse than me.' We *have* to refuse, we always can, in every situation, maybe by following the path of Miss Wolfson. Those who do not refuse (but they have to refuse right from the start, not put their hands to the machine) end up by giving in to the seduction of moving over to the other side: there they will find, at best, a deceptive gratification and a destructive salvation.

Cohn is guilty, but he has one mitigating characteristic: the generalized awareness that in the face of violence we should not yield, that we should resist, came later, but was not the case at the time. The imperative to resist began with the resistance and with the global tragedy of the Second World War. Before that, it was the precious patrimony of just a few. Nor does it belong to everybody even today, but today all of us have ears.

It is not necessarily the case that when we become fond of a book, or a person, we cannot see their defects. This book has faults, perhaps even serious ones. The style is tentative, oscillating between emotion and *badinage*. We often have the impression that the author Presser is not immune from the baroque literariness of his alter ego Henriques, with his mania for reeling off quotations even at the point of death. At times, in some harrowing moments, we find self-satisfaction where we would expect to find reticence and silence. All in all it is a questionable book, scandalous perhaps, but it is good that scandals come out because they provoke discussion and shine a clear light into our conscience.

From J. Presser, *La notte dei Girondini*, Adelphi, Milan 1976, pp. 11–15

14   Films and Swastikas

Do we really have to see the whole lot of them before we take a stand? By which I mean all the films whose posters show a naked woman against the background of a swastika? I do not think so; and besides, there is no sign of the phenomenon running out of steam. Its itinerary follows a classic path, beginning with a skilful cultural forgery, a work of art of reasonable level such as Liliana Cavani's *The Night Porter*; slipping down a few rungs we reach the more dubious craft of *Salon Kitty*, and then the doors are flung open to the cheapest brands, the plethora of Nazi-porn films.

To be sure, we cannot expect much from cinema producers. For the most part they are nothing more than short-sighted businessmen, happy enough if they strike it lucky every three or four years so they can pay off their debts (if they are lucky). Little else matters to them. Many of them make a living just by making porn films. This is unfortunate, but there is little to be done about it. It's a foolproof business: they are not difficult to make, they cost very little and bring good returns, for they have their own faithful viewing public made up of both young and old men who are timid, inhibited and frustrated.

In the short term there is nothing to be done. Invoking censorship would mean putting ourselves in the hands of inept and corrupt judges, breathing new life into a dangerous mechanism. We already have censorship, but it confiscates only films that are intelligent, if at times questionable. Obscene films, as long as they are idiotic, present no problem.

What is to be done? The best thing would be a boycott by the public. A sensible sex education policy in schools should have some result, but that would take another generation. For the moment all we can do is resign ourselves.

But please, all you cinema producers, leave the women's camps alone. They are not a proper subject for you, nor even for your most devoted clients, who are easy enough to please. They want the image of an object-woman since they can't have her in flesh and blood, but they have no interest in the context of the film. The most demanding of them, maybe, wish to be a spectator, for free or almost for free, at the sight of a virgin being tortured, but it's just a minor detail to them whether the perpetrator is a Nazi rather than a Saracen, a Philistine, or a Carthaginian. One is as good as the other, as long as the substance is there.

No, the women's concentration camps are not indispensable to you: you can leave them alone, and not be any the worse off for it. Besides, they are not a congenial subject for your boorish directors. Giuliana Tedeschi, who was there, has said it clearly. They were not back-street sex shows. People suffered there, yes, but in silence, and the women were not beautiful and they did not arouse desire; rather, they aroused infinite compassion, like defenceless animals.

As for the SS, most of them were not monsters, nor idiotic lechers, nor perverted dandies. They were functionaries of the State, more pedantic than brutal, and largely insensible to the daily horror amidst which they lived, and to which they quickly seemed to accustom themselves; not least because in accepting to guard the concentration camps, they avoided being sent to 'cover themselves in glory' on the Russian front. All in all, they were not elegant, stylish wild beasts but vulgar and cowardly little men. If they accepted this dismal profession they, too, must have been mentally damaged, as inhibited and as coarse as your clients. And I have often thought that they would have liked your porno-swastika movies.

La Stampa, 12 February 1977

15   Letter to Lattanzio: 'Resign'

Dear Minister,[*]
I am a survivor of Auschwitz, and I therefore know a good deal about Nazism: I know it from the inside, and I feel a deep revulsion for its followers, whether dead or alive. This includes Kappler. When I consider what he did (and I am thinking above all of the macabre gold trick in Rome), it seems to me that all attempts at excuses become futile. He was 'only' following orders: true, but he followed them willingly, and anyway, the mere fact of applying for entry into the SS placed him immediately in the position of someone who obeys without question. There were others more guilty than he was, as Giorgio Bocca has pointed out: true, and they, like him, should have been made to pay with life imprisonment, and only a distracted or perverted system of justice could have absolved them or sentenced them to anything less. He is sick: he should have been given medical treatment, and indeed he was, but no system of justice absolves the sick. Do you really think that Colonel Kappler ever bothered to find out if any of those on his list of victims was sick? He showed remorse: but to be satisfied with the verbal declarations of remorse of such a man is so ingenuous that even an ingenuous man like myself could not believe him, as indeed I did not believe him, and the facts have shown that I was right.

[*] Vito Lattanzio was Minister of Defence when Herbert Kappler escaped from the military hospital of Celio. Kappler (1907–1978), the former SS Colonel and head of the Gestapo in Rome, was responsible for the Ardeatine Caves massacre in October 1943, in which 335 Italians were shot in reprisal for guerilla action against German soldiers, following the fall of Mussolini. Kappler chose the victims along with Pietro Caruso, the Roman Chief of Police; Caruso was executed by the Italians in September 1944. Kappler helped organize the rescue of Mussolini by the SS, and was responsible for the deportation of about ten thousand Jews from Rome to concentration camps, after extorting their gold from them. After the war Kappler was handed over to the Italian authorities by the British. Tried by an Italian military tribunal, he was sentenced to life imprisonment. In 1977, after pressure from the government in Bonn, Kappler was transferred from the prison of Gaeta to the military hospital from which he escaped a few months later. The manner of his escape was never clarified. (Translator's note)

I therefore feel revulsion for Kappler. I would not be inclined to pardon him if it was within my power, and I am convinced that Gaeta was the right place for him. That said, I would like to add that his flight adds nothing to his guilt: it is natural for a prisoner to attempt to escape, as anyone who has ever been a prisoner (whether rightly or wrongly) knows full well. His flight adds considerably, however, to your burden of responsibility, Minister. The case of Kappler has been a topic of discussion recently: he had not been forgotten. You had most certainly given or confirmed orders for his custody, but you must be aware that not even a corporal, when his orders are not carried out, can get out of trouble by saying 'I gave the order, though'. A corporal or a general are subject to punishment. A minister, no: a minister resigns.

You should resign, Minister, even if you feel yourself innocent. Resign out of a sense of piety, of decency, of charity towards your country, your Party, and yourself. Of the many illnesses to afflict us, the most serious is the refusal to accept responsibility. Show us that you know this; let us see that you know that in any hierarchy the responsibility of the man lower down does not absolve the responsibility of the man above him. Resign, quickly and discreetly; do not miss this opportunity to restore your own dignity and that of the State.

La Stampa, 8 September 1977

16   Women to the Slaughter

When David Rousset coined the now famous term *l'univers concentrationnaire*, he knew what he was doing. It was indeed a matter of an endless and multiple universe, which even today has not been fully explored. In Italy at least, this book fills a gap, that of the deportation of women; it forms a significant triad with Nuto Revelli's *Il mondo dei vinti* ('The World of the Defeated') and Bianca Guidetti Serra's *Compagne* ('Comrades'), which also consist of testimonies left to speak for themselves. In all three books we hear the subdued and solemn voices of those who have acted and borne suffering with astonishing strength, those who have been modestly silent for decades, those who have not been able to speak.

The structure of the book is complex. There are two authors, Lidia Beccaria Rolfi and Anna Maria Bruzzone. It is Lidia, herself an ex-deportee, who offers the first testimony, which is also the longest and fullest, followed by the accounts of four other Italian women who were political deportees. Bruzzone is responsible for the dense and terse introduction, and she also edited the volume.

All these witnesses were deported to Ravensbrück, as were by and large nearly all the women 'politicals' from Nazi-occupied countries. This, indeed, was why Ravensbrück had been set up. Created out of nothing, it was an artificial city not to be found in any atlas, either then or now. It was the fruit of a monstrous plan, the only camp populated exclusively by women, who right from the start were 'hired out' by the SS to war industries and local farms as if they were so many domestic beasts. On page 16 there is a horrific piece of detailed accounting. How much money can be made from a human forced to work until dropping dead of exhaustion? The profit (according to SS sources) is on average 1631 marks, plus whatever 'can be gained from utilizing bones and ashes'.

The comparison to domestic animals is not a chance one, nor is it by chance that women deportees were treated deliberately more harshly than the men. In Nazi ideology any equivalence between men and women is deplored as decadent and bourgeois, and on this it is illuminating to read a little book which I suspect is no longer to be found today, *Educazione alla morte* ('Education to Death') by Zeimer, published in London (though in Italian) in 1944, and whose subtitle is *Come creare un nazista* ('How to Create a Nazi'). This book is a lucid compendium of how young men and women respectively were brought up and educated in Hitler's Germany.

The first duty of the German man was to fight and die for the Fatherland; that of the German woman was to sweeten the warrior's repose and to produce new generations of fighters. The foreign woman, especially if she is a presumed enemy or 'of inferior race', is of no use other than as a beast of burden. When the profit to be gained from her declines or ceases, there is the crematorium, and her ashes, mixed with the contents of the black pits of the camps, were distributed to agricultural enterprises.

All the witnesses in the book have benefited from their long silence. Lidia addresses this explicity on the last page of her account. She hesitated to tell her tale; her experience was too inhuman to be accepted by a normal listener; she feared she would not be believed; she felt around herself a 'wall' of incomprehension and facile pity. As an eighteen-year-old schoolmistress in a valley near Cuneo, nurtured in the school of Fascist rhetoric, she quickly understood the tragedy of the Albanian and Russian fronts, and after the armistice she naturally became a partisan.

After the trauma of arrest, the Carceri Nuove prison and the sealed freight car, this young provincial girl, with no political experience, with no faithful companions and no knowledge of languages, was tossed into the citadel of Ravensbrück, and it seemed to her she had 'plunged into another planet': she had not yet had either the time or the means to understand that this horrendous alienation is the ultimate aim of the concentration city, 'conceived, worked out and structured precisely in order to violate the person, to humiliate her, destroy her, turn her into an animal'.

But she was young, intelligent and endowed with a miraculous will to resist, to understand, to unravel the reasoning. She learned a little French, she got her bearings, she succeeded in making the great leap: from sub-proletarian, from 'Schmizstück' ('piece of filth', in the crude language of the camp, the term for women at their last gasp, destined to swift collapse through hunger, humiliation and ill-treatment) to 'proletarian', in other words, a worker in the Siemens factory.

This was the first step towards salvation. The second, and definitive, step was meeting Monique, an extraordinary character, lucid and tough, an expert French 'political', who took on the task of the 'political and social education' of the young Italian woman, *constructed* her, obliged her to study, to use her brain, explained to her 'why washing oneself. . . is part of the Resistance in the camps'. Monique transformed the victim into a fighter, alert and aware, capable of registering the horrors amidst which she was living, to glimpse a logic in it, the paranoid logic of profit above all else, of unbridled exploitation, of man reduced to a tool. I think that on this no reader will ever be able to forget the atrocious pages on the children born in Ravensbrück (from page 48 onwards), and the schoolmistress from Val Varaita became the historian of Ravensbrück. Ravensbrück was her university.

The other testimonies are shorter and more personal. As is the common experience of survivors, each woman lived through the camp in a different way. Bianca Paganini, a young anti-Fascist from La Spezia with Catholic roots, strenuously refused any compromise, yet glimpsed (significantly) signs of piety in the desperate women who surrounded her, and she herself felt pity for the German politicals. Her faith, which upheld her in the early days, largely collapsed when she saw the piles of dead bodies: 'it was difficult to come back to my faith: but little by little, I have managed it.'

Livia Borsi, class of 1902, socialist 'by birth' (she is the daughter of a docker in Genoa, illiterate but advanced in his views), was sustained before, during and after imprisonment by a natural, almost savage, energy which enabled her to insert herself into the savage life of the camp and to survive. She could bear everything, almost naturally, in her words there is no trace of self-pity, as if she drew strength from ancient experience of struggle. Generous and outgoing, she wept and sang, suffered and helped those who were suffering more than she was, 'invented' the sabotage of the work being done by the Germans; at no moment did she come close to collapse or surrender.

The final testimony, in the two voices of the Baroncini sisters, is perhaps the most moving. The entire family was deported, father, mother, and three daughters, and in the ingenuous and courageous words of the only two survivors surfaces the most atrocious grief, the grief of seeing members of your family die in front of you, day by day, beyond any possible help or succour.

This book is a timely confirmation of the dishonest and scandalous commercial operation that floods screens with Nazi sex films, and shows how little even the least shameless of them reflects the real condition of women in the camps. No, the female deportees were not sex objects. At best they were work animals driven to exhaustion; at worst, they were ephemeral 'pieces of filth'. This is confirmed by the very few women whose strength, intelligence and good fortune have made it possible for them to bear witness.

La Stampa, 10 March 1978

17   So that the SS do not Return

The violence we breathe in the air around us these days must not make us forget the violence of a recent past, which devastated Europe under the sinister sign of the swastika and the runic double S: for violence begets violence, and there is no such thing as good violence to counteract bad violence. I do not think we can fully understand the events of the last few months in Germany (but also in Italy!) if we ignore the fact that in 1977 alone, there were at least thirty rallies of ex-members of the SS corps – and this not only in all corners of Federal Germany, but in France, and in the very places covered in the blood of their actions. In Italy, too, there have been rallies, in Varna, near Bressanone.

We have fragments of information about an organization called the Hiag, the Cooperative of Mutual Help, the pious screen behind which ex-SS hide, duly organized into armed groups. Because a Hiag exists, in the Germany of Berufsverbot, in the Germany of prosperity, and it seems that nobody, or almost nobody, has any objection to this, even though Hiag lies behind the desecration of Jewish cemeteries, the threatening swastikas on the walls, the attacks on democratic institutions, in Germany and elsewhere.

The German government does not seem to realize the potential consequences of a renewed presence of Nazi poison in the body of the country, whether through the direct contagion of terrorist formations recruited amongst newer ranks, or the radicalization of groups who nominally declare themselves to be on the left.

In the light of this intolerable situation, European anti-Fascist organizations have launched an appeal from Brussels, signed by 84 associations of ex-deportees, partisans, those who resisted or were victims of the SS in 21 countries (including Israel and the countries of the Eastern bloc), requesting the dissolution of associations of SS veterans, under the terms of the Constitution of West Germany.

A smaller international committee, with Italy represented by the National Association of ex-deportees (Aned), has also decided to hold a large demonstration in Cologne on 22 April. This will naturally be attended by thousands of anti-Fascist Germans too: indeed, this initiative (the first to gather on German soil all the anti-Fascists of Europe) does not put itself forward as any kind of antithesis; rather, it sets out to recognize the merits of all those Germans who managed to stay faithful to the democratic ideal even amongst the shadows of Nazism, a conviction paid for with a heavy tribute of blood.

But it also aims to remind the current German government of the promises made time and again by all the Chancellors and all the presidents of West Germany: that never again, in no shape or form, will Nazism be reborn on German soil. We thus invite those in power to take some concrete political and legislative action.

Anti-Fascists are not asking for sanctions against individual veterans of the SS, but are demanding that their associations be eliminated from the life of the country, so that they no longer have a voice and can no longer pollute new generations with their 'messages'. No European has forgotten that the massacres of Marzabotto, Boves, Lidice, Oradour, of the Fosse Ardeatine, were the work of the SS, nor that the SS were entrusted with the task of running the forced labour camps from which they extracted enormous gain, as well as the extermination camps with their abominable machinery and their millions of dead. And the SS who still survive should stop bragging about all of this.

La Stampa, 20 April 1978

18   It Began with *Kristallnacht*

Probably only a few young people have read or heard about what happened in Germany exactly forty years ago. As soon as he reached power in January 1933, Hitler lost no time in showing his real character, as well as that of his regime. After just two months, Dachau, the first concentration camp, was already in existence; many others were to follow, with the purpose of eliminating and terrorizing the political opponents of Nazism. After just eight months, the exclusion of Jews from state employment and from the cultural life of the country had already begun.

Like every other absolute power, Nazism needed an anti-power, an anti-State, on which to blame all evil and all woes, whether past or present, real or imagined, suffered by Germans. The Jews, defenceless and seen by many as 'other', were the ideal anti-State, the focus for the convergence of the nationalistic and Manichean fervour which Nazi propaganda kept alive and well in the country.

In September 1935 the Nuremberg Laws were published, defining with maniacal detail who could be considered a Jew, who a half-Jew, who a quarter-Jew. This was the year of the 'Law for the defence of German blood and German honour'. There followed a whole raft of legal impositions, some cruel, others openly derisory in nature, all aimed at demonstrating the official position of Nazism: the Jews may be a shadowy universal power, the incarnation of Satan, but here in Germany, in our hands, they are powerless and absurd.

From the age of six upwards they had to wear the yellow star on their chest. They could only sit on public benches which had *nur für Juden* written on them. All men had to be called Israel and all women Sara. The Jews were not allowed to have their cow mounted by the communal bull. There was a census of all Jewish assets in April 1938, and of the commercial enterprises they owned in June of the same year; this was the prologue to their total exclusion from economic life.

Young Germans were encouraged to feel a visceral hatred, a physical repugnance, for the Jew, destroyer of the world and of order, guilty of all crimes. German Jews felt themselves on the whole to be profoundly German, and they reacted to this blanket propaganda by withdrawing into a dignified abstention, reduced to a marginal life of poverty, sadness and fear. Many terrorist acts had already been perpetrated, an obvious consequence and interpretation of the hate propaganda, but these were haphazard affairs. What the Nazis now needed was a pretext to move from individual efforts to organized terror, and the pretext was soon found.

In October 1938 around 10,000 Jews of Polish nationality were brutally expelled from Germany: men, women and children were forced to camp in no man's land, in wretched conditions, until Poland took them in. The son of one of the refugees, Herschel Grynszpan, had for some time already found refuge in Paris. He was only seventeen years old, a mystic and something of a hothead. Feeling called upon to take vengeance, on 7 November he killed the first German he came across, an attaché in the German Embassy in Paris. This was the gesture the Germans were waiting for, confirmation of the thesis of an 'international Jewish plot' to the detriment of Germany, and the response was immediate. The staging and the script had been ready for some time; the only thing now was for the show to start.

On the night between 9 and 10 November a pogrom broke out all over Germany. Seven and a half thousand shops and warehouses belonging to Jews were damaged and looted, 815 were completely destroyed; 195 synagogues suffered the same fate; 36 Jews were killed and 20,000 arrested, chosen from amongst the economic elite. During the first few hours the aggressors were in uniform, but then they were swiftly sent home to change into normal clothes; they had misunderstood their instructions; indignation should burst forth from the people, and was supposed to be 'spontaneous'.

Everywhere, the police stood and watched. Firemen intervened only where the flames threatened 'Aryan' buildings or property. Local officials carried out individual variations on a theme. In Krumbach, near Augsburg, Jewish women were dragged to the synagogue and forced to take the rolls of the Law out of the Ark and stamp on them, and they had to commit this sacrilege and sing at the same time. Those who refused to do so were killed.

In Saarbrücken Jews were made to carry straw into the temple, sprinkle it with paraffin and set it alight. Some of the 'indignant' went beyond the set programme and started looting for themselves, and then the police intervened, but the courts sent them home with a risible sentence. This was not the case for those zealots (or brutes) who raped Jewish women: they were thrown out of the party and severely punished; not because of the violence inflicted on their victims, though, but for contaminating themselves by contravening the sacred law of blood.

Day after day the destruction raged, and at the end of the 'week of crystal' the streets of all the cities were covered in shards from the broken windows. This damage alone, to the glass from windows, amounted to five million marks, and was covered by insurance. Would the damage be paid for? The solution was found by Goering, and was quite simple: the insurance companies would pay the Jews, but the State would intervene and confiscate the lot.

To cap it all, a fine of one hundred million marks was imposed on the Union of Israelite communities. This was the same sordid nexus of violence, disdain and fraud which we saw five years later, in Rome, with the macabre trick of the fifty kilos of gold which the Jews were to deliver to Kappler to avert deportation: but just a few days later the manhunt began anyway (and the hunt for women, the sick, children) and more than a thousand Roman Jews were deported to the death camps.

Shirer, who was witness to this barbaric outbreak, is perhaps right to see here 'a foretaste of a fatal weakness which in the end was to drag the dictator, his regime and his nation to utter ruin', identifying thus the first signs of Hitler's megalomania, a sickness which never fails to strike those who exercise unchecked power, whether on large or small scale.

The *Kristallnacht* opened the eyes of many, most notably of the British Prime Minister Chamberlain, who was finally convinced, although by now it was too late, that Hitler was not a gentleman with whom one could come to an agreement. Unfortunately it did not open the eyes of all, either in Germany or in Italy: if it had, the entire world would have been spared the horrors of the Second World War, and perhaps we would be living in a better society.

La Stampa, 9 November 1978

19   Jean Améry, Philosopher and Suicide

The appalling episode of the 'Temple of the People', the collective suicide of 900 followers of a mystic-satanic sect, is today still incomprehensible, and perhaps will always be so, if by 'to comprehend' we mean to identify a motive. And anyway, each and every human action contains a kernel of incomprehensibility. If this were not the case, we would be in a position to foresee what our neighbour is going to do. Clearly we cannot do this, and perhaps it is just as well that we cannot. It is particularly difficult to understand why a person kills himself, since generally speaking the suicide himself is not fully aware, or else he supplies both himself and others with motives that are consciously or unconsciously altered.

News of the massacre at Georgetown appeared in the papers alongside another less clamorous item: the suicide of a cantankerous and solitary philosopher, Jean Améry. This event is, on the contrary, absolutely comprehensible, and has much to teach us. Jean Améry was not his original name but a pseudonym, or rather a new name, chosen by the young Austrian scholar Hans Mayer in order to indicate that he had been forced to give up his native identity. Hans had both Christian and Jewish ancestors, but he was Jewish enough to be defined as such by the Nuremberg Laws. He was totally assimilated: in his house they celebrated Christmas, and his memory of his father, who died in the First World War, was not that of a wise and bearded Jew but of an officer in the Imperial Army in the uniform of the Tyrolese Kaiserjäger.

The Nazis poured into Austria: Hans took refuge in Belgium and became Jean, but in 1940 the Nazi tide washed over Belgium too and Jean, a shy and introverted intellectual but conscious of his dignity, joined the Belgian resistance. He did not fight with them for long. He soon fell into the hands of the Gestapo. He was asked to reveal the names of his colleagues and leaders, or else face torture. He was no hero; if he had known he would have told, but he didn't know. They tied his hands behind his back and hung him by his wrists from a ceiling hook. After a few seconds his arms were dislocated, sticking upwards vertically, behind his back. The torturers carried on beating the hanging body with whips and straps, but Jean knew nothing; he could not even take refuge in betrayal. He recovered, but 'legally' he was Jewish, and was sent to Auschwitz-Monowitz where he lived a further eighteen months of terror.

Liberated in 1945, he returned to Belgium and settled there, but he had no country to call his own and he was oppressed by his past. He wrote cold, bitter essays, called *How much country does a man need?*, *On the necessity and impossibility of being a Jew*, *Torture*, *At the Mind's Limits*. The last of these is a heartfelt and desperate meditation on 'how much use it was' in the camps to be an intellectual. It was of very little use, concludes Améry, indeed it was positively harmful: the intellectual tended not to adjust, not to accept that impossible reality, even as he did not have the strength (unlike those who held fast to their faith) to oppose it actively or privately. They are pages that we read with an almost physical pain, the testimony of a man cast adrift for decades, until his stoic end.

Elsewhere, Améry wrote: ' "Hear, Israel" is of no interest to me: only "Hear, world", only this warning could I offer with passionate anger.' But also: 'As a Jew, I go round the world like a sick man afflicted with one of those illnesses which do not cause great suffering but which lead inevitably to death.' And finally, like an epitaph: 'The man who has been tortured remains tortured . . .. Whoever has suffered torment will no longer be able to find his way clearly in the world, the abomination of annihilation will never be extinguished. Trust in humanity, already fractured by the first slap in the face and then demolished by torture, can never be regained.'

No, the death of Jean Améry is not a surprise, and it is sad to think that torture, which had disappeared from Europe some centuries ago, made its reappearance in our century, and is gaining ground in a number of countries', 'for the right reasons', as if suffering deliberately inflicted can give birth to anything good. It is unbearable to think that while the torture Améry suffered weighed down on him right to his death, indeed was for him an interminable death, it is more than likely that his torturers are sitting down in an office or enjoying their retirement. And if they were interrogated (but who is there to interrogate them?) they would give the same old answer with a clear conscience: they were only following orders.

La Stampa, 7 December 1978

20   But We Were There

So the operation has been a success. It was not enough to read the twaddle written by Darquier de Pellepoix* in *l'Express* last November, it was not enough to grant the assassins-of-old space and a voice in respectable magazines so that they could preach their truth with impunity: that the millions of dead in the camps never died, that the Holocaust is a fairy story, that in Auschwitz the gas was used to kill nothing more than fleas. All of this was not enough; evidently the time is ripe, and from his university lectern Professor Robert Faurisson has aimed to set the world's mind at peace: no, Fascism and Nazism have been denigrated, tarnished, slandered. Let us speak no more of Auschwitz, it was all a charade: now we shall speak of the lie of Auschwitz. The Jews are crafty, they've always been crafty, so crafty that they have themselves made up a massacre that never happened in order to throw mud at innocent Nazis: so crafty that they

---

* From 1942 to 1944, Louis Darquier was the French cordinator of Vichy's anti-Jewish operations. Darquier assisted in the Nazi deportation of Jews and worked closely with the German Authorities in Paris. His administration was marked out by its brutality. (Translator's note)

themselves, *après coup*, built the gas chambers and crematoria in the camps.

I do not know who Professor Faurisson is. It is possible that he is a madman; he would not be the first professor to be insane. But there is another more likely hypothesis, which is that he was one of those guilty at the time, as Darquier was, or that he is the son or friend or supporter of those responsible, and that he is doing his utmost to exorcise a past which, despite the laxity we see today, weighs him down. We are very familiar with certain mental mechanisms: guilt is burdensome, uncomfortable at the least; in times now far off, in Italy and France, it was even dangerous. We begin by denying it in the courts, we deny it for decades, in public, then in private, then to ourselves, and hey presto, the spell has worked, black has become white, what was crooked is now straight, the dead are not dead, there is no assassin, there is no more guilt, indeed there never was any. Not only did I not commit the crime, but the crime itself no longer exists.

No, Professor, this is not the way. The dead were there, including women, including children: tens of thousands in Italy and France, millions in Poland and the Soviet Union, and it is not that easy to shake them off. It doesn't take a great deal of effort to find out, if you wish to find out. Go and ask the survivors: they are there even in France; hear from their lips what it is like to see your companions die around you one by one, to feel yourself dying day by day for one, two years; to live without hope in the shadow of the crematoria chimneys, to return (those who returned) to find your family destroyed. This is not the way to cleanse yourself of guilt, Professor. Even for someone speaking from a university lectern, the facts remain stubborn enemies. If you deny the massacre carried out by your friends of old, you need to explain to us how the seventeen million Jews in 1939 were reduced to eleven million by 1945. You have to say that hundreds of thousands of widows and orphans are lying. You have to say that each and every survivor is lying. Come and discuss this with us, Professor: you will find it harder than preaching nonsense to your ill-informed students. Ill-informed to the point of accepting everything you say? Did not one of them raise a hand in protest? And in France, what did the university authorities and judicial authorities do? Did they just let you, in denying the dead, kill them a second time?

Corriere della Sera, 3 January 1979

21   Concentration Camp at Italy's Door

Mondadori is about to publish a book full of shame and grief. The author is the Triestine Ferruccio Fölkel, and the title is *The Rice Mill of San Sabba – Trieste and the Atlantic Coast during the Nazi Occupation*. In the autumn of 1943 this rice mill, an old factory formerly used to lay out and dry rice, was taken over by a section of highly specialized senior and junior officers of the SS. These men were expert in the art of collective and secret assassination, starting with the German centres that practised euthanasia on the mentally feeble, and moving on to the total extermination camps in Poland.

One of them, for example, was Franz Stangl, who was personally responsible by his own admission for 600,000 deaths, and whose chilling statement we read in the book by Gitta Sereny, *In quelle tenebre* (Adelphi, 1975; English translation *Into That Darkness*). They had successfully fulfilled their mission in Eastern Europe, but on the newly-occupied Adriatic coast there was plenty of work for them: an ever-growing number of Istrian, Slovene and Croat partisans, not to mention a few thousand Jews. Besides, their presence was not particularly welcome in the German motherland. They were a bunch of corrupt and untrustworthy plotters, but above all they shared a secret which, in the ever more likely hypothesis of military defeat, could become awkward for many senior Nazis already prepared to offer themselves to the British and Americans as anti-Soviet mercenaries in an expected overturning of alliances: this was the secret of the gas chambers and crematoria in Sobibor, Treblinka and Auschwitz.

Nonetheless in a peripheral area such as the *Adriatisches Kustenland*, the Adriatic coast annexed to the Reich, and with their tried and tested techniques of spreading terror while throwing a veil of mystery over the most sinister details, their work could still serve a purpose. So with the help of auxiliary Ukrainians and also Italians, one of the sheds at the rice mill was transformed into a gas chamber, and the drying room into a crematorium. This small Italian annihilation camp, rudimentary but ferocious, operated for more than a year, scything down victims whose numbers are unknown but who probably numbered around five thousand.

This is not the first time the rice mill has been spoken of, but until now the subject has always been circled around. In Trieste in 1976 those reponsible for its running were made to stand trial, thanks to the diligence of one magistrate, and an appeal was heard in the early months of 1978. But this legal process was inconclusive (how could it have been otherwise, since they had to stand in judgement on events of almost thirty years before?), and took place in almost total silence: the same silence which had blanketed the massacre itself.

Why this silence, then and now? There are many reasons, connected to each other. Because before fleeing, the Nazis took precautions, in San Sabba as elsewhere, destroying the machinery of collective death, doing everything to make it unrecognizable. Because the victims of the rice mill were for the most part Slav partisans, and Tito's warriors were not welcomed by the temporary Anglo-American administration in Trieste; nor for many years, after Tito's schism, were they welcome by the Soviets or the Italian Communists. And because local Fascist functionaries were also party to what was going on at the rice mill.

But all these reasons for silence are brought together by a further more general reason, the sense of guilt of an entire generation. Guilt is burdensome, and rarely leads to expiation. Those weighed down by it tend, by various means, to free themselves of it: forgetting, denying, falsifying, lying to others and to themselves. It is an opportune moment for this book, the result of the author's personal investigations, to be read: it might function as an antidote. Indeed in these last few months, by a strange coincidence, very different 'testimonies' have been published. Irving, an English historian, has put forward the deranged thesis that Hitler not only did not order, but (until 1943) did not even know about, the Holocaust of the Jews in Europe: as if Hitler had never read the *Stürmer*, every issue of which was an incitement to purifying massacre.

Other voices come from France, and put forward a new and strange thesis. In all of the trials to have taken place so far (the Nuremberg trials; the Auschwitz trial which took place in Frankfurt in 1965; the Eichmann trial in Jerusalem), the few guilty people who have been dragged into the courtroom have justified themselves in the usual manner: they did not commit any of the crimes with their own hands; they were forced to; they were bound by an oath of loyalty, by their duty as soldiers, by loyalty to their leaders; but they never dared to deny the reality of mass exterminations. But two Frenchmen have been so bold as to do just that, perhaps trusting in the fading of memory after thirty-five years, perhaps hoping that in the meantime survivors and witnesses, who were few but rather awkward, had disappeared from the scene.

The first of these can be dealt with in just a few words. Louis Darquier de Pellepoix, Special Commissioner for Jewish affairs in the Vichy government, and as such directly responsible for the deportation of 70,000 Jews, is now almost 85 and plainly senile. Interviewed (but why? Why, my French journalist colleagues, do you let yourselves be drawn into these shady operations?) by *l'Express*, he denies everything: the photographs of piles of bodies are montages; the statistics of millions of dead have been fabricated by the Jews, always avid for publicity and pity; deportations took place, but he didn't know where to, or what the outcome would be; yes, there were gas chambers at Auschwitz, but they were only used to kill fleas and anyway (note the coherent argument!) they were only built after the end of the war. It is not difficult, indeed it is an act of charity, to see in Darquier the typical case of the man who is accustomed to lying in public and ends up by lying in private too, even to himself, constructing a comfortable truth that enables him to live in peace.

The case of Faurisson is less clear. Robert Faurisson is fifty years old and teaches French literature in the University of Lyons II, but for eighteen years now he has cultivated an innocent mania: he has set himself the task of demonstrating that gas chambers never existed in the Nazi concentration camps. This is his life's aim, and in order to achieve it he has risked (or is risking) his academic career. Indeed, after some initial hesitation the Rector, worried by his aberrant claims and the reactions he has provoked amongst students, has suspended him temporarily from all teaching duties, and has even forbidden him to set foot in the university.

But Faurisson will not give up so easily. He besieges *Le Monde* with letters, protests because they are not published, accuses the Rector of mounting a persecution campaign against him, of denying him a promotion he should have had years ago. On 12 December last year he writes once more to *Le Monde* in haughty tones and issues an ultimatum: he expects 'a public debate on a topic being manifestly avoided: that of the "gas chambers". I ask *Le Monde*, whom I have been urging for four years now, finally to publish two pages on *La Rumeur d'Auschwitz*. The moment has come. The time is ripe.'

At this point anybody can plainly see that this is a frustrated man, afflicted with a monomania verging on paranoia: but *Le Monde* publishes the two pages just the same, on 29 December, promising a rebuttal, which duly appears the following day, and prefacing it with a curious comment: '. . . however misguided it may appear, the argument of Monsieur Faurisson has spread a sense of unease, especially amongst younger generations who are unwilling to accept acquired ideas uncritically'. The reasoning of Monsieur Faurisson is as follows: there were no gas chambers in Orani-enburg, Buchenwald, Bergen-Belsen, Dachau and so on, *therefore* there were none anywhere. The chambers described by Höss, Commandant at Auschwitz, are not credible because Höss made his statement to the 'Polish and Soviet judicial apparatus' (not true: Höss had earlier made a statement also to an Allied commission). The chambers in Auschwitz had a floor area of 210 square metres; how could upwards of 2,000 people be placed in there? Well, they were indeed placed in there, savagely crushed together; indeed, we were in there. I did not go into the gas chambers (those who went in never came out to tell their tale) but, waiting for a selection for the gas chambers, I was shoved into an area of seven metres by four together with 250 companions, and I spoke of this in *If This is a Man*.

The poison used in the chambers could not have been eliminated so swiftly, and would have killed the 'Germans' (this is what Faurisson says, after eighteen years dedicated to studying this problem, in an interview with Radio Lugano) detailed to clear the bodies. Faurisson has never noticed that these workers were not Germans but other prisoners, for whose well-being the Germans cared little; and in any case, the poison, cyanide acid, was extremely volatile under the conditions in which it was deployed (it boils at 26°C; in the chambers, heaving with human beings, the tempera-ture was around 37°C) and besides there were efficient ventilators, documented not only by witnesses but by commercial order sheets and invoices.

Faurisson is not personally guilty: so who is behind him, who is encouraging his fixations? Why does *Le Monde* publish him, after his Rector has suspended him, expressing doubts as to his intellectual balance? Perhaps precisely to spread 'unease' amongst young people? If this is the aim, it will certainly succeed. The very enormity of geno-cide nudges us towards incredulity, towards denial and refusal. Behind these efforts at reshaping the truth there lies concealed not only the need for journalistic scandal but also France's other soul, which sent Dreyfus to Guyana, which accepted Hitler and which followed Pétain.

La Stampa, 19 January 1979

22   No Return to the Holocausts of the Past (Nazi Massacres, Crowds and the TV)

I have not been able to see the whole of the TV series *Holocaust*. I have seen just a few episodes, and those before it was dubbed. I attended the screening with some misgivings, the same misgivings felt by all witnesses from those times, in the face of the many recent and less recent attempts to 'utilize' their experience. This experience was so singular, and so far off the normal human scale, that it constituted a dangerous temptation for many writers in search of prime matter to be fashioned into literature or spectacle, or worse, transformed into a horror show: these are our own, private affairs, and it causes us great unease to see them tampered with.

I also found it hard to step away from my specific reactions to various moments of naivety or lack of precision. It was not like that *there*, the striped clothes were not clean but filthy, the overcrowding was always horrific, every moment of day and night, leaving little space for feelings or thought; the prisoners' cheeks were not so well shaven, nor were the women waiting in line for the gas chamber so well fed.

And yet these are not significant comments. Even if the film came about as a business proposition with a colossal budget, on the whole it seems to me to display good faith, decent intentions and results, a discreet respect for history and a simple gaze (simplifying, if you like) that renders it close to parts of Victor Hugo's *Les misérables* and guarantees its popular success. We should expect neither subtle emotions nor psychological shading: it does not depict them, and did not set out to do so.

The astonishing success that *Holocaust* has had in the countries where it has been shown – the United States first of all, West Germany, France and Israel – is a matter of public record, and is already a subject of debate for sociologists. This success can be traced to obvious and broad reasons: the unique and pitiless way in which the Jews were persecuted, the enormity of the scale of persecution, its brutal stupidity and senseless fanaticism. And in part the film's success is due to the specific way in which each separate country experienced the events reproduced in the film at the time.

Today the United States are the cultural centre of Judaism. 'Operation' *Holocaust* was conceived and developed according to a traditional American format and with a televisual language all too typically American. Israel is the direct descendant of the part of Eastern European Jewry to escape massacre, coming into being to redeem the exile and long slavery of the Jewish people, and its younger generations harbour a profound sense of shame and disbelief at how easily massacre was perpetrated. France is a separate case, a country as split now as it was then: divided between the sting of the lost war and the obedience offered to occupying Germany, pride at the freedoms won with the Revolution, and the persistent rumblings of the gross and nationalist xenophobia which lay behind the Dreyfus affair. We should not be surprised that the most alarming signs of a new anti-Semitic wave come from France.

As for Germany, seeing this film must clearly have given quite a jolt to a country where there are still many thousands of bureaucrat-assassins from those days who have never been punished, protected as they are by a vast wall of silence, and hundreds of thousands of citizens who are obsequious before the law (present as well as past!), who have saved their souls by stubbornly refusing to know or to understand what was happening all around them. They have persisted in an equally stubborn silence about what by chance they might have known or realized, even with their own children. If this film had been shown in Germany fifteen years ago rather than now, it would most likely have come hard up against the same wall of wilful deafness that a whole generation of people who were directly involved cower behind, and the film's success would have been considerably reduced.

It is difficult to predict what resonance *Holocaust* will have in our own country, where Fascists did not intend the Jew hunt to be any less vigorous than in allied Germany, but where it was widely hindered by the human sensibility of the Italian people, by the political inefficiencies of the time and by the discredit which by then dogged the Fascist regime.

We should make two observations on the multifaceted, sometimes polemical but always profound interest that *Holocaust* has aroused. First of all, anti-Semitism is an ancient and complex fact, with barbaric or indeed pre-human roots – there is, notoriously, a zoological racism, seen indeed in social animals. But at intervals it is aroused by a calculated cynicism which reasons that in moments of political instability or turmoil it is useful to find or to invent a scapegoat on which to heap past, present and future woes, and unleash the aggressive and vindictive tensions of the people. The Jews, dispersed and defenceless, were seen as ideal victims after the Diaspora, and this is how they have been treated in many countries over the centuries. Weimar Germany was unstable and in turmoil, and in need of a scapegoat: but even today Italy is unstable and in turmoil.

Secondly, in all countries the film was seen by tens of millions of people, not *even though* it was a story, but because it *is* a story. Hundreds of books have been written on the Nazi genocide, hundreds of documentaries screened, but none of them has reached a number of readers or viewers equal even to one per cent of *Holocaust*'s viewing public. These two associated factors, the story format and the vehicle of television, clearly demonstrate their colossal power of penetration.

In this particular instance this is a positive phenomenon, serving to bring to people's attention the events of a tragedy still unique, even in the bloody history of humanity, when for too long vested interests have imposed silence. In doing so, it lends new weight to the arguments of those in Germany and elsewhere who believe it wrong that Nazi crimes are beyond our knowledge. We can only be glad of this, but we cannot suppress a shiver of alarm at the hypothesis of what might happen if the chosen theme had been different or opposite, in a country where television was the voice of the State alone, neither subject to democratic controls nor accessible to the criticisms of the viewers.

La Stampa, 20 May 1979

23   Images of *Holocaust*

In the beginning there is show business, the gigantic machine of the American cultural industry. As an industry it is not exempt from the rules, laws and habits of any other industry. It requires forecasts, market research, programmes of expenditure and funding, together with carefully calculated publicity campaigns, and its aim is profit. Like any other industry, it makes capital out of previous experience, its own and that of others, and experience teaches that the highest profit is gained from a judicious balance of innovation and conservatism. These are the utilitarian and reasoned premises from which operation *Holocaust* was born, just as, shortly before, *Roots* was born, as well as the colossal biblical films cinema produced right from its earliest days. These enterprises are at once cynical and pious, and this contradiction should not surprise us, given that the author is not a single individual. The authors are in fact many, and amongst the many there are, indeed, those who are cynical and those who are pious. I do not think we can make serious objection to this; since the time of Aeschylus, public spectacle has drawn on the sources which move the public the most, and these are crime, destiny, human pain, oppression, massacre and insurrection.

Thus the film *Holocaust* was born as a marriage of interests, but not all marriages of interest are doomed to failure. I should say straight away that the first triumphal reviews in the press filled me with unease and distrust. I feared that the cynicism would be the larger part, and that the piety would be marginal. As we know, right from the very early years following the war the subject of Hiter's massacres and the concentration camps had willingly lent itself as a topic to be explored in literature, and not only in literature; it was self-evident that the blood, massacre, and intrinsic horror of the events that unfolded in Europe during those years would attract a host of second-rank writers in search of subjects with easy solutions, and that this immeasurable tragedy would be picked apart, hacked into pieces, arbitrarily distorted, in order to extract from it fragments deemed fit to satisfy the murky taste for the macabre and the sordid which is believed to lodge deep within every reader and consumer. This desecrating 'utilization' manifested itself promptly, and not only through the pens of dozens of writers: we only have to think of *The Spark of Life* by Erich Maria Remarque, an eloquent example of how a deeply false novel can be constructed on true events, to the point of casting a shadow of incredulity over the very events it sets out to describe. The same, or almost the same, can be said of the sado-pornographic school, whose cornerstone is probably the abominable *Casa di bambole* ('Doll's House'), even though it was written by an ex-deportee; unfortunately no law of the human soul prescribes that all those who live through an experience, terrible and fundamental as it may be, possess the spiritual resources required to understand, judge, to grasp its limits, in order subsequently to transmit it. 'Doll's House' describes a brothel within a concentration camp. Brothels did exist in some camps as a not particularly tragic marginal accessory, but packs of crows have fed on this detail, filling half the world's screens with a flood of indecent films purporting that all the women's camps, far from being places of suffering, death and growing political maturity, were nothing more than theatres of refined (and not always refined) sadism.

My distrust was somewhat allayed when I learnt of the film's audience figures in the United States, France, Israel, Germany and Austria. A higher viewing figure by itself proves nothing. At most it proves that the television public was interested in the show, and says nothing about that show's quality. But then it emerged that after each episode the channels were inundated by tens of thousands of phone calls, that the broadcast prompted serious debate. Chancellor Schmidt took part in one of these debates, which lasted for several hours. Despite the geographical and ideological distance of the United States, a commentary guide was printed for use in schools there, together with an in-depth bibliography. It must, then, be something rather more than simple entertainment; in some way, at some level, the spectator is becoming involved.

I tried to watch *Holocaust* with the eye of the neutral spectator, not letting myself get involved but putting aside preconceptions, 'defending' myself insofar as I could from my reactions as an ex-deportee, and I think I succeeded in this. And having thus calibrated and filtered out my personal emotions, and erased my moments of violent identification with some of the characters, I can say that the film is decent and of a consistently high standard; above all, it does not abuse the sensational material on which it is based. Its authors were measured, and did not give space to the promptings of the macabre, the obscene or the horrific, even though the horrific, notoriously, 'pays'. This much we can see in their efforts not to slip into stereotype and in the attempt to endow the characters with individuality. On the other hand its historical depth is slight, inadequate, and here matters become more complicated.

The roots of Nazism, of Nazi anti-Semitism and the parallel yet different popular anti-Semitism of the Russians and the Poles (frequently mentioned by the film) are complex and go far back in time; they cannot be understood without reference to the sermons of nineteenth-century German philosophers, the tortured story of European Jews from as long ago as the destruction of the second temple and the theological doctrines spread by the Catholic, Orthodox and Reformed churches alike.

We cannot understand Hitler if we know nothing of the wound inflicted on German pride by the defeat of 1918, the successive attempts at revolution, the disastrous inflation of 1923, the violence of the guerrillas and the vertiginous political instability of the Weimar Republic. I do not mean to say that everything that came before is sufficient to explain Hitler, but it is certainly necessary, and there is no mention of this anywhere in the film; the spectator is given the impression that Nazism burst out of nowhere, the devilish work of cold fanatics such as Heydrich or sinister brigands with swastikas on their sleeves, or else it was the fruit of an intrinsic and ill-defined wickedness on the part of the German people. The episode of the revolt in the Warsaw ghetto can similarly be taken to task for lack of political motivation and an analogous over-simplification. This memorable and desperate struggle, which will be remembered down the centuries, and is portrayed in the film with a very high level of dramatic tension, was more than a heroic attempt to reaffirm the dignity of the people and victims; in its turn it was the overturning of ancient and multiple oppressions, and here bloomed the stoic virtue of the defenders of Massada against the overwhelming armies of Tito, the millenarian and messianic impetus of early Zionism, and the interpretation of the Marxist word by the Jewish proletariat of Warsaw, doubly oppressed in that they were both proletarian and Jews.

On the other hand, justice asks us not to demand too much. The ferocity and sheer excess of the Holocaust brought about by the Nazis, and depicted in a number of scenes with shocking realism, harboured an enigma as yet unresolved by any historian, and this explains the countless telephone calls besieging the broadcasting stations of the countries where this film has been shown so far. For the most part they were viewers wanting to know 'why', and this is a huge 'why', as ancient as humankind itself. It is the why of the evil of the world, the why that Job futilely addresses to God, and which we can answer with a number of half answers: but the global, universal answer, the one to bring peace to the spirit, is unknown and perhaps does not even exist. We can explain, and sociologists, politicians and ethnologists have explained, why minorities are hated and persecuted, and why the Jewish minority in particular was persecuted in Germany, but we cannot explain why the Nazis were concerned to hunt out the old and sick as well, transport them halfway across Europe to Auschwitz, and there reduce them to nothing but ashes. We cannot explain why, in the tragedy and chaos of a war by now lost, convoys of the deported had precedence over troop and munitions transports. Above all, and this is outside anything known in the animal world, nobody has yet understood why the desire to suppress 'the enemy' went hand in hand with an even stronger desire to make him undergo the most unimaginable suffering, to humiliate and vilify him, to treat him like a filthy animal, or worse, like an inanimate object. This is the unique feature of the Nazi persecution. The film seems to me to have attempted to portray this, and in large part to have succeeded.

There is much that could be said about the general framework of *Holocaust* and its adherence to historical truth. There are features that seem to be 'quoting' from illustrious origins; unconsciously possibly, thanks to the miraculous vitality of the classics, or perhaps deliberately. The revolt in the ghetto is a page from *Les misérables*: the barricades are here, Gavroche too, and the flight through the sewers. When little Peter, Erik Dorf's son, first sees his father in the uniform of the SS, he cowers back crying, terrified by his father's proud armour, just like Astianatte when he sees Hector returning from the field of war still in his battledress. Erik's wife, Martha, is as implacable as Lady Macbeth in spurring the ambition of her ambivalent husband, and in urging him on from crime to crime, right to the end.

Erik Dorf is the central character in the story, or at least the most complex and rounded, and a multiple ambition burns in him: he is a fearless and open careerist, then an astute and cruel Councillor, and finally a slightly vulnerable but nonetheless fearsome member of the Nazi elite, lacerated by intrigues and jealousies. The film sets out to model him as a concrete portrayal, an inverted and emblematic instance of the German man blinded by the Nazi myth, and he thus loses some of his human quality. As a young lawyer in Berlin, frustrated, poor and insecure, Erik allies himself with the almighty

Heydrich; he is fascinated by the man, but even more fascinated by the power emanating from him that Erik wishes to share. A 'confused and uncertain' bureaucrat, he is torn between his own moralistic education and the fascination of active and passive authority. The latter swiftly prevails, however, and Erik becomes a fraudulent Councillor, indeed, 'the' Councillor of the Nazi court. After the *Kristallnacht*, he is the one who remembers his law studies and advises Heydrich that the insurance companies should be encouraged to pay the Jews for damage done to their property, but that the government should then 'confiscate these payments, on the pretext that the Jews themselves incited the riots and had therefore forfeited any right to recompense'. He is the man to suggest that the burning and destruction of Jewish property should be carried out by Nazis in ordinary clothes rather than uniform, to make their actions appear spontaneous. Later, he is the one to invent the well-known euphemisms under which extermination masqueraded, 'resettling' meaning 'deportation', 'final solution' meaning massacre and 'special treatment' meaning killing by gas. It will be his suggestion to use Zyklon B in the gas chambers, or cyanide acid, instead of carbon dioxide. He even has attributed to him the hope of being able to persuade future public opinion that no harm was ever done to the Jews, through clever manipulation of propaganda. Overwhelmed by the military collapse of Germany, and by the defection of his leaders, Erik is interrogated by an American officer and in the course of this interrogation he kills himself, swallowing a phial of poison. Throughout his whole career of unwholesome power and intimate servitude, Erik, who is excellently acted by Michael Moriarty, shows occasional outbursts of humanity, which indeed culminate in his suicide. But while he is acceptable on a dramatic level, the figure of Erik seems to me to be undermined by his historical impossibility. In this character we see repeated, it seems to me, the error of those who tend to concentrate the whole responsibility of Nazism onto one or a few persons, or indeed the Devil, leaving out of count its historical causes and the wide consensus of the German people. Clearly the programme sought to make of him a symbol of the very many Eriks who formed the backbone of Germany at the time, but I would be concerned that many viewers who see him on the screen, alongside historical and single figures such as Himmler and Eichmann, might believe that he, too, is a historical and single figure.

A parallel symbolic weight hangs over the Weiss family: these are assimilated Jews *par excellence*. Doctor Weiss, a Jew of Polish origin, feels himself profoundly integrated into German society. When the first racist skirmishes take place he tends to underestimate them, saying that 'it will pass', and his wife agrees: after all, Germany is the country of Beethoven and Schiller, is it not? A refined pianist, she will seek an illusory refuge in music while all around them, from 1935 to 1939, Nazi barbarism begins to unleash itself. They will not attempt to emigrate: step by step, including heroic participation in the revolt in the Warsaw ghetto to which the doctor has been relegated as a native of Poland, they draw closer to the gas chambers of Auschwitz. Their eldest son Karl will also die at Auschwitz, sent there as punishment for trying to leave some witness for 'future memory' of the horrors taking place in the ghetto of Theresienstadt. Anna, the younger child, is raped, loses her mind, and vanishes to Hadamar, one of the sinister 'hospitals' in which the mentally infirm were secretly killed with poisonous gas.

The sole survivor of the family is Rudi. Rudi is an athlete, inclined by nature and by education to give blow for blow. Rudi cannot bear to be suffocated in the net of persecution. He escapes into Czechoslovakia, then to the Ukraine, where he joins a group of Jewish partisans and, albeit reluctantly, learns to kill. He is captured and taken to the concentration camp in Sobibor. There, together with a group of Soviet soldiers, he scrambles over the fence and finds once more the freedom in which he, alone in his family, had never failed to believe. He willingly agrees to take a dozen Jewish children from Thessalonika, who have survived the camps, to Palestine, violating the English blockade as clandestine immigrants.

There has been much debate, and there will be a great deal more debate, about the 'truth' of the events depicted in *Holocaust*. There is no place for such a debate; the fundamental events are absolutely faithful to the truth, documented by countless historical sources, the most important of which are the confessions of the perpetrators, captured by the Allies and brought to justice at the end of the war. What is more, a good part of the dialogue, the more or less secret meetings of the Nazi leaders, the secret and public orders, the proclamations, the biographical details, are taken from German documentary sources, or reconstructed faithfully on them. The authors had no need to turn to fantasy: *Kristallnacht*, the elimination of the feeble, Buchenwald, Theresienstadt, the horrendous mass grave at Babi Yar, the women heaped together waiting unknowingly (sometimes knowingly!) for death by gas, the hopeless insurrection of the Jews in Warsaw, the bloody and victorious revolt of Sobibor, all took place, and took place as depicted here. These are historical truths, to be disputed only by the guilty parties who still feel burdened by guilt, or by madmen incapable of looking reality in the face; and since the guilty and the mad do exist, these truths are sometimes – laughably – contested. We do not need to waste many words on this subject: let them explain to us where the six million Jews who had diappeared by 1945 had gone, and the question will be resolved. Nor is there much to be added about the inevitable imprecisions and naivety in the film, such as the rather too well-shaven beards of the rioters, the over-clean huts in Auschwitz, the surprisingly large rooms in the ghetto. These things come from the film-makers' residual faith in the humanity of the time and the place, rather than from negligence.

We can anticipate that there will be much debate in Italy, too, over the appropriacy of transmitting 'horrors like these' to a vast television audience. We would do well to remind those who do not know, or who choose to forget, that the Holocaust extended as far as Italy, even though the war was by now drawing to a close, and even though the majority of the Italian people showed themselves immune to racist poison. Around 8,000 Jews out of the 32–35,000 who lived on Italian soil at the time were deported, and only three or four hundred returned. The round-ups were by order of the occupying German forces, but were frequently carried out by the police and the Fascist militia, not unwillingly as far as we can tell, since each Jew captured was worth a financial reward. Why should we stay silent about this?

I have discussed this television programme, making the occasional criticism, trying to bring out its good and weaker points and without trying to conceal the mixture of unease and respect that it aroused in me. I would like to add a final observation. The Weimar Republic that gave birth to Fascism was characterized by political instability, growing violence and a widespread hope in a messianic and irrational solution, in the intervention of the much-needed Hero, the saviour of Germany foretold by Nietzsche. In parallel fashion, Nazi doctrine inculcated into people's consciences an equally irrational and much more insidious certainty: that the ills of Germany, of the whole world indeed, sprang from a single source, from the Superenemy, the incarnation of evil, that were the Jews. Once this scapegoat had been slaughtered, Germany would be triumphant. Well, the scapegoat was slaughtered in the Holocaust in Europe, but alongside the six million murdered Jews a pitiless war saw the deaths of fifty million other

men, women and children, and more than ten million of these were
German.

'The images of *Holocaust*: from Reality to TV', in *Special Edition of
Radiocorriere TV*, edited by Pier Giorgio Martinelli, Eri, May 1979, pp. 2–5

24   Europe in Hell

Forty years on now from August 1939, the way we thought and
behaved at the time can only astonish others as well as ourselves. By
'us' I mean the Jewish minority in Italy, who were artificially fenced
off from the rest of the country at the time, thanks to the racial laws,
who for over two years had been the constant target of a propaganda
campaign, insulted, relegated to the margins of society, slandered
and humiliated. This is of course an unhistorical astonishment,
belonging to the kind of optical illusion whereby once the future has
become the past, we imagine that even when it was an authentic
future, it was as decipherable and readable as the past itself. This is
of course the wisdom of hindsight, the phenomenon whereby when
matters have come to an end everyone feels themselves retrospect-
ively gifted with foresight, and blames others for not having been so
endowed.

When I think of the wilful blindness which has prevented the
Germans, both then and now, from scouring to the depths the dark
abyss of Nazism, I glimpse a paradoxical analogy with the parallel
blindness of many European Jewish communities. Both perpetrators
and victims have refused to acknowledge the truth.

Certainly the reasons for this refusal have been different. The
Germans preferred to keep their eyes tightly shut so as not to feel
caught up in the guilt of Nazi crimes, stubbornly denying all the
evidence right until the end of the war, and with some of them denying
it even now. Jews threatened by Nazi invasion largely refused to
take stock of the danger for a number of reasons that differed
from country to country. If we stick to the situation in Italy at the time,
we might well say that the lack of seriousness with which the Fascist
government applied the race laws was disastrous for many: the winks,
the complicity, corruption and easily purchased indulgence led the

majority of Italian Jews to believe that things would carry on in the same way indefinitely, affirming and denying, prohibiting and conceding, in a *laissez faire* atmosphere that became even more marked as the Fascist regime lost credibility. Nor can we deny a certain logic to this way of seeing, or foreseeing; it was not illogical to expect that Fascist Italy, all too obviously unprepared for war, would conduct herself as indeed Franco conducted himself in Spain, with prudent ambiguity.

There were other reasons, too, for this deliberate refusal to know. The majority of Italian Jews possessed neither the courage nor the means necessary to emigrate and, as often happens, the sense of powerlessness this engendered was suppressed, distorted even: 'I can't' was transformed into 'I don't want to' like Aesop's fox faced with the unreachable grape. What's more, integration with the Catholic majority was profound and went back a long way, resulting in a reciprocal acceptance that was perhaps unique in the modern world. And finally, news about the anti-Jewish atrocities already under way in Germany (the *Kristallnacht* had been read about in the Fascist press) was censured and then repressed precisely because of its intrinsic horror, just as many people censure and repress the knowledge that they are faced with an incurable disease.

At the time I was only twenty years old, and I was naive, both morally and politically. I had not been able to combat this dangerous blindness either in myself or in others, in friends or family. News of the Ribbentrop-Molotov pact, the news which followed soon after of France and England's entry into the war, and the lightning German advance into Poland, were a brutal and painful awakening, and only then did we realize that from spectators we might very well soon be turned into protagonists, as resisters or as victims, as indeed happened immediately following the armistice of 8 September 1943. I remember very well my own irrational and symbolic reaction when news of the war was broadcast on the radio. My family, with my seriously ill father, was on holiday in the upper Valle di Lanzo. We decided to return to Turin but, instead of waiting for the terribly slow bus, I grabbed my bicycle and hurled myself down the twisting curves of the steep descent, like someone seeking to flee before his own destiny.

La Stampa, 27 August 1979

25   Anne Frank, the Voice of History

The strategy always seems to be identical. Last year 'someone' in France unearthed an ill-equipped little professor who was very ambitious and a little bizarre, and entrusted him with a noble mission. This was to demonstrate that the gas chambers of Auschwitz had never existed, or rather, they did exist but were only used for killing fleas; all the massive documentation of the Nazi genocide, whether papers or objects, memorials or museums, was the work of falsifiers and as a consequence all those accusing testimonials are a pack of lies. The central argument of the little professor was remarkable: some have claimed, falsely, that gas chambers existed in Oranienburg and in Dachau, but there were none there; therefore, there were none anywhere, and the massacre is an invention of the Jews.

Now we read that a seventy-seven-year-old pensioner in Hamburg, clearly prompted by 'someone', has taken it upon himself to sue the editors of Anne Frank's diary, casting doubt on its authenticity because in the famous notebook found in the clandestine lodgings some passages have apparently been written in ball-point, and were therefore added later, because in 1944 ball-points did not exist. The strategy, as I said before, is always the same. Find a small crack, stick a knife in it and lever it open. You never know, may be the whole building will come tumbling down, however robust it may be. Now, it is perfectly possible that some additions were made to the diary. This was common editorial practise, even if inappropriate from a philological point of view. As far as the person making the changes was concerned, they helped to make a connection, to fill a gap, to sharpen the focus of the historical background. It is certainly deplorable that the additions are not acknowledged, if for no other reason than the doors would not thus be opened to manoeuvres such as those of our Hamburg pensioner.

It is a manouevre that arouses disgust. Anne Frank's diary made the entire world weep because its authenticity is self-evident. There is no faker capable of creating a book such as this out of nothing. He would have to be at one and the same time a historian of customs, with a minute knowledge of the details of daily life in a little-known time and place, an expert psychologist able to reconstruct states of mind at the limits of the imaginable, and a poet with the candid and mercurial soul of a fourteen-year-old girl.

It takes a good deal of obtuseness and bad faith to maintain that these pages have been put together at a desk, but even if the experts of the Hamburg Court of Appeal were to declare the entire diary false, the historical truth would not change one iota; Anne would not come back to life, nor would the millions of innocent people the Nazis wilfully slaughtered rise up with her. Perhaps it is not by chance that this squalid affair, which brings to mind the New Testament story of the speck and the beam, should have been stirred up only after the death of Anne's father, himself an ex-prisoner, whom I came across in Auschwitz for just a few moments after Liberation, as he searched for his two missing daughters.

It is doubly alarming to read about this effort today, after 'someone' did not think twice about snuffing out unaware and innocent lives in Bologna, then in Munich and Paris. The scale is different, for the moment at least, but the style and the aims are always the same, and theirs is the monstrous ideology that the world neither could nor would eradicate.

La Stampa, 7 October 1980

26   Seekers of Lies to Deny the Holocaust

In Torrance, near Los Angeles, the 'Institute for Historical Review' has been set up with the remit of revising the official history of the Second World War. We would take no exception to such an enterprise, were it not clear from the Institute's proceedings that this revision is one way only: its sole purpose is to deny, or at best minimize, Nazi crimes. We should not be surprised to read of a seminar held in Torrance and attended by an expert in this particular branch of history, the same Professor Faurisson who desperately sought to get himself in the news last year when he claimed that the gas chambers in Auschwitz never killed a soul; indeed, they were built after the war in order to defame the Nazi regime. The Torrance Institute has recently offered a prize of fifty thousand dollars to anyone who can prove 'irrefutably' that the Nazis murdered Jews in the gas chambers.

It is worth noting that this particular prize has been announced at the same time as the trials for the Varese affair and the bomb in Copernico Street in Paris are taking place. Everything is happening together as if someone were crying out, demanding to be believed: 'There was no massacre, but we wish there had been and that it was still going on'; or else 'There was no massacre, but we're doing our best to make one happen.' Can we have a little coherence in all this, please? If you like massacre, why do you deny that it took place? And if you don't like it, why do you imitate it, and act as apologists for it?

It is a pretty safe bet that this provocative prize will stay within the coffers of the Institute. It takes very little courage or even money to set up initiatives of this kind, only endless arrogance and bad faith. There would be no risk in setting up a prize, of fifty million dollars even, to be bestowed on anyone who can demonstrate 'irrefutably' that between 1939 and 1945 a gory war was fought on the face of this planet. Anyone turning up with witnesses, documents and site evidence in order to claim the prize could be rebutted with arguments analogous to those stubbornly put forward by their forerunner, Faurisson. These arguments state that the Maginot and Siegfried lines never existed; the ruins still standing were constructed years later by specialist enterprise, using plans supplied by obliging scenery designers, and the same goes for the war cemeteries. All photographs from the time are fake. All statistics on the victims have been massaged, the work of terrorist propaganda with vested interests. Nobody died in the war because there *was* no war. All the diaries and memoirs published in the many countries caught up in the supposed conflict are a pack of lies, or the work of the mentally defective, or extorted by torture or blackmail, or simply paid for. Widows and war orphans are subsidized bit-players, or else simply paranoid.

What can an Institute not deny? Ariosto, who knew about these things, ironically recommended that princes stay on friendly terms with writers, poets and historians, because they are the fabricators of truth. Whoever wants to know the truth should not trust Homer, who was corrupted by the Greek establishment with gifts of palaces and villas: 'And if you wish the truth not to be hidden from you/Turn history on its head;/Say that the Greeks were broken and Troy victorious/And that Penelope was a whore.'

This is the historical truth that the Torrance Institute would have stated had it been around at the time of Homer, and which it proposes to restate today.

La Stampa, 26 November 1980

27   To the Visitor

The history of the Deportation and of the extermination camps, the history of this place, cannot be disentangled from the history of Fascist tyrannies in Europe. An uninterrupted line runs from the first fires at the Camera di Lavoro in Italy in 1921 to the book-burning in the squares of Germany in 1933, ending with the obscene flames of the crematoria at Birkenau. Those who burn books end up by burning men, for violence is a seed that flourishes all too easily. This is ancient wisdom, and the poet Heine, who was both a Jew and a German, had already sounded the warning.

Sadly we are compelled to remind both others and ourselves that the first European experiment in the suffocation of the workers' movement, and the sabotage of democracy, was born in Italy. This was Fascism, thrust to power by the crisis following the First World War, by the myth of the 'mutilated victory' and nurtured by long-term misery and guilt. Fascism gives rise to a growing delirium, the cult of the providential man, organized and enforced enthusiasm, each and every decision entrusted to the whim of a single individual.

But not all Italians were Fascist, as is witnessed by those of us who were Italian and who died here. Alongside Fascism another continuous thread was born, first in Italy then elsewhere: that of anti-Fascism. And bearing witness alongside us are all those who have fought against Fascism and suffered because of Fascism, the martyred workers of Turin in 1923, those who were imprisoned, sent into internal exile, exiled abroad, our brothers of all political faiths who died to resist the Fascism restored by the National Socialist invader.

And other Italians also bear witness with us, those who fell on the fronts of the Second World War, fighting against their will and in desperation against an enemy who was not their enemy, and realizing too late the deceit practised upon them. These men, too, are the victims of Fascism, unknowing victims. We were not unknowing. Some of us were partisans and engaged in a political struggle; these men were captured and deported during the last few months of the war, and they died here, as the Third Reich teetered on the brink, lacerated by the thought of the liberation just beyond their grasp.

The majority of us were Jews. Jews from all cities in Italy, as well as foreign Jews, from Poland, Hungary, Yugoslavia, Czechoslovakia and Germany, who in Fascist Italy, under the yoke of Mussolini's anti-Semitic racial laws, had discovered the benevolence and civil hospitality of the Italian people. They were rich and poor, men and women, healthy and sick.

There were children amongst us, and old people on the point of death, but we were all loaded like cattle onto the freight cars, and our fate, the fate of those who crossed the threshold of Auschwitz, was the same for all. Not even in the darkest of centuries did it ever happen that human beings were exterminated by the million, like troublesome insects, or that children and the dying were sent to their deaths. We, the children of Christians and of Jews (but we do not like these distinctions), from a country that had been civilized, and which returned to civilization after the night of Fascism, we bear witness to this. In this place, where we innocents were killed, the very depths of barbarity were reached. Visitor, look at what remains of this camp and ponder. Whichever country you come from, you are not a stranger. Let your journey be not in vain, let not our deaths be in vain. May the ashes of Auschwitz serve as a warning to you and to your children; ensure that the horrendous fruit of hatred, whose traces you have here seen, do not give up new seed, tomorrow or ever.

Text published for the inauguration of the Memorial in honour of the Italians who died in the Nazi concentration camps. Edited by the National Association of ex-Political Deportees to the Nazi extermination camps, April 1980

28   You Tell Me if This is a Fortunate Jew

Memoirs of a Fortunate Jew: the title of this intelligent, thoughtful book is subtly ironic: is it enough to escape massacre, to escape suffering and grief, to define ourselves as fortunate? In a relative sense it certainly is; in an absolute sense, I leave it to the reader to judge, and in particular to those who are like the author in his book, young Italians of today, whose life is secure and whose identity is certain.

And indeed, this is what this book is about, on almost every page, a continuous and always inconclusive search for identity. Vittorio Segre, the author, is nowadays a famous academic, diplomat and journalist with a vast experience of humanity and politics behind him, but the book shows how much this has cost him. Atypical amidst the atypical Jewish experience in Italy, he was born in Turin in 1922, 'one month after the March on Rome'. His father was a survivor of the Great War and a rich landowner who merged unproblematically with triumphant Fascism. The young Vittorio knows nothing else, and sees in Fascism 'a natural form of collective life'.

Judaism, in his family, is nothing more than a few vague relics: the odd solemn prayer, or food custom. His pale, beautiful mother was brought up in a Catholic convent and is permanently hesitating between the two faiths, both of which attract her romantic spirit. There is not a trace left of Jewish culture; Vittorio finds it 'more convenient' to be Jewish than to be Christian, because this means he can avoid the boredom of Sunday mass.

Vittorio, too, is childishly romantic. He likes skiing and climbing, and he has inherited both his father's love of action together with his mother's contemplative fragility. And precisely because this family is so well assimilated, the racial laws of 1938 strike them with the force of a hurricane. Vittorio has never been a Zionist, indeed he hardly knows the meaning of the word, but he is drawn to adventure. At seventeen he tries in vain to enrol in the Foreign Legion. He is one of the first Italian Jews to leave for Palestine, at that time under British mandate.

At this point the book becomes both tense and illuminating. The country where the young man disembarks is hardly the 'land of milk and honey'. It is poor and divided, hot and humid, full of flies, sand and wind. Here, side by side, there are still traces of the disastrous Ottoman rule, an age-old Arab poverty, the inheritance of the Crusades, the haughty (but efficient and just) English administration, and the indomitable stubbornness of the Zionist colonies of Russians, Poles, and Germans. At times we find the intensely composite environment and equanimity of judgement that dictated Forster's *Passage to India*.

The young Italian, a political virgin, an ex-avant garde Jew without roots, speaks English badly and Hebrew and Arabic not at all: but even the best of polyglots would feel lost in this linguistic, ethnic and religious Babel. He enters a kibbutz and follows courses in agriculture, but he finds the discomfort and especially the lack of action hard to bear. The world is at war, the Jews of Europe are condemned to death. It's their own fault, the Zionists tell him, they should have made up their minds sooner and 'ascended' to the Land of Israel like us. But Vittorio cannot accept their certainties and feels guilty.

Even Israeli Jewry, united in frenetic activism, is desperately fractured at an ideological level. There are the orthodox Jews who reject the lay state of the general Zionists; the Socialists who see the kibbutz as the first, exhilarating egalitarian experiment; the nationalists, Communists and revisionists who preach violence against Arabs and English alike, princes and servants, false philosophers and real priests.

Vittorio is alone, uprooted, disoriented: he wants action, but senses that he seeks in action some sort of compensation for his lack of cultural awareness. In this confused country the English are a solid point of reference: he admires them in that they represent order and the law; he loathes them because they have blocked Jewish immigration; he envies them because they are waging a fierce and stubborn war against the Satan of Berlin. He is not yet twenty years old; he is afraid, but he is also afraid of being afraid. In 1941 he brings his dreams of glory a little closer by enrolling in the clandestine Jewish army, and soon afterwards, in the British army.

It is a disappointment. His status is that of 'colonial volunteer'. The discipline is not inhuman, but the uniform is ridiculous, the duties are tiresome, the English refuse to engage 'indigenous' troops in battle and his sense of guilt increases. Perhaps only at this moment do we see the 'fortune' indicated in the title of the book: Vittorio speaks Italian well, and the Intelligence Service selects him as radio announcer. He no longer has to live in the barracks and can find a room to rent in Jerusalem.

It is a decisive step, and even more decisive is the meeting/collision with a woman, the first in his life. Berenike stands out amongst the thousand figures who make this book memorable. She is described with a delicate and steady hand, and with the sober elegance of a great writer. She is twenty years old but already an adult, mature even. Nourished on Freud and Marx, she rejects sentiment and practises sex with the ascetic nonchalance of a nurse, offering her body to the needy as if she were handing out a pill. No love: love is 'a form of spiritual delinquency' at a time when entire nations are in their death agony. Only at the end of this episode do we learn that Berenike, a German Jew, was raped by the Nazis in 1937, and for this reason is no longer 'capable of loving, only of offering some sort of service.'

With Berenike, and with another lively and suffering female figure, the story ends in the aura of liberty in 1945, in a Yugoslav scenario of unspeakable horror. Indeed, it does not conclude, but leads us rather to be curious about what came after, and to ponder what came before. Israel is probably the most complex and dramatic country in the world, and this book, written with the humility of a confession and the honesty of one who bears witness, is of fundamental help in understanding its excesses, its victories and its difficulties.

'Tuttolibri', *La Stampa*, 15 June 1985

29 The Pharoah with the Swastika

By 1943 I already had my chemistry degree and was working in Milan. I was living in a kind of commune (though we didn't call it that at the time) of young, financially independent Jews, brought together by lively intellectual interests and by an aversion to Fascism that was more ironic than violent.

For four years now the Fascist racial laws had expelled us from the context of society and had stamped us as biologically inferior. Not a day went by without newspapers and journals defining us as foreign to the tradition of the country, different, harmful, abject, enemies.

Jews had been chased out of all state employment, teaching, administration, the armed forces; Jewish doctors and lawyers could not have 'Aryan' clients; no Jew could own a radio, employ a Christian in their service, run an industrial company, own land, publish books.

The drip-drip effect of slanders and prohibitions, some of them cruel, others simply absurd, but all of them bitter and hurtful, went on from month to month. How could we defend ourselves? By gathering together, cultivating the friendship of many Aryan anti-Fascists or non-Fascists, forcing ourselves to laugh and to ignore what was coming.

We were all from middle-class families; none of us had inherited the seed of active resistance and revolt; none of us knew how to use a weapon. With hindsight, we were plainly ignorant, inept and badly informed; as, indeed, were the vast majority of Italians.

It astonishes me to recall that in August 1943, so pregnant with tragedy, we went up for a trip in the mountains without troubling ourselves too much about the future. We didn't think there was very much we could do about this future. As far as Fascist Italy was concerned we felt a shadow of sharp resentment, of bitter vindication. Italy had expelled us? Fine, let her go to meet its own destiny, whatever that might be, but we would have nothing to do with it.

Besides, we had spoken with anti-Fascist friends who were older and more experienced than us, and they had put our minds at rest. Goodness me, Badoglio was not born yesterday, there were a number of armoured divisions in the Brenner pass and elsewhere, and even if Italy sought armistice from the Allies the Germans would not be able to break through, while those who were already in Italy would find themselves caught in a bottleneck. We should not be afraid; there would be a separate peace settlement and the Allies would arrive in the Alps in the blink of an eye. We left Milan during a violent bombing raid and went on holiday with the easy conscience of fatalists. By 8 September we were already back in the city. News of the armistice filled us with stupid joy; there, peace was here, and with peace a return to just laws, to equality and fraternity, and not even Hitler could hold out much longer, given the enormous hole that had opened up on the southern front.

So the war was about to come to an end, and with the war Nazism and Fascism would come to an end, together with discrimination, humiliation and slavery. We felt ourselves in the same state of mind as our distant ancestors after the waters of the Red Sea closed over the Pharoah's war chariots. Some of us swiftly began to make plans: we would be able to resume our suspended studies, aspire to professions which had been closed to us.

Both our joy and our plans were short-lived. News came thick and fast: the king and Badoglio had fled Rome, leaving no orders for the armed forces; the Italian soldiers were disarmed by the Germans, loaded by the hundred thousand onto troop trains and deported to Germany; Mussolini was liberated with derisory ease from his prison on the Gran Sasso.

Germany was neither dead nor dying. A bare three days after the armistice the grey-green snake of Nazi divisions had invaded the streets of Milan and Turin. The game was over and Italy was an occupied country, like Poland, like Yugoslavia and like Norway.

During the forty-five days of Badoglio's government, some of us had had confused political contact with the Partito d'Azione, which had just emerged from clandestine status, but there had been no time to organize a network of political and military resistance. With no clear idea in mind, I left Milan, joined my family, who had been evacuated from the city into the surrounding hills, and then went up to the Val d'Aosta to join friends.

The situation was desperate, and the spectacle unforgettable: remnants of Italian troops who had occupied southern France were flooding back into Italy in disorderly fashion through every crossing place; few soldiers had wished or been able to keep their weapons, everybody was desperately hunting for civilian clothes. They avoided the railway and the roads along the valley floor, marching on interminable journeys along the highest mule-tracks, from hamlet to hamlet, like a flock of sheep with no shepherd. They were tired, demoralized, hungry; they asked for bread, milk, polenta, and all they wanted was to return home, even if they had to cross the whole of the Alps on foot. They wanted nothing more to do with the uniform they were wearing – what good was it? None, except to make it easier for them to fall into the hands of the Germans.

I spent a few weeks in a state of indecision. It was my overpowering duty to take part in the fight against the Nazis: they were my enemies, the enemies of humanity, now the enemies of Italy too, and Italy, Fascist or not, was still my country. On the other hand, my experience as conspirator and soldier was zero: I was not trained to fight, to shoot or to kill; nobody had ever taught me; these things were miles away from everything I had thought and done up to now. But then

I met other young people who were barely more experienced than me, but much more decisive. We had few weapons, no money and minimal organizational contact; nonetheless we declared ourselves partisans *in pectore*. We would find weapons, and money, while experience could be gained in action.

In wartime, lack of preparation, incompetence and imprudence exact a high price. In the valley our little group was spoken of much more than it merited. Certainly the Fascists of the newborn Republic must have overestimated us, because three hundred of them came looking for just eleven of us, and we were for the most part almost unarmed. We did not even attempt to defend ourselves, and my history as a partisan finished prematurely on a hill covered in the first snows. From there I was taken as prisoner to Aosta: in Aosta I was acknowledged as a Jew, and taken to the concentration camp at Auschwitz.

La Stampa, 9 September 1983

30   Preface to H. Langbein's *People in Auschwitz*

Literature on the National Socialist concentration camps can be roughly divided into three categories: diaries or memoirs of the deported, literary depictions and sociological and historical works. The book presented here belongs to the last category, but is clearly set apart from other works to appear on the subject so far by its extreme attempt at objectivity. It helped that it was written late on, only in 1972, allowing thus for a dispassionate serenity of judgement that would have been impossible in the years immediately following the war when, as is hardly surprising, shock, indignation and horror were paramount.

The original title, *Menschen in Auschwitz*, is full of meaning, anticipating both the proposition and the specificity of the work, for *Mensch*, in German, means human being. Highly significant is the moment the author himself speaks of in his introduction: he was spurred into finally writing this long-planned book by the comparison between

Nurse Klehr of Auschwitz, a self-proclaimed doctor, 'omnipotent, the terror of the hospital', whose appalling deeds are recounted in the text, and the aged, coarse rather helpless prisoner whom Hermann Langbein met during the great trial of Auschwitz which came to an end in Frankfurt in 1965. At that moment his vague intention acquired a precise outline. Langbein, a political fighter in Vienna and Spain, a prisoner at Dachau, Auschwitz and Neuengamme (but even in Auschwitz he was active in the 'Auschwitz Combat Group', a secret self-defence organization), a committed Communist who left the party after the invasion of Hungary in 1956, decides to tackle a problem which provokes real fear. Not only will he describe Auschwitz, but he will try to clarify to himself, to his contemporaries and future generations, the sources of the barbarism of Hitler's era, and how Germans were able to sustain and follow it through to its extreme consequences. Since Auschwitz is the work of man and not of the devil, he will move aside the tombstone; he will probe the very depths of human behaviour at Auschwitz, that of the victims, the oppressors and their accomplices, during the time of the camp and after.

The theme of the book, then, is Auschwitz, *anus mundi*, the concentration camp in its complete and exemplary form, fruit of the accumulated experience of almost ten years of Hitler's terror. And indeed, drawing on the author's personal memory and on numerous other sources, the book contains everything we might wish to know about the camp: its history and geography, its size and population, its complex sociology, its machinery of death, the infirmaries, the rules, the exceptions to the rules, the few ways to survive and the many to die, the names of the Commandants. But Langbein's particular perspective makes this book unique in a number of ways, and increases its weight and its universality.

The book's perspective is threefold. A brave and able man, Langbein was at one and the same time member of the clandestine resistance movement in Auschwitz, and secretary to Dr Wirths, a medical man, one of the most powerful SS officers in the camp. Later, after the liberation, he had access to the documents of the most important trials of high- or low-ranking bureaucrats, many of whom he had met before in the exercise of their duties. By these three routes he was able to obtain a vast amount of information, and he dedicated the rest of his life to the study of man living under extreme conditions. Such are prisoners behind barbed wire, but such also are those in the constellation of torturers, for they too, willingly or otherwise, have reached the extreme edges of what a man can commit or feel. With austere curiosity Langbein casts his eye over these men, not just to condemn or absolve them, but in a desperate attempt to understand how such a point can be reached. He is perhaps unique among modern historians in dedicating so much attention to this topic. His conclusion is disturbing. Those most responsible are *Menschen*, too; they are made up of the same prime matter as we are, and to trans- form them into cold assassins of millions of other *Menschen* did not take great effort or real coercion: a few years of perverse schooling and the propaganda of Dr Goebbels were quite enough. A few exceptions aside, they are not sadistic monsters, they are people like us, en- meshed in the regime because of their smallness, their ignorance or their ambition. Very few of them are also fanatical Nazis, for the period Langbein spends at Auschwitz, the period 'most dense with events', from 1942 to 1944, is also the time when Hitler's star begins to wane in the face of military defeats.

Langbein studies the lives of these ministers of death, before, during and after 'service', and the picture to emerge is very different from the one constructed either by regime propaganda or the folkloric historiography of the post-war, or of the sadistic Nazi line of films. The SS of the camps are not supermen faithful to their oath of loyalty, neither are they savage beasts in uniform. Rather, they are squalid, insensitive and corrupt individuals who much preferred surveillance in the camps to the 'glory' of battle, who were careful to enrich them- selves stealing from the warehouses and who plied their abominable trade more with obtuse indifference than with either conviction or pleasure. National Socialism had embedded itself deeply, extinguish- ing in them from a young age any normal moral impulses and con- ceding to them in return a power of life and death they were not prepared for, and which intoxicated them. Wittingly or otherwise they had taken a risky path, the path of obsequies and consensus, from which there is no turning back. Totalitarianism, any totalitarianism, is a broad path that leads downwards; the German version, Langbein tells us, was 'a path from which, step by step, it became more and more difficult to turn back, and which in the end led to Auschwitz'. And just a little further on:

> The lesson of Auschwitz is that the very first step, the acceptance of a type of society that seeks to dominate men in total fashion, is the most dangerous one. When a similar regime has embraced the idea of annihi- lating 'inferior beings' – and they don't necessarily have to be Jews or Gypsies – and a man wears its uniform (which might have for decoration

symbols different from the runes and skulls of the SS), at that point he has become its tool.

Another lesson to be learnt, we might add, is that although it might be difficult, it is necessary to judge. The enormity of the events recounted by this book imperiously compels us to take a position, with regard both to the worst Nazi criminals and to their collaborators, down to the grey band of the Kapos and the prisoners with privileged status. Now, it is a feature of despotic regimes that they restrict individual freedom of choice, making their own operations ambiguous and paralysing our faculty of judgement. Who should shoulder the blame for the evil committed or permitted? The individual who has let himself be convinced, or the regime that has convinced him? Both, certainly, but the respective measure of blame should be adjudged with caution, and case by case. This is precisely because we are not totalitarian, and the global labelling so dear to totalitarian regimes repels us. This book is a vast anthology of complex human cases, and is strewn with invitations (one, quite justified, addressed to me) to refuse facile generalizations. In Auschwitz not all 'criminals' marked with the green triangle behaved like criminals; not all the 'politicals' behaved like political prisoners, and not all the Germans hoped for German victory. Not for nothing does the book begin with the quotation: 'Only those who were interned there can know what Auschwitz was. Nobody else.' But Langbein, an attentive and comprehensive investigator of many cases of conscience, here is transformed into rigorous and tenacious accuser in the face of proven crime, and he is a severe critic of the pretexts and lies adduced by the guilty to ease their conscience.

From H. Langbein, *Uomini ad Auschwitz*, Milan 1984, pp. 5–7

31 Why See These Images Again?

There have been many times when those of us who survived the Nazi concentration camps have realized how useless words are to describe our experience. Words do not work, because of 'poor reception', because we live now in a civilization of the image, recorded, multiplied, broadcast; the public, especially the young, are more and more unwilling to turn to written information. But neither do they work for a different reason, because of 'poor broadcasting'. In all our tales, verbal or written, there are commonly expressions such as 'indescribable', 'inexpressible', 'words are not enough to . . .', 'it would take a new language to . . .'. That indeed was our everyday sensation when we were there. If we returned home, and if we tried to speak, words would fail us, for everyday language is suited to describing everyday things, but this was another world; here it would take a language 'of another world', a language born in that place.

Fully aware of the power of the image, with this exhibition we have tried to adopt its language. As anyone can see, the photographs are skilfully done but are not touched up, not 'artistic'. They depict the camps, in particular Auschwitz, Birkenau and the sinister rice mill of San Sabba, as they appear to the visitor today. They seem to me to demonstrate the claim of information theory: given equal space, an image 'tells' twenty, one hundred times more than the written page, and what is more it is accessible to everybody, including the illiterate or the foreigner. It is the best form of Esperanto. These are not new observations, but were formulated long ago by Leonardo da Vinci in his *Treatise on Painting*; but applied to the ineffable universe of the camps, they acquire even stronger resonance. Better and more strongly than the word, they reproduce the impression that the camps, more or less conserved, more or less transformed into sanctuaries or places of reverence, exercise on the visitor. And it is a strange fact that this impression is deeper and more disturbing for people who were not there than for the few of us who were.

For many of us the old trauma still prevails over reverent emotion, the ulcer of memory, and thus the need to repress. If we had been asked as we were liberated: 'What do you want to do with these infested huts, these nightmare barbed wire fences, these multiple cesspits, these ovens, these gallows?' I think most of us would have said, 'Away with it all. Flatten it, raze it to the ground, together with Nazism and everything that is German.' This is what we would have said, and what many did say as they pulled down the barbed wire and set fire to the huts. But we would have been wrong. These were not horrors to be wiped out. As the years and decades go by, those remains lose nothing of their meaning as both monument and warning: indeed, they become more meaningful. Better than any treatise or memorial they show the extent of the inhumanity of Hitler's regime, even in its scenographic and architectural choices. Over the entrance to the Birkenau camp, so well depicted here in the squalor of snow and the timeless bareness of the landscape, we read a Dantesque 'Abandon all hope', and nothing could portray better than this image the repetitive obsession of the searchlights lighting up the no man's land between the electric fence and the barbed wire. The photographs of the rice mill are different, but no less suggestive. It was in fact nothing more than a rice mill, a plant for the industrial treatment of rice, built in the days when a good part of the crops imported from the far East were unloaded in Trieste. But we see a theatrical and malign imagination at work in the transformation of this mill into a place of torture. Not by chance were the walls made so high, so solid and so blind. Visiting it today, and seeing the images reproduced here, we are reminded that as well as being a megalomaniac fanatic, Hitler was also an architect *manqué*; the backdrop of the oceanic walls was an essential part of Nazi ritual, and its attraction for the German people. Speer, that ambiguous genius of organization and official architect of the Thousand Year Reich, had been the most intimate confidant of the Führer and the organizer of the ferocious exploitation of labour supplied by the camps.

Triangolo Rosso, n. 3–4, March–April 1985

32   Preface to R. Höss's *Commandant of Auschwitz*

Usually someone who agrees to write the preface to a book does so because he likes the book, finds it pleasant to read, of high literary level such as to arouse sympathy or at least admiration for the person who wrote it. This book is at the other end of the spectrum. It is full of vileness recounted with a disturbing bureaucratic obtuseness. Reading it is oppressive, its literary quality is base and its author, despite all his efforts to defend himself, comes across just as he is, a stupid, verbose scoundrel, a coarse braggart whose mendacity at times is more than obvious. And yet this autobiography by the Commandant of Auschwitz is one of the most instructive books ever to have been published, describing as it does with the utmost precision a human journey which is, in its own way, exemplary. In a different climate from the one in which it was his lot to grow up, Rudolf Höss would have become a grey, anonymous bureaucrat, with discipline his duty and order his love – at the most, a careerist of moderate ambition. But instead, step by step, he transformed himself into one of the greatest criminals of human history.

Those of us who survived the Nazi camps are often asked one symptomatic question, especially by young people: what were they like, who were 'the ones on the other side'? Were they really so wicked that human light was never to be seen in their eyes? This book answers the question exhaustively, showing how easily good gives way to evil, is besieged and finally overwhelmed, to survive only in tiny grotesque glimpses – an ordered family life, a love of nature, a Victorian moralism. The author is hardly a man of culture, and for this very reason he cannot be suspected of colossally and knowingly falsifying history – this would have been beyond him. In his pages, rather, we see the flowering of mechanical reversions to Nazi rhetoric, lies both big and small, attempts at self-justification, attempts to gloss over certain matters, but they are so ingenuous and transparent that even the least resourceful reader will have no difficulty in identifying them: they stand out in the fabric of the tale like flies in milk.

The book, then, is a largely truthful autobiography, and it is the autobiography of a man who was not and never became a monster, not even at the peak of his career, when on his order thousands of innocent people were killed in Auschwitz each day. By this I mean that we can believe him when he claims that he never found any pleasure in inflicting pain or in killing. He was not a sadist, there is nothing satanic about him, although there are hints of the satanic in the portrait he sketches of Eichmann, his equal in status and his friend. But Eichmann was much more intelligent than Höss, and we have the impression that Höss took at face value certain of Eichmann's boasts which do not in fact bear close scrutiny. Höss was one of the greatest criminals who ever existed, but he was not made of different clay from any other member of the bourgeoisie in any other country. His guilt, which is not inscribed in his genetic patrimony nor in the fact that he was born German, lies in not having been able to resist the pressure which a violent environment had exercised on him, even before Hitler came to power.

If we want to be absolutely honest, we have to admit that as a young man he had a bad start in life. His father, a businessman, was a 'fanatical Catholic' (although we have to be careful here because in the language of Höss, and the language of Nazism generally, this adjective always has a positive connotation) who wanted his son to become a priest, but at the same time subjected him to a rigid, militaristic education. The young boy's tendencies and inclinations were of no account. It is understandable that he felt no affection for his parents, and that he grew up closed in on himself, introverted. He was orphaned at a young age, went through a religious crisis and when the Great War broke out he did not hesitate: his moral universe was by now reduced to a single constellation – Duty, the Fatherland, Courage. He volunteered, and the seventeen-year-old boy was flung out to the Iraqi front; he killed, was wounded, and felt he had become a man, in other words a soldier, for in his mind the two terms were synonymous.

War is the worst type of school, and while this is true everywhere it was particularly so in a defeated and humiliated Germany. Höss made no attempt to reinsert himself back into normal life. In the dreadful climate of post-war Germany, he enlisted in one of the Volunteer Corps whose role was substantially repressive; he was involved in a political assassination and sentenced to ten years in prison. The prison regime was hard, but it suited him. He was not a rebel, he liked discipline and order, he also liked expiation: he was a model prisoner. He displayed worthy sentiments: he had accepted the violence of the war because he had been ordered by Authority, but he was disgusted by the violence of his prison companions because it was spontaneous. This was to be one of his constant themes: order is needed, in everything; directives must come from above and are by definition good. They should be carried out conscientiously and without discussion. Initiative is admissible only if it serves the purpose of a more efficient execution of orders. Friendship, love and sex are suspect: Höss was a man alone.

After six years he was given an amnesty. He found work in a farm community, he married, but he confesses that he never managed, either then or later, when his need would have been greatest, to communicate fully and openly with his wife. It is at this point that the trap was opened before him. He was invited to join the SS, and he accepted, drawn by the 'prospect of a rapid career' and by the 'financial advantages connected with it'. This is also the point where he tells the reader his first lie: 'Reading Himmler's call to join the SS on duty in the concentration camps, I had never reflected in the least on the real truth of those camps . . .; it was an absolutely unknown concept to me, nor could I imagine what it would be like.' Come off it,

Commander Höss, it takes more mental agility than that to lie: we are in 1934, Hitler is already in power and has always spoken clearly. The term 'Lager' in its new sense was already well known; few people knew exactly what went on there but everybody knew they were places of terror and horror, all the more so within the circles of the SS. The 'concept' was anything but 'unknown'; indeed it was already clinically exploited by the regime propaganda: 'Toe the line or you'll end up in the camps' was an almost proverbial expression.

His career was indeed rapid. His prison experience was not wasted; quite rightly, his superiors saw in him a specialist, and they refused his feeble requests to return amongst the troops: one type of duty is as good as the next, the enemy is everywhere, at the frontiers and inland; Höss should not feel any the less for this. Höss accepted that if his role was to play the jailer, he would be a jailer with all possible diligence: 'I must confess that I carried out my part with all conscience and care, I never had any consideration for the prisoners, I was severe and often hard.' Nobody doubts that he was hard, but that his 'mask of stone' concealed an aching heart, as he claims, is a lie not only indecent but childish.

His repeated claim that once you were part of the machinery it was hard to get out again is not, however, a lie. There was no risk of death, nor even of harsh punishment, but moving away was objectively difficult. The SS militia included intensive and skilful 're-education' which flattered the ambition of the disciples who, largely uncultured, frustrated, rejected, felt themselves valued once more, exalted. The uniform was elegant, the pay was good, the power almost unlimited, impunity guaranteed; if today they were the masters of the country, tomorrow, as one of their hymns went, they would rule the entire world. At the outbreak of the Second World War, Höss was already *Schutzhaftlagerführer* in Sachsenhausen, which is not nothing, but he deserved a promotion. He accepted with surprise and joy the elevation to Commandant, in a new camp, still being built, far from Germany, near a small Polish town called Auschwitz.

He really was an expert, and I say it without a trace of irony. At this point his pages become urgent and full of participation. The Höss who writes has already been condemned to death by a Polish court. This condemnation comes from an authority and is therefore accepted, but that is no reason to renounce describing his finest hour. He gives us a veritable treatise on town planning; he addresses us from the lectern; his knowledge must not be lost, nor should his heredity be dispersed. He teaches us how a concentration camp is to be planned, constructed and run in a way that will work, *reibungslos*, despite the ineptitude of those beneath him and the blindness of his superiors, and disagreements when they send him more trains than the camp can handle. And what about him, the Commandant? Well, he can get on with it. Here Höss becomes epic: he asks the reader for admiration, praise, commiseration even; he was an exceptionally competent and diligent bureaucrat, he sacrificed everything to *his* camp including days and nights of rest and family affections. The Inspectorate had no consideration for him, they did not send fresh supplies, to the extent that he, model servant of the state, caught between the two jaws of Authority, had to 'literally go out and steal the amount of barbed wire that they most urgently need . . . I had to take things into my own hands!'

He is less convincing when he sets himself up as scholar of the sociology of the camps. He deplores with virtuoso disgust the fights between the prisoners: what scum they are; they know neither honour nor solidarity, the great virtues of the German people. But just a few lines later he lets slip the admission that 'these struggles were care-fully cultivated and encouraged by those in charge', that is, by him. He describes with professional haughtiness the various categories of prisoner, interpolating his old, long-standing contempt with discord-ant notes of retrospective hypocritical piety. The political prisoners were better than the common criminals, the Gypsies ('they were . . . for me the most precious of prisoners') better than the homosexuals. The Russian prisoners of war were like animals, and he never liked the Jews.

The discordant tones become more strident when he talks about the Jews. There is no question of a conflict here: Nazi indoctrination does not find itself in collision with a new and more human vision of the world. Quite simply, Höss has understood nothing, he has never overcome his past, he is not cured. When he says (and he says it often) 'Now I see . . .. Now I understand that . . .' he is blatantly lying, just as today all the political *pentiti*, the grasses, are lying, and all those who express their repentance with words rather than actions. Why does he lie? Perhaps to leave behind a better image of himself; perhaps simply because his judges, who are his new superiors, have told him that the correct opinions are no longer those of before, but different.

It is the theme of the Jews which demonstrates the extent to which Goebbels's propaganda weighed down on Germany, and how difficult it was, even for a submissive individual such as Höss, to ward off its effects. Höss admits that the Jews were 'quite' persecuted in Germany but moves swiftly to add that their entrance *en masse* into the camps had a pernicious effect on morality there. The Jews, as everyone knows, are rich, and everyone has his price, even the most moral officers of the SS. But the puritan Höss (who in Auschwitz had a woman prisoner as lover, and tried to free himself of her by sending her to her death) does not agree with the pornographic anti-Semitism of Streicher's *Stürmer*; this newspaper has 'caused a great deal of mischief, and done nothing to help serious anti-Semitism'. But that is no surprise since, Höss improvises, 'it was edited by a Jew'. It was the Jews who spread (Höss can't bring himself to say 'invented') news about the atrocities in Germany, and for this they should rightly be punished, but Höss the virtuoso is not in agreement with his superior Eicke, who would strangle the leakage of news with the intelligent system of collective punishment. The campaign on atrocities, Höss notes, 'would have been carried out *even* if hundreds and thousands of people had been killed'; the italicized *even*, a real gem of Nazi logic, is mine.

In the summer of 1941 Himmler 'personally' told him that Auschwitz would be something more than a place of affliction: it was to become 'the greatest centre of extermination of all time'; together with his collaborators he should set about finding the best technique. Höss did not bat an eyelid; it was an order like any other, and orders are not questioned. There had already been experiments carried out in other camps, but machine-gunning a mass of people or lethal injections are not really suitable for the purpose: what was needed was something quicker and more efficient. Above all 'blood baths' were to be avoided because they demoralized the executioners. After the most bloody operations some SS committed suicide, others drank methodically. What was needed was something aseptic, something impersonal, to safeguard the mental health of the military. Collective asphyxiation with the gas from engine exhaust was a good start, but it needed to be perfected. Höss and his associates had the brilliant idea of using Cyclon B, the poison used for rats and cockroaches, and everything seemed set fair. After the successful trial on 900 Russian prisoners, Höss felt 'a great comfort'; the mass killing went well, in terms of both quantity and quality – no blood, no trauma. There's a huge difference between machine-gunning naked people on the edge of a pit which they have dug themselves and tossing a small container of poison into an airway. His greatest aspiration was realized, his professionalism clearly demonstrated: he is the technical master of massacre. His envious colleagues were roundly beaten.

The most repugnant pages of the book are those in which Höss lingers over descriptions of the brutality and indifference with which the Jews charged with clearing out bodies go about their work. They contain a sordid accusation, a sidelong sneer, almost as if those unfortunates (and were they, too, not simply 'following orders'?) could shoulder all the guilt of the person who had invented them and given them that role. The kernel of the book, and its least credible lie, is on page 136. Watching the killing of children, says Höss, 'I felt such immense pity that I would like to have disappeared from the face of the earth, yet I was not permitted to show the slightest emotion'. Who was stopping him from 'disappearing'? Not even Himmler, his supreme boss who, despite the flattering treatment he gets from Höss, emerges from these pages in his double aspect of demi-god and pedantic idiot, incoherent and impossible to deal with.

Not even in the final pages, which take on the tone of a spiritual testament, does Höss succeed in measuring the horror of all that he has done, nor can he find the tone of sincerity. 'Now I understand that the extermination of the Jews was an error, a colossal error' (error, mind, and not crime). 'Anti-Semitism got us nowhere; on the contrary, Judaism was enabled to take a further step towards its final goal.' Just a little after that he claims to feel 'faint' on 'learning what frightful tortures were carried out in Auschwitz and in other camps'. If we think that the writer of these lines already knows he will be hanged, we cannot but be astonished by his stubborn lying right to his final breath. The only possible explanation is this: Höss, like all men of his kind (and not only Germans; I'm thinking of the confessions of the turncoat or dissociated terrorist) spent his whole life making his the lies which impregnated the very air around him, and thus lying to himself.

We might wonder, and someone will certainly wonder, what reason there might be for reprinting this book now, forty years after the end of the war and thirty-eight years after the execution of its author. To my mind there are at least two.

The first reason is contingency. A few years ago an insidious operation began: the number of victims in the extermination camps was claimed to be a great deal smaller than stated by 'official history'; toxic gas would never have been used in the camps to kill human beings. On both these points the testimony of Höss is complete and quite explicit, and it is impossible to see why he should have formulated it in such a precise and thorough manner, with so many details matching the information of survivors and the physical evidence, if he had found himself as constrained as claimed by the 'revisionists'. Höss frequently lies in order to justify himself, but never on matters of fact. Indeed, he appears proud of his organizational skills. They would have to have been far more subtle, he and the people apparently behind him, to create edifice so coherent and believable out of nothing. The confessions extorted by the Inquisition, or in the Moscow trials of the thirties, or the witch trials, had a different tone altogether.

The second reason is a matter of essence and is permanently valid. Many tears are shed these days over the end of ideologies, but this book seems to me to show in exemplary fashion where an ideology can lead when it is accepted as radically as it was by Hitler's Germans, and by extremists in general. Ideologies can be good or bad; it is good to know them, to compare them and attempt to evaluate them; it is always bad to take one on completely, even when it is decked out with respectable words such as Fatherland and Duty. Where duty blindly followed leads us, that is to say the *Führerprinzip* of Nazi Germany, is clearly demonstrated by the story of Rudolf Höss.

March 1985

From R. Höss, *Comandante ad Auschwitz*, Einaudi, Turin, 1985, pp. v–xii

33   The Black Hole of Auschwitz

The current polemic in Germany between those who are inclined to banalize the Nazi massacres (Nolte, Hillgruber) and those who claim its uniqueness (Habermas and many others) cannot be a matter of indifference to us. The thesis of the former is scarcely new: there have been massacres down the centuries, above all at the beginning of our own century, especially against the 'class enemy' in the Soviet Union, and thus near the German borders. Over the course of the Second World War we Germans did no more than adopt a practise that was dreadful, but by now well established: an 'Asiatic' practise of massacre, mass deportation, merciless exile to hostile (inhospitable) regions, torture and the splitting up of families. Our only innovation was a technological one: we invented the gas chambers. We should say in passing that it was precisely this innovation that was denied by the school of 'revisionists', the followers of Faurisson, and thus the two positions complement each other in turn in a system of interpretation of history which can only set alarm bells ringing.

Now, the Soviets cannot be absolved. First the massacre of the kulaks, then the iniquitous trials and the innumerable and cruel acts against real or presumed enemies of the people are very grave indeed, and have led to the political isolation of the Soviet Union which in various guises lasts to this day. But no legal system absolves a killer because there are other killers in the house over the road. And besides, it is beyond doubt that these were matters to do with the internal affairs of the Soviet Union, which nobody from outside could have opposed except through a generalized war.

The new German revisionists, then, tend to present Hitler's massacres as a preventive defence against an 'Asiatic' invasion. This seems to me an extremely fragile thesis. It remains to be demonstrated that the Russians were intent on invading Germany; on the contrary they feared her, as is shown by the hurried Ribbentrop-Molotov pact; and they were right to fear her, as the later, sudden, German attack in 1941 was to show. Besides, it is not clear how the 'political' massacres operated by Stalin could find their mirror image in Hitler's massacre of the Jewish people, when it is well established that before Hitler rose to power, German Jews were profoundly German, intimately integrated into the fabric of the country and considered as the enemy only by Hitler himself and the few fanatics who first followed him. The identification of Judaism with Bolshevism, Hitler's *idée fixe*, had no basis in objective fact, especially in Germany where notoriously the vast majority of Jews belonged to the bourgeoisie.

It is true that 'the Gulag came before Auschwitz' but we should not forget that the aims of these two infernos were not the same. The first was a massacre between equals; it was not based on racial supremacy, nor did it divide men into the superman and the subhuman; the second was based on an ideology imbued with racism. If it had prevailed we would find ourselves, now, in a world split into two, rulers on the one hand and everybody else in their service or else exterminated because racially inferior. This contempt for the fundamental equality of rights amongst all human beings showed through in a host of symbolic details, from the tattooing at Auschwitz to the use, in the gas chambers, of a poison originally produced to disinfect ships' holds infested with rats. The wicked exploitation of the dead bodies and their ashes remains a unique characteristic of Hitler's Germany and still today, notwithstanding those who would seek to soften its contours, constitutes its very emblem.

It is indeed true that the death rate in the Gulag was frighteningly high, but it was, so to speak, a by-product, tolerated with cynical indifference. The primary aim, barbaric as it was, had a certain rationality and consisted in the re-invention of a slave economy destined to 'Socialist edification'. Not even the pages of Solzenitsyn, which quiver with well-justified furore, suggest anything similar to Treblinka or Chelmno, which did not produce work, were not concentration camps, but 'black holes' destined for men, women and children guilty only of being Jews, where people arrived by train only to go straight into the gas chambers, from which no one ever came out alive. The Soviet invaders of Germany, after the martyrdom of their own country (do you remember, amongst the myriad details, the pitiless siege of Leningrad?), were thirsty for revenge and tarnished themselves with dreadful crimes, but there were not amongst them the *Einsatzkommandos* charged with machine-gunning the civilian population and burying them in vast common graves frequently dug by the victims themselves; furthermore, they had never planned the annihilation of the German people against whom they understandably harboured a justified desire for reprisals.

Nobody has ever stated that in the Gulag 'selections' were carried out as have frequently been described in the German camps, where a quick look front and back was enough for the SS doctors (doctors!) to decide who could still work and who should go to the gas chambers. And I do not see how this 'innovation' can be considered marginal, or be attenuated with an 'only'. These were not imitations of 'Asiatic' methods, they were decidedly European; the gas was produced by reputable German chemical factories, and it was to German factories that the hair of massacred women was sent, while the gold extracted from the teeth of the dead bodies was destined for the German banks. All of this is specifically German, and no German should ever forget it; nor should he forget that in Nazi Germany, and only in Nazi Germany, children and the sick were also sent to an atrocious death in the name of an abstract and ferocious radicalism which has no equivalent in modern times.

In the ambiguous polemic now under way, the fact that the Allies bear a heavy portion of blame has little weight. It is true that no democratic state offered asylum to threatened and expelled Jews. It is true that the Americans refused to blow up the railway lines which led to Auschwitz (while they carpet-bombed the neighbouring industrial zone); and it is also true that probably the Allied failure to provide relief was due to sordid reasons, in other words the fear of having to take in and feed millions of refugees or survivors. But this is not the same as speaking of a genuine complicity, and the moral and legal difference between the one who acts, and the one who turns a blind eye, remains colossal.

If Germany today desires the position which is rightfully hers amongst European nations, she cannot, and must not, whitewash her own past.

La Stampa, 22 January 1987

34   Preface to *La vita offesa*

Not all books can defend themselves against a question, often asked quite openly of the author: why does this book exist? Why did you start work on it, what drove you, what was your aim? I think this anthology resists this question, just as it resists the converse question: why only now? Why has it taken so long?

Yes, it has taken a long time. If the collection and recording of these stories had begun earlier, the memories of those interviewed would have been fresher and their number greater; many of our fellow ex-deportees have disappeared along the way. It is late for organizational reasons, but also because in Italy as elsewhere, only recently have people fully begun to realize that mass political deportation, along with the drive to massacre and the reprise of a slave economy, is central to the history of our century, together with the tragic emergence of nuclear arms. It is also central in the memory of the survivors: almost all those interviewed, even those who suffered less, even those whose health or family ties were not permanently damaged, even the few who (for reasons that we fully respect) have refused to speak, know this, feel it and have said as much, more or less explicitly. This modern return to barbarism is central, finally, to the consciences both of the guilty parties and to their heirs. If things were otherwise we would not have had to witness the ugly rant of the revisionists, the young historians who have emerged over the past few years and declared themselves politically white, blank sheets, impartial, neutral, open to all the pros and cons, but who dedicate page after page of polemical acrobatics to demonstrate that we did not see what we saw, and we did not live through what we lived through. Even if not openly declared in the *incipit*, this anthology of deliberately inflicted brutality and pain is dedicated to them.

The testimonies gathered here differ in register, tone and historical value. Nor could it have been otherwise: those who were deported were men and women, intellectuals, workers and peasants; partisans, resistance fighters with a strong backbone of political belief, ordinary folk rounded up by chance in the street; believers and unbelievers; Christians and Jews. Nonetheless, in certain key areas the accounts are substantially in agreement, in a way that distances them from the accounts of war veterans or former prisoners of war, accounts which are often just as painful and dramatic. Ever present is the trauma of dislocation, of feeling violently uprooted, and this is described with candour and surprising expressive power. The sealed train (another constant element, to the point that it has become the very symbol of deportation) tears you rudely away from your environment, your climate, town, family, job, language and friendships, and tosses you into an alien environment which is foreign, incomprehensible and hostile. Sometimes the deportee does not even know which country he has ended up in. The camp, the KZ – these are new terms for him, he has never heard them before. In a way, it is the world turned upside down, where honesty and mildness are punished, where violence, spying and deceit are rewarded. Here, unsurprisingly, destinies and stories diverge: there are those who give in straight away, adapting out of pure instinct to a subhuman level of existence; some attempt to understand and to respond; some seek and find comfort in faith; others (and this is the case particularly of the 'politicals', especially the Communists) perceive around them the strength to resist, an indomitable will to carry the struggle forward, an experience of international solidarity which mitigates the material and moral sufferings of the new arrivals. Later events similarly diverge: there are those who go back to find their families, their home, love and affection, their job, and for these liberation is a moment of joy, without shadows and without problems; but there are those who go back to find their family has been exterminated, their house destroyed, the world around them indifferent and deaf to their anguish. They have had to make a huge effort to rebuild a new life for themselves on the rubble of their previous one. For this man, or this woman, the mourning has never ended.

Another feature common to all these testimonies is their spontaneity, the good will with which they have been given. We almost have the impression that the desire to speak, to find an attentive and sympathetic listener, is an ancient one, and that the opportunity to give written form to these now long-past experiences has been long awaited. Many statements bear the same characteristic trait: the need to 'tell', to 'talk about it', can be traced back to the time of imprisonment; at times it is almost a vow, a promise made by the believer to God and by the unbeliever to himself: if I return I will speak of this so that my life will not have been without purpose. The hope of survival, in other words, coincides with the obsessive hope of letting others know, of sitting by the fire, around the table, and telling the story: like Ulysses in the court of the Phaeacian king, like Silvio Pellico who survived the squalor of Spielberg jail, like Ruzante returned from battle, like the soldier spoken of by Tibullus, who narrates his endeavours and 'on the table paints the encampment with wine'; and like the other unforgettable soldier described by Eduardo de Filippo, who returns to the starving and *milionaria* Naples of the immediate postwar period, searching in vain for someone to listen to him. The survivor's story is a purely literary genre.

For the survivor, to tell his story is both an important and a complex undertaking. It is perceived at one and the same time as a moral and civil obligation, as a primary, liberating need, and as social capital: a person who has lived through the camps feels himself a repository of fundamental experience, inserted into the history of the world, and he is witness by both right and duty, frustrated if his eyewitness account is not sought out and received, rewarded if it is. As such for many of us the interview which served as prelude to this anthology was a unique and memorable occasion; a moment waited for since the day of liberation, and which has given sense to liberation itself.

Many of us (but each year our number dwindles) remember the specific way in which we feared death, *there*: if we die here in silence as our enemies wish us to, if we do not return, the world will not know what man has been capable of, what he is still capable of: the world will not know itself, it will be more exposed than ever to a repeat of National Socialist barbarism, or to any other equivalent barbarism in whatever actual or declared political framework.

It is this impulse to live in order to speak, this consciousness of a clearly-defined historical responsibility which flourished in the rare moments of truce, that gave many the strength to resist, day after day: from the reasoned need to bear witness was born the idea of this book.

Those who conceived the book, financed and promoted it, the young researchers who lent a patient ear to our memories, often confused and shaken as we often were by recalling our suffering, those who laboured to reconstruct them, are all owed the grateful acknowledgement of survivors who are no longer young, who have not forgotten, and who are not always heard.

From *La vita offesa*, edited by A. Bravo and D. Jalla, Franco Angelini, Milan 1987, pp. 7–9

35   To Our Generation

To our generation has fallen the unenviable lot of living through events rich in historical significance. In saying this I do not mean that nothing else has happened 'afterwards' in the world: natural catastrophes and collective tragedies brought about by man have occurred everywhere, but despite all omens nothing comparable to the Second World War has happened in Europe. Each of us is, therefore, a witness, whether we wish it or not. The Region of Piedmont was both correct and timely in its decision to document the memories of deportation survivors, since this was unique in history, so far at least, both in its scope and in the number of its victims.

I was called upon to speak in my dual role as witness and as writer. I am honoured by this, and at the same time burdened by responsibility. A book is read, it can please or otherwise, it can teach or otherwise, it may or may not be remembered or reread. As a writer of the deportations this is not enough for me. From my very first book, *If This is a Man*, I have wanted my writings, even if the name on the front cover is mine, to be read as collective works, as a voice that represented other voices. And even more than that, I wanted them to be an opening, a bridge between us and our readers, especially if they were young. It is very agreeable for us ex-deportees to sit round a table and tell each other of our far-off adventures, but it serves little purpose. As long as we are alive, it is up to us to speak, but to other people, to those who were not yet born, so that they know 'how far it can go'.

It is not then by chance that a good part of my current work consists of a kind of uninterrupted dialogue with my readers. I receive many letters full of 'why?'; I am asked for interviews; and I am asked two fundamental questions above all, especially by young people. How could the horror of the death camps come about? Will it happen again?

I do not believe in the existence of prophets, readers of the future; those who put themselves forward as such usually fail miserably, covering themselves in ridicule. I am far from feeling myself to be a prophet, or indeed an authorized interpreter of recent history. Nonetheless, these two questions are so pressing that I have felt it incumbent upon me to attempt a reply, or rather, a cluster of replies, and for the purposes of this conference copies of them have been distributed. Some respond to Italian, American and English readers; others, and these seem to me the most interesting, are the fruit of an extensive correspondence that over the years has brought me to confront the German readers of *If This is a Man*. These are the voices of the children and grandchildren of the people who did those things, or who allowed them to be done, or who never bothered to find out about them. There are also a few German voices of a different sort, of those who did as little or as much as they could to undermine the crime being committed by their country. It seemed right to me to give space to both these groups.

We survivors are witnesses, and in law each witness is called upon to respond with the truth, and the whole truth. But in our case there is also a moral duty, because our ranks, which were never full, are dwindling. I tried to address this duty in a recent book, *The Drowned and the Saved*, which some of you may have read, and which will soon be translated into English and German. This book, too, made up of questions about the deportations (not only the Nazi deportation) and attempted answers, is part of a dialogue that has lasted over forty years now, and I feel it to be profoundly in harmony with this conference. I hope that readers will judge it to be in line with the theme of the conference itself: that it will, in other words, contribute in some modest way to our understanding of the history of our age, whose violence is born of the violence that we were so fortunate to survive.

In *Storia vissuta*, Franco Angeli 1988

Part II   Other People's Trades

36 The Writer Who is Not a Writer

It is not my intention to say that in order to write a book you have to be a 'non-writer', but simply that I came to be a writer without choosing it. I am a chemist. I came to be a writer because I was captured as a partisan and ended up in the concentration camps as a Jew.

My first book is the story of my year in Auschwitz, and the story of the book is long and strange. Despite my fear, I had made an effort to write even when I was still a prisoner: just a few lines, annotations, notes for my family written with a pencil stub and immediately destroyed, because there was no way of keeping them, except in your mind. To be found with them on you was deemed an 'act of espionage' and was therefore punishable by death. But such was the need to transmit the experience I was living through, to make others share in it, to tell a story, in other words, that I already started to do it there. I hoped, we hoped, to live 'in order to' tell of what we had seen. This was not just my desire, but everybody's, and was reflected in the form of a dream, which for many of us was exactly the same; recently I chanced to read the same thing in a book by a deported Frenchwoman. It was a double dream. In the first we dreamt of fatty, succulent food that smelled appetising; but every time we were about to put it in our mouths something went wrong: either it disappeared, someone took it away from us, or else a kind of barrier sprang up between the hungry person and the food, making eating impossible. The other dream was of telling our story, usually to someone dear to us. But here, too, we never managed to finish. Our interlocutor was indifferent, was not listening, and after a while would turn his back, walk away and disappear.

The symbolism of this double dream was very simple. I only mention it to underline the fact that the need to eat, and the need to tell our story, were on the same level of primordial necessity. Food placed beyond our grasp, and the tale stopped before reaching its end, display the same anguish of unsatisfied need.

When I returned I carried this primordial and violent need to speak back with me. There were two reasons why I started writing straight away, constructing the tale around those lost notes. First, because everything I had seen and lived through was a heavy weight on my mind, and I felt an urgent need to free myself of it all; second, to fulfil a moral, civil and political duty to bear witness. Out of eight thousand deported Italian Jews who ended up in the camps together with millions of other Jews from all over Europe, whose only crime was being born, just a few dozen were lucky enough to survive; out of my convoy of 650 people, just fifteen went home. People knew little, or knew only in the vaguest of terms. I myself did not know the scale of the extermination carried out on the basis of a crazy ideology that sought to suppress whatever was different, just because it was different.

But in writing *If This is a Man* I had no literary ambitions; I didn't set out to write a book, much less to become a writer. So much so that I didn't write in logical order but out of urgency, starting with the final chapters, and I didn't even bother about structuring it or making its fragmentary nature more coherent. As soon as it was finished I took up my work as a chemist once again. For ten years. Only in 1958, when *If This is a Man* was republished, did I feel the desire to write again. As for the book, it was published at the end of 1947 by a small publishing house after everyone else had rejected it, with a print run of 2,500 copies. It was well received by critics, but forgotten just a year or so later – even though here in Turin, particularly, a few small groups of people continued to talk about it, particularly people who had been touched by the events recounted in *If This is a Man*. Thinking back, it is understandable that the book was not judged readable, and that it found few listeners. Times were hard. Life was a struggle, the wounds of war were wide and deep, people thought only of reconstructing on the ruins and wanted nothing more than to forget and go forward. But by 1955–56 the climate had changed: people had read Vercors, Russell, Poliakov and others; they had seen the documentaries filmed at the liberation of the camps, and a broader interest was developing in the phenomenon of the camps.

A prestigious publishing house agreed to reprint *If This is a Man* in 1958. It was immediately translated; young people read it and were interested. They asked me to talk about it, to explain it; they asked questions. And so my third trade was born, for if I had accepted all the requests that came from schools I would have had no more time for anything else. This put me into contact with a new reality, with the generation just starting out on life. In the end I collected all the children's questions, at least those that had some kind of answer, into another school edition of *If This is a Man*, and this volume will come out soon.

With a book now making its own way in the world, I realized I had a new instrument in my hands, one made to weigh, divide and verify, like instruments in a laboratory, but agile, swift and gratifying. I had told a story – why not tell another? The bug of writing had got into my blood. And so *The Truce* was born, where I told of my return from Auschwitz. In the first book I had paid attention to 'things'; I wrote the second one fully aware that I could transmit experiences, but with a single aim: to write clearly in order to seek out contact with the public. There is very little reward or use in writing and not communicating. This was the gift my first book had made me, with the readership it had gained, the understanding that if to speak obscurely can be to speak for posterity, the important thing in order to be understood by those for whom the page is written is to be clear. Writing serves to communicate, to transmit information and also feelings. If it is incomprehensible it is useless, it is a cry in the desert, and while the cry may be useful for the person who writes, it is not for the person who reads. Maximum clarity, then, and, rule number two, minimum waste baggage: it should be compact, condensed. The superfluous also damages communication because it is tiresome and annoying.

Contact with readers has enriched my life and brought me joy. But a reader is an insubstantial, vague spectre. I have formed a 'perfect' one who has the same relationship to the real reader, as 'perfect gas', defined by physicists and subject to simple laws, has to real gas. I write for him and to him, not for critics who read under compulsion, and not for myself. When I write I feel him alongside me, this reader; he comes to me willingly, he follows me and I follow him; I want him to receive what I am transmitting without anything being diminished or lost along the way. At the same time as *The Truce*, and long before that too, I wrote short stories, drawing on a technical idea for each of them, born in the laboratory or in the factory. The world around us is extraordinarily fruitful and thus I began to think about producing a 'crossover', a kind of meeting point between writing and my experience as a chemist. With regard to the short stories, many people have asked me if in giving form to the small or large cracks in our world and our civilization, I was trying to allude once again to the concentration camps. I can answer that this was certainly not deliberate, in the sense that writing deliberately about a reality in symbolic terms is not part of my intention. Whether or not it is possible to see some continuity between these institutions and the camps, I do not know with any precision. It does not depend on me. 'I', as Palazzeschi used to say, 'am only the author.'

This writing of short stories, too, was a writing of 'things'. But I felt myself indebted to my daily work, and it seemed to me a wasted opportunity not to speak of my experience of work which many think is dry, mysterious and suspect. I felt there was a certain partiality in the books I read. It was an impression I had long carried around inside me, and which was confirmed over and over. Everybody knows how a corsair lives, an adventurer, a doctor, a prostitute. But there is little trace of us chemists, transformers of matter, a trade with an illustrious ancestry; it seemed right to me to 'plug the gap'. And so *The Periodic Table* was born. The title is undoubtedly a provocation, as is giving each chapter the name of an element for its title. But it seemed opportune to me to explore the chemist's relationship with matter, with the elements, as the Romantics in the nineteenth century explored the 'landscape': the chemical element became a state of mind, as the landscape was also a state of mind. Because for those who work with it, matter is alive: mother and enemy, indolent or an ally, stupid, inert, dangerous at times, but alive, as was well known by the founders of our discipline, who worked alone, unrecognized, without support, with reason and imagination. We are no longer alchemists, but anybody who has had anything to do with matter knows these things. So why not create a drama where the characters are the elements of which matter is composed? Young people write to me: 'If chemistry was as you say it is, I would be a chemist.' This is one of the compliments that mean most to me. And entering the literary arena as a chemist, I was also fulfilling a vow. I owe my life to my work. I would not have survived Auschwitz if after ten months of hard manual labour I had not entered a laboratory, where I continued to do manual labour, but with a roof over my head. My qualification as chemist, inserted alongside my name for that year, in other words my number, and hence into the organism of the Buna factory which was part of the IG Farben Industrie, also perhaps protected me from 'selection' for, as chemists, we were considered 'formally useful'. And chemistry provided my subject matter for a book and two stories. I feel it in my hand as a reservoir of metaphors: the further away is the other field, the more taut the metaphor. But mine is not the only case of this kind. Huxley and Proust did it. The fact is that anyone who knows how to reduce and concentrate, to distil and crystallize, also knows that laboratory operations have a long symbolic shadow.

There, I've had a look into my workshop. I would add that my model of writing is the 'report' that we write in the factory at the end of each week. Clear, to the point, comprehensible to everybody. It would seem to me an unpardonable rudeness to the reader to present him with a 'report' that he cannot understand. This is not to say that the language of my unconscious is that of the reader's unconscious. But I think it right to transmit to him the largest quantity possible of information and emotion.

I also owe my work everything that makes a man mature, succeeding and failing, the two necessary experiences of adult life – the expression is not mine, it is Pavese's – in order to grow. The laboratory-based chemist needs both, and the militant chemist is familiar with them both: to make a mistake and put things right; to take blows and deal with them; to face a problem and solve it or else withdraw defeated and immediately begin the battle again.

And so my chemist, too, has a long symbolic shadow; taking on matter, through successes and failures he is similar to Conrad's sailor, taking on the sea. He is also like a primitive hunter. In the evening when he draws the formula for the molecular structure he will have to build tomorrow, he carries out the same propitiary rite as the hunter of Altamira who 50,000 years ago drew on the cave walls the elk or the bison he would have to kill the next day: to appropriate it, to make the antagonist his. Both are sacral gestures. I am almost sure that the chemist's experiment is the same as man's distant past, guided by the same purpose that led him to embark on the long road leading him to civilization. That is all. That is why, I've said it many times but I will repeat it here, today, when someone asks me 'Why are you a chemist who writes?', I answer 'I write because I am a chemist.' It is my profession that helps me to communicate my experience.

Associazione culturale italiana, 19 November 1976, published in G. Poli and G. Calcagno, *Echi di una voce perduta*, Milan 1992

37   Racial Intolerance

Let me begin with a declaration of humility.

We live in strange times, times in which all sorts of people will explain everything to you; this is the age of the explainers, whose purpose is to make everything clear, to go deeply into things, the whys and wherefores. We cannot deny that this is a laudable aim. But to believe that everything has been unravelled and laid bare, or that we have brought to light the essential 'why' of historical phenomena and the motives behind the inevitable consequences, the link between cause and effect that is the foundation of the sciences, is somewhat rash.

We should admit that this way of explaining does not work terribly well for the phenomena addressed in this series of lectures. It is utterly naive to think we can explain everything in the manner of determinism, and it is an utter deception if we lead others to believe us, if we convince audience and listeners that the answer they are hearing is both satisfactory and total.

For this reason everything I will say this evening will be only an attempt at an explanation, a proposition only, or a series of propositions.

The very fact that phenomena connected with prejudice and intolerance have given rise to not one, but many, explanations does not mean there are indeed many explanations; the explanation, the full and complete motivation, has not been found, does not exist, or else has rooted itself in the very deepest layers of our minds, perhaps even beyond our minds, in some darker place.

Intolerance, and in particular racial intolerance, my topic for this evening, is a multifaceted phenomenon, as is everything that concerns man, his mind and his history. They are subjects under which we can never draw a line, and which we could argue about for ever.

Racial intolerance – as the words themselves state – is intolerance between human races. Here there is no room for discussion – human races exist. There is no doubt that the skin of a negro is black, or darker than the skin of a white man, there is no doubt that the eyes of the Japanese and people from the East are shaped differently from ours, nor is there any doubt that some human races are taller, while others are shorter. But when we try to define the human races, their distinctive features, the lines of demarcation between one race and another, and above all which race, or races, a people or even an individual belong to, we immediately run into difficulty.

The history of humankind is fantastically complicated. I mean by this written history, history which is to some degree documented, if not materially with writings, then at least with remains, with what has been left behind. This history goes back about six thousand years.

But there is no doubt that long before any traces were left, long before any documentation, there was not just one human species in existence but numerous human races, distinct from each other and almost certainly in competition with each other.

Man has existed for at least a million years and every year we witness a dizzying retrogression of this date. Now we speak of three million years, and with each passing year our ancestors are ever more distant. There are new archaeological discoveries all the time and our origins, Adam and Eve, are rooted in an ever more distant past. There is absolutely no reason to doubt that just as there were different races, there was also friction between one race and another.

It is a sad fact that the majority of skulls found by archaeologists in excavations, currently in Western Africa, are skulls that have been smashed in. And somebody has smashed them in.

The history of Neanderthal man is pretty well known. He was a human being, not *homo sapiens* but very similar to *homo sapiens*; he certainly had the same technological abilities as us, as our distant forebears. He lasted up to ten or twenty thousand years ago and then he was exterminated, probably by us, by *homines sapientes*. This much is testament to the fact that the dark instinct of aversion that drives men to recognize themselves as different from each other has very ancient roots.

Coming up to more recent times, towards an age which has left a record of itself behind, it has been observed that in Egyptian paintings and drawings the most humble workers are painted in black; they are Nubians, Ethiopians, Sudanese.

In the Song of Songs it is written *Nigra sum sed formosa*, 'I am black *but* beautiful', not 'I am black *and* beautiful', and this is an important clue. Even more important is the story we read in the first chapters of Genesis, when the story of Noah is told, the invention of wine, and the bad son, the son named Cam. This perverse son who discovers his father drunk and naked, has a name, Cam, which in Hebrew means 'the burnt one', the tanned one, the one with the dark skin. It is not said explicitly, but in the genealogy which follows the peoples said to descend from Cam are the peoples of black Africa. It is remarkable that even before such things were rationalized, hatred for the dark-skinned man sought and found justification in the fact that he had broken a taboo, violated a sexual taboo; and this is by and large one of the most common accusations still made against black men.

The black man is a violator, a violator of sexual taboo in particular, and he contravenes the law. 'I don't hate him because he's black, but because . . .' and so on. This is biblical history, as far as Cam is concerned.

It would be untrue to say that this deep aversion is universal or that it infects all civil societies. It should be noted that the Roman Empire was virtually free of it; Latin historians speak of enemy peoples, black or white, as having more or less the same physiognomy; they draw very few differences between them and they do not speak of the Nubians as inferior people to, say, the Parthians or the Britons.

Other civilizations and empires on the other hand have been deeply infected by a profound antagonism to what is different. We only have to think that this same myth of Cam is to be found in the term 'camite', in inverted commas; we still speak of camitic languages. It is not a very scientific term, but it has endured. It has been adopted for different purposes and different periods, and was deployed during the long centuries of black slave trading, a trade that was not just marginal but of vital importance, involving as it did the merchant fleets of England, Portugal, Spain, the Arab world, Holland; indeed, more or less the whole of Europe.

A figure is bandied about, though there is no way of verifying it: around fifty million slaves were deported over the Atlantic, after the discovery of America. And it is not just white-skinned men who deserve our censure here. The slave trade was carried on by blacks themselves. Coming from the middle of Africa, slaves passed from hand to hand, from the black sovereigns who sold them to other sovereigns who then sold them on the coasts to the Arab or European merchants, and they finally landed with a terrifying crash on the shores of America. And if North America has a racial problem today, a black problem, it is due above all to the fact that this trade lasted so many centuries and involved such conspicuous numbers, largely depopulating the continent of Africa.

In the case of racial tension, and of the racial oppression of the black by the white, it is often difficult to unravel racial intolerance from a number of other interconnected and complicating factors: factors of economics, language, religion, level of civil society and so on. And for this reason I call once more on the declaration of humility I made at the beginning; often it is not at all easy to unravel the causes and almost impossible to find just one, single reason for racial intolerance.

The case of South America is similar and different at the same time.

Europe, the European peoples and the Mediterranean people had known of the existence of Africa since time immemorial, for there had always been some sort of contact, since the dawn of time. After Christopher Columbus, however, they found themselves faced with a surprise, a new continent that was not India, having to deal with unknown peoples, societies and inhabitants. Here, too, the problem of contact between European civilization and this new central and South American civilization was immediately further complicated not only by economic interests but also by religious ones. There were those who argued about whether these Indians, these Indians who were not Indians, had a soul or not. If they had a soul they must be converted to Christianity; if they did not have a soul they could be exterminated, or used as domestic beasts.

Following a lengthy debate on the subject, two solutions were found: full and thorough extermination, still ongoing, and at the same time the attempt to give them some culture, in other words to convince them of the superiority of European culture.

Different again is the case of the Australian aboriginals because they were, indeed they are (and there are still a few of them left), tremendously different. They are so different that they raise the question as to whether they really belong to the same species as us. And this makes us think of the other side of the coin; that even when there is a genuine desire for integration, for assimilation, we can stumble against objective difficulties. For often those who are not tolerated cannot, in their turn, tolerate the people or the civilization that sweeps over them. It is an explosive process; one intolerance leads to a second intolerance, the dividing line splits and doubles, there is deliberate non-acceptance, refusal matches refusal.

This is a catalytic chain effect, leading to situations beyond remedy. I mentioned before the difficulty of identifying causes. Last Monday Norberto Bobbio concluded his lecture by saying that prejudice is born in the mind of man, and just as the mind of man has created it, so the mind of man can extinguish it. I do not completely agree with this. It is clear that cultural prejudice, religious prejudice, religious intolerance and linguistic intolerance are human phenomena, human in inverted commas, insofar as they are a characteristic of man and belong to the civilization of man, for better or for worse.

I think, rather, that racial prejudice is something barely human, I think it is pre-human, that it precedes man, and belongs to the animal world, to the animal rather than the human world. I think it is a feral kind of prejudice, the kind that belongs to wild beasts, and this for two reasons. First, because we find it, in fact, in social animals and I will come back to this point; second, because there is no remedy. We can protect ourselves from religious prejudice by changing religion; against linguistic prejudice, against linguistic diversity there is shelter – it can be painful, but by assimilating the language of the other we lose our own characteristics of difference; but against racial prejudice there is no defence. The black man stays black, his children remain what they are; there is no defence. And so there is no salvation; in the events which took place, and to which I will return, intolerance turned to hostility and then to massacre, and there was no refuge.

In my view, then, racial prejudice – and here I propose a solution to the problem – is of animal origin; and indeed we see it amongst the majority of social and gregarious animals, animals that like man cannot live alone but must live in a group. Amongst these animals we encounter many phenomena that are typically human. We almost always see a division into caste, typically in the hymenoptera, in ants and bees, where caste division is fundamental, and where individuals are born already stratified into different castes.

We find the need for hierarchy. This is very strange, and not easily amenable to explanation, but everybody can see it: even domestic animals demonstrate this need. Amongst the cows in the herd there is always a cow who is Number One. In all the valleys of the Val d'Aosta, for example, there are competitions which cows willingly take part in. Even amongst these animals that have been so profoundly modified and diverted from their original condition into farm animals, that have been in the service of man for thousands of years, there is still this primitive need for hierarchy.

In the coops, amongst the hens, there is a pecking order. After a certain number of preliminary pecks, a precise order emerges in which there is one hen who pecks all the others, a second hen who pecks all the others except one, and so on, right down to the last hen in the coop who is pecked by all the others but can peck none of them.

This phenomenon is utterly chilling because it is very similar to the one we are talking about.

Alongside these phenomena, which we might call phenomena of animal intolerance, we find others that can only be described as the parallels of racial intolerance.

In the books of Konrad Lorenz, Nobel Prize winner, founder of ethnology and writer of some wonderful books of popular science, especially *On Aggression*, there is a chapter on rats which I think will serve perfectly to explain and justify my statement that racial intolerance has long-lost origins that are not only prehistoric but pre-human, and that it is is indeed enmeshed in particular primordial instincts of mammals, but not only of mammals.

By this I am not claiming, and indeed I would be most careful not to claim, that racial intolerance is an evil we cannot eradicate. If we are men it is because we have learnt to seek shelter, to transgress, to put an obstacle in the way of certain instincts that are our animal inheritance.

Lorenz tells us that rats divide spontaneously into tribes; the rats of a particular group, a particular cell, are a different tribe, hostile to the rats living in nearby cells. If we take a rat from cell number one and drop it directly into cell number two, it is torn to pieces. If on the other hand we take it and put it into cell number two, but inside a protective cage, after three or four days it is accepted, perhaps because the others have learnt to recognize it visually. It is impossible not to think of human analogies, to think of the immigrant who until he has acquired, perhaps not the smell, but at least the accent of the country in which he has settled, is recognized as other. He is not usually torn to pieces, luckily, he is not always torn to pieces – although this has happened – but at the very least he is seen as different, he is marginalized, and obstacles are put in his way.

I have talked about a pre-human, prehistoric racial intolerance, an intolerance that is distant history (such as the slave campaigns) and now I would like to speak of modern racism.

The nineteenth and twentieth centuries have been the great centuries of Europe, when great philosophical systems have been constructed, when awareness of this intolerance was born, and tolerance has been preached.

Yet with all this, at the heart of Enlightenment thought and the later theories of Positivism, there was still an effort to justify this anything but rational instinct, to uncover a rational motivation for it. It is curious to read now books by scientists who were at the time in utter good faith, people both admired and worthy of esteem, and who are still worthy of esteem today.

I recently reread a book by a famous astronomer, Flammarion, a noted popularizer with a great deal of humanitarian spirit. In this book on the world before the creation of man, he speaks of the brain, its development from the animal world, from invertebrates indeed. He relates a continuous chain of cerebral capacities; there are mammals, then monkeys as such, then anthropomorphous apes, then the blacks, then the whites – in other words the French. This is quite remarkable; Flammarion was French, and for him the best brain was the French one; no other brains are quite on a par, they are a little less complete, a little less weighty than the brains of the French. When the anthropologist was English on the other hand, he was in no doubt either, the best brain was the English one. And he stopped to measure not only the weight of the brain but its mass, the number of convolutions, the surface of the cerebral cortex, the diameter of the cranial skull and, above all, the angles of the facial bones.

The facial angle had become of the utmost significance. It was found that the facial angle of the negro was at exactly mid-point between the facial angle of the gorilla and that of the Frenchman, or the Englishman, or the German, naturally. This was absolutely key; they had found what had been missing, they had found the missing link of evolution, the link that explained the transition from animal to man. It had been found, and it was the negro, or the Australian aboriginal, or anything else – not the European, no, Europe was different. In a word, we might note that the superior race is always the race of the person doing the theorizing, and there has never been a case where the anthropologist noted in terror and humiliation that his race was not the superior race, but was in fact an inferior species.

Even Hegel, the famous founder of Idealism, comes up with statements about black people which nowadays would make our hair stand on end. He says that negroes are outside the civilized world; they are part of nature, they are uncontaminated, uncorrupted nature, they are, and please excuse the play on words, nature in its natural state, they are part of the earth, part of vegetation indeed. And as they are what they are, they will never be acceptable – they are a different race.

At this point I should say that despite the best efforts of all the anthropologists, no serious anthropological study has ever succeeded in identifying a difference of any value between human races, once racial factors have been taken out of the equation: in other words, cultural factors. It is quite clear that there are those who are black, white, yellow and so on. They are different in their appearance, in their build, but when we come to speak of 'value', in other words of good or bad, these differences vanish into thin air. We have to accumulate a colossal heap of lies, including scientific lies promulgated in good faith, if we wish to demonstrate that one race is worth more than any other race.

There has been much discussion, for example, about psychological testing. In North America it has been claimed that psychological tests, dreamed up by white people, give blacks a different IQ.

But when they did the opposite, in other words black scientists applied their own tests to white people, the same thing happened, in other words the whites came out with a lower IQ.

Despite all these efforts it is clear that any attempt to measure intelligence is an act of great presumption and not as neutral as it claims, and is in its turn an instrument which seeks to rationalize. If we talk about learning languages, for example, it was held, and some people still believe this, that there is such a thing as a black accent. Thus blacks in America, or transplanted into France, Italy and so on, all speak with a different accent. Until a few decades ago it was thought that there was nothing to be done about this, it was a fact of anatomy: the black glottis and larynx were different. For this reason a black man would never be able to speak properly with a correct accent any language other than his own.

This is totally false, and we can counter this prejudice, because it is pure prejudice; a black man who studies at Oxford, who has lived in England since he was a baby, speaks with the best Oxford accent imaginable. Blacks who study in Italy, provided they are separated from their background from the age when language is learnt, acquire perfect Italian, without any trace of an accent.

We only have to think of sporting competitions. Maybe some still remember the scandal which broke out in 1936 at the Berlin Olympics, in Hitler's racist Germany: a black, a North American black, Jessie Owens, won the hundred metres' sprint. How could the racist National Socialists get round that one? They just had to put up with it. Here was the demonstration that in this test at least, the test of the hundred metres' sprint, there was a black man who was worth more than a white man.

If we look at the list of Nobel Prize winners, for example, we see men of all races. I'm not speaking of the Nobel Prize for literature, which is a very contrived affair, but the Nobel Prizes for medicine, physics, chemistry and so on, which are a serious matter; and here we find that no race has a monopoly on Nobel Prizes, no race has a monopoly on scientific knowledge.

The most fraudulent strand of racism is the one which talks about crosses between races. A fundamental component of German racial theories was the conviction that a cross was a half-caste, a hybrid, a bastard in other words (for these were euphemisms for the word 'bastard'), and that to cross two races was to pick up on the worst aspects of each and so produce something inferior. The consequence was that there could not, and should not, be mixed marriages, which were indeed prohibited by law.

But objective reality is otherwise, and easily proven. If there is something to be gained from modern genetics it is that between different species – 'species' in the strict sense of the word – a cross is not possible. As we all know, it is impossible to mate a horse and a cow and have them reproduce, or at least amongst very close species they can reproduce but the result, the mule, cannot then reproduce in turn. Within the species, it is always possible to reproduce, and the best demonstration that the difference between human races is not a difference of species is that all human races can reproduce with each other. And if there is anything to be learnt from this, it is that the most favourable crosses occur when the two creatures come from far apart. This is the result of natural selection, not only in animals but also in plants. All animals and all plants are endowed with mechanisms for dispersal; for example, the very phenomenon studied by ethnologists and Konrad Lorenz, aggression between the species, whereby wolf pack fights wolf pack and dog fights dog (not, generally, to the point of death), whereby there are competitions between male stags, whereby the birds sing (in order to send the competitor bird packing), consists in dispersal, in the spreading out over the maximum area of surface, in order to encourage distant crosses and not, in other words, mate amongst their own. Nature herself advises, prescribes even, through natural selection, that these crosses occur, and that they occur through dispersal, over a wide area. This motif, this myth of the cross as taboo, the cross which should never take place, which produces the bastard, links back to ancient and mysterious archetypes and to the idea of purity. There is a great deal of talk about racial purity, and there has been a great deal of talk about racial purity, especially in Nazi Germany, as I will describe in just a moment. As if it were a demonstrable fact that the Indoeuropean race – as it was called at the time – was pure, and being pure, was good.

Now, in that place the Indoeuropean race was not pure, because nothing points to that; any human race could be as pure, any human people.

Here I must make an aside.

The very term 'race', which I find myself compelled to use, has been greatly discredited, given the manner in which it was deployed for the purposes of one of the greatest massacres of the century. Yet I am compelled to use it; I use it as it were in inverted commas, but always with the warning that in Europe, for example, it is almost impossible to speak of human races other than as some broad and obvious subdivisions.

With regard to Europe itself, and Italy in particular, the little that we know of recent, let alone distant, history tells us that over a period of two thousand years, from Rome onwards, Italy has been the theatre of extremely complex historical events, of invasions, occupations, migrations in both directions, both in and out of Italy, and thus to speak of an Italian or European race makes absolutely no sense, in the racist sense of the term.

We can say that Italians generally have white skin, but all other definitions slip from our grasp. If we cast about for precise criteria by which to affirm racial unities in Italy or in Europe we come up empty-handed; or rather, only now can we uncover something.

A very interesting and complex branch of genetics is developing which allows us to follow with great precision a particular genetic characteristic, albeit by means of very costly research; to date this has led to what we might expect, in other words an enormous confusion dating back to remote and distant times. This means that the same characteristic found here is also found in Ireland, in Finland, and so on.

I said before that racial myth holds it as self-evident that the white race is by definition superior.

This position was the starting point for a more restrictive concept, born in Germany before Nazism, the fruit of work by German philologists who had noted a strange analogy between the grammar and lexis of neo-Latin languages, Germanic languages, Slavic languages and Sanskrit, found in ancient Indian documents, variants of which are still spoken in India. From this discovery they fashioned a precise theory of race, which they labelled the Indo-Germanic race for two reasons – one obvious, the other less so. The obvious reason was that India and Germany were the two extremes of a race which spoke a certain language and which had spread across or occupied an area which stretched from India to Germany. But more meaningfully, this Indo-Germanic definition enabled them to state that Germany was the heir to India, in other words the heir to Aryan civilization, which had risen in remote times in India, birthplace of humanity, and had elected Germany itself as its new seat. Thus Germany was a privileged country, heir to an ancient civilization.

By the way, the swastika itself, the sign which you can still see sometimes daubed on walls, was a sacred sign in India, and it was no accident that Hitler and the National Socialists chose it as the new symbol of Germany, heir to this ancient civilization. A civilization pure by definition, there was no argument because that was civilization *par excellence*. It was simply itself. The swastika had emigrated from India to Berlin.

At this point we come to the most terrible and dreadful of ideological mystifications tied to the myth of race. It is paradoxical that the most murderous racism amongst all historical racisms had in effect no concrete foundation, less of a basis even than the Portuguese had when they destroyed the Brazilian Indians. This is because they spoke not in more general terms of one or more non-Indoeuropean races, but of one race in particular, that of the Jews.

It took all the fascination which Hitler by all accounts exerted over his public to get away with such a gross piece of nonsense – for if there is a race which is a 'non-race', it is that of the Jews.

If we read what is left of the documentation, the Bible, the Old Testament, we can see that even then this people called the Hebrews in the biblical text were a vanished people, who did nothing other than assimilate other peoples, split into different groups, occupy other lands, mix with other populations, and send their offspring out far and wide. In historical times there had been one community in Egypt, another in Babylonia; it's difficult to believe even then that this race had remained pure.

Without doubt it was already a non-race in those times; but three-and-a-half millennia have passed since then, and this race that is a non-race has become ever more contaminated.

A remarkable but surprisingly little known episode took place during the Kazar Empire in the Ukraine. Around the sixth century AD, a great kingdom within the borders of modern Ukraine converted to Judaism. The king converted, and since in those days the principle held sway that *cuius regio, eius religio*, of him to whom belongs the kingdom, of him is its religion, the entire Kazar population converted, or were converted. It is difficult to say how many of them there were, but they were several million to be sure, and it is almost certain that the greatest nucleus of Hebrews in Europe, the Polish and Russian Jews, are the descendants of these Kazars. In other words they have nothing to do with the Jews of Palestine, even if we go back to the myth of blood. Despite this, it was against this race which was not a race that the most savage of racial campaigns was unleashed.

In this case, too, it is somewhat difficult to uncover the reason. Certainly this was fertile territory, because before Hitler there was in Germany an intense nationalism tied to events of the Risorgimento, the difficulties of German unification, the insecure frontiers to the east and west; in other words there grew up a nationalism against all others, *erga omnes*, and in particular against the Jews, once again for a number of reasons both apparent and less apparent. It most certainly had to do with the destiny of the Hebrew people; the Hebrews of Palestine had been occupied by the Romans, and had resisted the Roman occupation with vigour and tenacity because the Romans intended to assimilate them culturally and, above all, religiously. This was not to the liking of the Hebrews. The Hebrews had, and to some extent still have, an extremely rigid religious and traditional code which does not permit idolatry, and for them it is a rigidly prescribed taboo not to bow down before idols. Hence they rebelled many times against the Romans, and were largely exterminated or condemned to exile. They settled all around the Mediterranean basin, nonetheless maintaining amongst themselves, between communities and within communities, a profound tie which was religious in origin. These meant they remained largely strangers. These nuclei, coherent within and between themselves, were connected by a religion that became a detailed, very precise ritual code, and a tradition, which made them utterly different, and it was for this reason that as the centuries went by they were continuously driven out of one country to be hurled into another where they were once more strangers, even more than before; whatever they had assimilated from a certain culture became redundant and they had to acquire a whole new culture.

This is what happened to the Spanish Jews who were driven out in 1500, to the English Jews expelled around 1300, and so on. And so, despite their geographical dispersal, they became a people who were coherent yet nomadic, as with each expulsion they were once more declared to be strangers.

This is certainly one of the reasons why nationalist, chauvinist Germany felt them to be foreigners; they very usefully served as scapegoats for all the sins that the German people could not themselves take on board.

Against this background emerged the figure of the political agitator Adolf Hitler, who was furiously anti-Semitic.

Dozens of volumes have been written as to why Hitler was anti-Semitic, and anti-Semitic to such a degree, and their very number point up the difficulty, once again, of explanation. His was certainly a personal obsession, and while many theories have been advanced, nobody knows why he had this obsession in particular.

It has been said that he feared Jewish blood ran in his own veins because one of his grandmothers fell pregnant while working in a Jewish household. He carried this fear with him as long as he lived, because while he was obsessed with purity, he feared that he was not himself pure.

Other explanations are offered by psychoanalysts, the type that explain everything. He is said, or has been said, to have paranoid traits, perverse traits in himself, and thus projected them onto the Jews in order to expel them from his own self. I give you this explanation as I read it, and understand it, which is not very well. I'm not familiar with the language of psychoanalysis, so maybe somebody else could put it better than I can, but nonetheless this is also an outline of an answer. Then there are the economic explanations. It certainly cannot be denied that at the start of the century the Jews belonged to the German bourgeoisie and had relatively powerful positions in finance, the press, culture, the arts, cinema and so on, and so were most certainly the object of some jealousy.

But we come back to what I said before, which is precisely the inextricable confusion between a racial motivation and other causes.

Some have said that the racial war was the only war Hitler won, and indeed, he did win it. Savage war was waged first against German Jewry, then step by step in all the countries occupied by Germany; it was waged without mercy and was carried out with the talent for thoroughness and detail that characterizes the Germans in good as in evil. It led to massacre, to the deaths of six million Jews out of a global population of seventeen million, something approaching a third, and in countries such as the Ukraine, Lithuania and Poland, Jewish culture was practically wiped out. If this did not happen elsewhere too, it was only because the Germans didn't get that far, but the intention was there. It's worth remembering the testament dictated by Hitler when the Russians were just eighty metres away, an hour before his suicide: it ends with a sentence that says 'Above all I leave to you, my successors, the task of completing the racial campaign, of exterminating the Jewish race that is the cause of all humanity's woes.' This seems to me proof enough that the need of Hitler the man to heap all possible sins onto a scapegoat was beyond reason, beyond the reasonable: and this scapegoat was, of course, the European Jews.

It was not just a question of killing, and this too seems to me to contribute to the savage, animal character of this kind of racial hatred.

The act of killing can be done in a spirit of mercy. A man condemned to death is more often than not killed in a merciful manner, pity is felt for him and he is allowed to express a last wish. The massacre of the European Jews on the other hand, and in Eastern Europe in particular, took place with senseless cruelty, killing children before their mothers' eyes, bringing about death only after inflicting

prolonged and useless pain, superfluous humiliations, demoraliza-
tion and deportation – and to this I can bear personal witness.

We need to think what it meant to be loaded onto a train, into the
freight cars. Fifty to sixty people, men, women and children, were
forced to stay five, ten days (or even fifteen when trains left for
Auschwitz from Thessalonika), all shoved in together with no food, no
water, no sleep, in the bitter cold of winter and the atrocious summer
heat, in freight cars that were never opened; thus before death came,
in the concentration camps or as often as not in the trains themselves,
there was a process of brutalization, with the precise objective of
demolishing the human in man even before killing him. And I believe
that, even in this bloody history of our humanity, this is something
unique.

Another personal testimony. I was in a concentration camp, in
Auschwitz, and I worked in a factory that was bombed at intervals, and
we were made to clear away the rubble.

We had been prisoners for several months, a year almost (others
had been prisoners for over two years) and we were certainly not pretty
to look at; we had long beards, rags for clothes, our heads were shaved,
we were dirty, many did not speak German. Next to the bombed
factory there was a camp of Hitler Youth, children who were about
fourteen and who corresponded to the young avant-garde in Italy.
They came from all social classes and were doing a pre-military camp,
as it were, a sports camp under canvas, close to us.

They were brought on a guided visit to see us shovelling up the
rubble; their instructors didn't even bother to keep their lesson secret
or speak it quietly, and it was this: You see, obviously we keep them
here in the concentration camp and make them work, because they're
not men, are they? Their beards are long, they don't wash, they're dirty,
they can't even speak properly, they're only good to work with pick and
shovel, we have no choice but to treat them like this, as you would treat
a farm animal.

This turning upside down of cause and effect was quite typical,
because clearly those were the effects of imprisonment and not the
cause; and it is evident in all corners of the earth where racial prejudice
exists. The 'other' is persecuted and then they say: 'Of course we per-
secute them, you can see what they're like, can't you? They're like
animals, they're worth less than us, they don't have our culture, of
course we want them to do hard labour, the most unpleasant labour . . .'

Obviously I don't want to draw too many parallels because the
persecution of the Jews in Europe was much more thorough, more

terrible, widespread and bloodier than all other persecutions, but for this reason it can stand in some way as an example.

At this point, what can we say about today?

This was yesterday, thirty, thirty-five years ago. Does racial discrimination still exist? Certainly it does.

Italy is in some measure a privileged country precisely, perhaps, because it is a country of mixed blood, and in recent times, too, blood has been mixed.

In Italy we are so aware of not being an Italian race that we are barely sensitive to frictions with other races, and I believe that to this extent Italy really is a privileged island in Europe. And it is also for this and other reasons that the Italian Jews have suffered moderate persecution and humiliation throughout the ages, but almost never has this reached the point of spilling blood, other than under German occupation.

I would say that racial intolerance in Italy is so slight because Italy is a sceptical nation, fanaticism is unusual in Italy and it is hard for us to believe in the 'prophet'. If another prophet such as Mussolini were to appear in Italy today, now that we have been vaccinated against him, I believe he would get short shrift.

But Italy is not the only country in the world; those of you who have watched on television what has been happening in Iran can see persecution, racial or otherwise (as I said before, the confusion is permanent). There the persecution is nominally religious, because the Kurds are of the same religion as the Iranians, and yet they are persecuted. There are many Iranian Jews of Hebrew race and origin but of Muslim faith, and they are equally persecuted.

And with this, seeing what is happening as we speak, in a country that is hardly far off, for nowadays no country is far off, I have to say that optimism would be, to say the least, imprudent.

Text of a talk given as part of a series of lectures organized by the Council of Turin, entitled 'Turin Encyclopedia', November 1979

38   Preface to L. Caglioti's *I due volti della chimica* (The Two Faces of Chemistry)

Twenty years ago, around 1960, Italy, Europe and the world were sailing along in a diffused sense of euphoria, just barely troubled by the clouds appearing to gather over some recently decolonized countries. The common view, barely open to dissent or discussion, was that with the end of the Cold War between the United States and the Soviet Union, with the acceptance of nuclear equilibrium and the first signs of detente between the two superpowers, the sinister inheritance of the Second World War might be overcome and banished to the past, and the world could move forward with hope towards a future of increasing production, increasing consumption and increasing well-being. Once the dangers of a political kind had vanished or at least faded, the only dangers for humanity on the horizon seemed to be the distant ones connected with overpopulation.

Ten years ago, the picture was already different. A number of voices, some of them timid and others authoritative, had been raised, warning of the difficulties of carrying on like this indefinitely: paradise, yes, but on all fronts? And up to what point? Had the moment not come for a worldwide reckoning, to put a brake, if not on consumption, at least on waste, on artificially stimulated needs, and on the pollution of earth, sea and air? The entire world was brought sharply and suddenly to the realization that the moment had indeed come, in the autumn of 1973, over the few days of the 'minor' war between Egypt and Israel, the Yom Kippur. Oil, the principal source of energy for all industrialized countries, source material for thousands of products, tacitly assumed to be in inexhaustible supply, could on the contrary disappear temporarily because of one individual's arbitrary and autonomous decision. Indeed, a slightly closer look showed that within a few decades it could disappear altogether: or rather, it would dry up because the oil fields would be exhausted. This sudden awareness of an end point, which could be delayed but not put off for ever, was in many ways salutary, because it made clear to everyone the need to resolve, in an intelligent manner and on a global scale, a number of problems that had been building up. An alarm bell rang: the oil will run out, it is already coming to an end, and with it will end the age of cheap energy, the *belle époque* of careless waste, of oil flowing like water, hardly more expensive indeed than mineral water. And sooner or later not only oil will run out but also many metals, whose consumption is growing exponentially at the expense of limited resources. In short, we have been marvellously ingenious in the short term, in the solution of perhaps complex but temporary and marginal problems, while we have been astonishingly feckless when it comes to larger problems that stretch out in space and time, and on which depend nothing less than the survival of our civilization, or even of our species.

And so another blow was dealt to the Enlightenment concept of progress. From the start of the century, with the First World War, progress began to be talked about with some circumspection: progress, yes, but only in scientific and technical fields, certainly not in moral terms, and perhaps not even in culture and art. Today there are thinkers (and many non-thinkers) who cast doubt on scientific progress itself: the industrial revolution has given rise to two worldwide, bloody wars; chemistry has given us dynamite; out of Einstein and Fermi came Hiroshima; from weedkillers we got Seveso; from tranquillizers the tragedy of thalidomide, cancer comes from colourants. Enough, we should call a halt, turn the clock back.

Except that we cannot turn the clock back, or at least we could, but only at the price of a massacre of unheard of proportions; going backwards would mean opening the gates once again to epidemics and infant mortality; halting the production of chemical fertilizers would reduce agricultural production to a half or even a third, condemning hundreds of millions of people to starvation, over and above the number who are already starving. Humanity finds itself today in a new and critical situation so complex that it would be ingenuous to seek to resolve it on the basis of a single general criterion. We cannot continue to 'progress' indiscriminately, but neither can we stop or retreat on all fronts. We need to deal with the problems one by one, with honesty, intelligence and humility: this is the delicate and formidable task of today's and tomorrow's technicians, and this is the theme around which this book revolves.

I would be so bold as to say that rather more than a compendium of chemistry, this book is a little manual of practical behaviour. It is right, and it is fundamentally important, that the many, serious problems of a technical nature that we face should be separated from emotions and economic interests, and set out as competently and honestly as possible. There are very few solutions offered here: sometimes a balanced examination of the facts shows that the problem does not exist, or else it exists but the solution could be found only through disproportionately expensive research, or else (as in the case of the 'saccharine mess') the truth can drown in a sea of contradictory experimental data. This, of course, is an extreme case, due to the fact that the product is characterized by only modest risks and benefits, both of which are ill-defined. A different matter of more universal importance is the problem of food additives, because we are all consumers of food, and the majority of human beings now consume food which has been altered or conserved in some way. There are useful, even indispensable additives, such as those which protect food longer and more safely from decomposition; others, such as colourants, serve a merely commercial purpose and therefore satisfy false needs, created by habit and by marketing. It would hardly be impossible to become used to eating grey salami or colourless jams (or rather, 'naturally' coloured), but 'the resistance of the consumer has so far been decidedly against' these innovations, however logical they may be. It would be very fitting if the same propaganda weapons called upon to promote totally futile and sophisticated needs could be deployed against the use of pointless additives. Indeed, in the light of the most careful and intelligent ecological balance that this book sets out to promote, pointless means harmful: if there is no benefit we should make a presumption of harm, however small. We need only take, for example, the case of nitrates and nitrites which for centuries have been added to sausages, to brighten their colour, and which have recently been suspected of favouring the development of cancer through complex and unsuspected transformations that they seem to undergo in the organism.

Equally sensitive is the problem of medicines. Hippocrates already knew full well that every drug was a potential poison, as demonstrated by the semantic ambivalence of the Greek word. We learn that 'between 3 and 5 per cent of hospitalizations in the United States are caused by a bad reaction to a form of medication', and there is great uncertainty about what happens when a patient is prescribed two or more medicines about whose compatibility and mutual interaction the practising doctor, or the pharmacist, know practically nothing. And what should we make of the case, all too common now, in which medicines are consumed by the patient without medical prescription, on the basis of other people's experience, or hearsay? Here we need to evaluate the risk–benefit equation, with intelligence and skill, and aside from any emotional response. But in the majority of cases this evaluation far exceeds the capacities of the layman, and we are all laymen: it is a matter of chance that each of us manages to achieve some kind of competence in one of the infinite problems we find ourselves faced with. But it is difficult to divest ourselves of our emotional reactions. The press, and the mass media, bombard us with increasing quantities of information that is imprecise, twisted, partial, frequently ill understood by those who are telling us, and almost always polluted by vested interests or preconceived ideologies. The question of tobacco is exemplary, and is here dealt with at length. It is certainly true that a general awareness is forming that 'smoking is bad for you', but it is salutary to see it clearly stated that in West Germany, for example, each year tobacco earns the state 9 billion marks, but brings with it a social cost of 20 billion marks for the treatment of the illnesses directly or indirectly caused by smoking; or that tobacco kills four times as many people as do road accidents.

It is a difficult matter to pronounce judgement on the toxicity of chemical elements, traces of which are present (and always have been: the sea contains almost all of them, but their concentrations have grown and new ones have appeared) in the environment we live in and in the foods we eat. We have known for a long time that arsenic and selenium are 'toxic', are in other words harmful or deadly if absorbed in high quantities: but what does 'high' mean here? Only the most modern and subtle methods of chemical analysis have allowed us to establish that in very low doses, both are, on the contrary, necessary or at least useful: arsenic as a growth factor; selenium as antagonist of mercury. We might add that the dosages in which they (together, probably, with other elements and compounds) are useful vary considerably from species to species, and more than likely from individual to individual. It would therefore be prudent to reduce their presence in the environment; but it would be foolhardy to eliminate them altogether. Where is the line of demarcation between wisdom and stupidity?

The author points out that this uncertainty and confusion reaches its high point on the question of energy; and yet this, interwoven with all the other problems of today (including political ones), is the problem of problems, the kernel of our survival, before which all other questions should pale. The threatening title of a book by Fred Hoyle is *Energy or Extinction*, quoted here. It is also the problem about which we are least informed, because the solution that seems most plausible to us, in other words recourse to nuclear energy, does not rest, like others, on the experience of decades or centuries; it transcends the confines of classical physics and chemistry, and comes up against old habits and disturbing mental associations: for many, plutonium is Pluto, and the atom is Hiroshima. The 'two faces' to which the book's title alludes, risks and benefits, are both masked and camouflaged, sullied, too, by the enormous financial interests at play. There is no unanimity as to their objective evaluation, not even amongst people working in the field. And yet the problem cannot be ignored, for a failure of energy would lead to a massacre of unimaginable dimensions; nor can we delegate the resolution of the problem to the next generation, as we would be punishing it for our own improvidence. But once again, to solve it requires intelligence, culture and honesty.

From all that we have said here, and from the many other vital themes dealt with in the book, there is a very clear need, a moral obligation indeed, not to be gullible, impulsive or ignorant. Never before has there been such a great need to be informed, and never as now has schooling, in Italy at least, been so poor at educating us. We should welcome those who, like Caglioti, set out to fill these gaps. There are knotty problems which will not be resolved by yelling for and against, or with demonstrations and processions, but rather with concrete actions and faith in human reason, because there are no other suitable tools. If we oppose a necessary and urgent decision, we must have an alternative and better option to propose. If we speak of 'new models of development', we must know what this expression means. In a word, we need to know; not to give way to the enthusiasms and catastrophe-mongering of others, and not to satiate ourselves or others with words.

Beneath the technical information and inevitably weighty quantitative data, a silent current of wisdom flows through this book, of moral tension and a desire to educate. It does not proclaim solutions, but the very way it sets about its task teaches us the most opportune state of mind to find these solutions. Each and every citizen can find in it material for meditation, and indeed it is a book which should be immediately adopted as a textbook for schools.

From L. Caglioti, *I due volti della chimica*, Milan 1979, pp. 9–13

39   We See No Other Adam in the Neighbourhood

It is a pity, but we see the same thing all the time: the fact that a statement is believed by countless people over countless years, is no proof whatsoever of its truth. How many hundreds of years did schools spend teaching us that worms are born from rotten meat? How many hundreds of years did doctors maintain that malaria comes from bad air, and that bleeding cures all diseases?

In the same way, the ancient credentials of the belief in 'inhabited planets' are no evidence of its truth. This view, and its opposite, that life exists only on earth, have both been held for thousands of years with extreme vigour but feeble argument. Perhaps no other philosophical dilemma has provoked a polemic more long-lasting and more vague in substance. It persists, and will continue to persist, because it consists of two repeated and opposing arguments that are, in brief, the following:

1   Only the earth is inhabited because the earth is the centre of the universe. We have reluctantly been compelled to renounce this view in its material form; we have admitted that it revolves around the sun, that the sun is not the centre of the galaxy, that it is nonsense to speak of the geometric centre of the universe, but we believe nonetheless that the earth is a privileged place because on the earth we human beings live, and we are privileged in that we know good and evil and we have been granted divine revelation. Naturally, there are no signs of extraterrestrial life. Clearly it does not exist, and even more clearly there cannot exist any form of intelligent life.

2   Other inhabited worlds exist for reasons of symmetry and economy. Only life, and especially conscious life, can be the goal of creation, and creation cannot have had any other goal. An endless universe in which only insignificant earth nurtured life and consciousness would be an illogical and wasteful universe. For the moment there are no signs of extreterrestrial life, but its precursors have been discovered on our very neighbours in the solar system; all the more reason to expect that we will find them on the stars, if and when we will be able to explore them. Perhaps

the stars are not infinite in number, but they are certainly so numerous that millions of planets could be the backdrop to the emergence of life, and the path of life is inexplicable and senseless if it does not lead to consciousness. It is therefore self-evident that intelligences other than ours exist in the Cosmos.

In reality, there is just one thing that is self-evident in this dispute, and that is prejudice. If we reduce the two arguments to their most profound essence we should then express them like this: 'I, man, do not wish to have any competitors in creation', and 'I, man, fear solitude, and desire companionship and guidance.' These are sentimental positions and therefore unimpeachable: they are desires in the form of beliefs. Now, the leaps made by astrophysics over the past few years have produced breathtaking results, and making metaphysical hypotheses about things which are now within reach of our instruments has become a vaguely irritating exercise. Man has stepped on the moon, he has analysed the soil of Mars and the infernal atmosphere of Venus, he has photographed the volcanoes of Io and the hydrocarbon rains on Titan: the heavens have more imagination than we had foreseen, but there are no signs of life, either past or present. There is no other Adam, at least in our neighbourhood, nor is there his most rudimentary progenitor: there are only moderately complex carbon compounds, in other words the clay with which to make him.

How things might be further afield, in the near and more distant stars, we have no idea, nor can we tell if we will ever be able to know. For the moment all we can say is that extraterrestrial life is possible, probable and desirable to varying degrees given the sentimental and theological prejudices that each of us unconsciously preserves, but it is rather less evident to us than to our scientist and positivist fathers.

Article published with the launching into orbit of satellites Pioneer 10 and 11, carrying on-board information about the environment and the nature of man. *Tuttolibri – La Stampa*, 3 January 1981

40   Horseshoe Nails

A book has just been published that is in many ways remarkable, and is on sale in the main bookshops: by Luciano Gibelli, it is called *Prima che scenda il buio – Dnans ch'a fàssa neuit* ('Before night falls'). It is remarkable because it is a bilingual work in parallel text, Italian and Piedmontese; because, despite the elegant presentation, it has been published at the author's own expense; and above all because of its subject matter. This is indicated in the subtitle: 'Tools, instruments and objects from the past, collected so that we do not forget'.

The book places itself therefore in the academic field of cultural materialism, the link between anthropology and history, but it is far removed from any academic pretence, from any abstraction or any school of thought.

The author, Luciano Gibelli, from Canelli, is a man in his fifties, a gentle enthusiast with no scholarly credentials. He is a curious, precise amateur, motivated by the desire to prolong the life, at least in our memory, of a civilization on the verge of dying out. It is a civilization captured in the objects that only the most elderly amongst us have had occasion to see, or have heard described by their father and grandfathers. Gibelli has had little recourse to library research but instead has entrusted himself to the willing conversation of elderly village folk, giving each object a philologically complete picture, with names, origin, usage and drawings he has done himself and which are carefully calculated to the millimetre.

He has found many of these objects in the country lofts so dear to Gozzano, 'where age-old refusal sleeps'; others, no longer to be found but of which a memory trace persists, he has reconstructed himself, with the woods and metals of old, in order to look at them, feel them in his hands and see for himself how they work. This has been an almost religious enterprise of devoted patience and a high level of manual skill: but we can also glimpse the pious effort of the artist who paints from memory the portrait of the beloved who has since disappeared.

Nonetheless, this rigour goes together with a pleasurable freedom in the format of the book. Perhaps it would be more accurate to say that the book has no overall design; topics lead one to the other as in a conversation, a chat amongst old friends around the hearth. From the House we pass to the Bricks, the Tiles, and by analogy to the Braziers, to Fire and the various archaic (but not all that archaic!) ways of lighting it. From Weights and Measures we pass to long-gone bureaucratic customs, to instruments for writing, to inks, seals and so on. The author has no fear of digression; indeed he is at his sparkling best here, in the affectionate description of family customs, festivals and now extinct customs. Read, for example, the pages in which the technological description of church bells merges into a nostalgic discussion of the various ways in which they were rung with their peels, harmonies and melodies: voices now hushed, or else kept alive artificially.

Who would know how to prepare a goose quill these days? There is a drawing of the seven stages, while another shows us the Temperer, a multiple device which served solely to cut pens and sharpen them; besides which we learn that because of their different curvature, the most prized quills were those taken from the goose's left wing. Quills from the right wing hindered the writing, because their tip was too close to the writer's eye. After this we are given a list of no less than ten accessories indispensable to the scribe, from the portable ink-pot to the 'dust', precursor of the blotting paper, also made redundant by the invasion of the ball-point pen.

Through the six hundred entries in this book we learn that not so long ago, in cases of emergency, copper spectacles were used. These were circles of copper with a tiny hole in the centre which, by reducing the amount of light to the pupil, also reduced in equal measure all the defects of the eye. If the light was good at least they allowed the wearer to thread a needle. We also find the objects and rules of forgotten games, such as the spinning top, tip-cat (*cirimela*) and shooting games.

We learn that the blacksmith had at least three types of nails for horseshoes: normal ones, nails for going uphill and others for ice. Before undertaking a long trek uphill the carter would often have to substitute one with the other, as we do now with snow chains. We read with nostalgia and curiosity hundreds of recipes for food made of lowly ingredients, among them no less than a dozen for waffles (*Canëstrej*) in which the main ingredient, to be added to the flour, ranges from chocolate to garlic. Also described and illustrated is the metal waffle pan, without which they cannot be made.

Recipes, cooking implements and edible herbs take up over a hundred pages. There are more than a hundred herbs described, and it is interesting to see amongst them many supposed 'weeds', and we might think of the skinny young girl mentioned by Manzoni, who steals wild herbs from the heifer, herbs 'which hunger had taught could also be eaten by men'. Those were times of famine, but then it was almost always a time of famine. Rather than a direct description, from these entries we see a portrait of a time when the kitchen was the heart of the house and meals were a ritual; the rhythm of life was poorer than ours, more precarious, but also more convivial and more human.

And so before the darkness of forgetting (*dësmèntia*) descends, it is good that the forms of petrol lamps have been recorded, of the threshing belts, the sundials, the wine kegs, the winnowing-fans, and of hundreds of other objects shaped by the experience of centuries, and which have now disappeared or are in the process of disappearing. Our spirits inhabit not only the illustrious works of individual creativity but also these humble tools which accompanied our forebears in their path through life.

La Stampa, 22 March 1981

41   Let's See How Much has Come True

In my view, science fiction can and should invent everything. This is its vocation, and to impose limits of verisimilitude on it would be to clip its wings. The only admissible limits are not those of the possibility and feasibility of its inventions, but their 'comic power'. In other words, science fiction can propose anything it likes for the future, plants that learn to speak, hybrids (fertile, maybe) between man and machine, new methods by which word or thought can be incarnated directly into fact or object, inversions of past and future, folly and wisdom, inner and outer and so on, as long as the themes are stimulating, rich and above all new, which is already to ask a great deal.

By way of comparison, and also provocation, I would suggest we shift the question onto adjacent territory and ask not what science fiction, but what science and technology, can still invent. This is a matter of serious prophecy, and prophecy has always been a dangerous art. Thus, prophets all down the ages have prudently taken two wise precautions: they have used obscure language (which has given them the added advantage of appearing inspired) and they have placed their predictions not in the immediate future but in a far off, distant and indefinite future so that they would be dead by the time anybody challenged them.

Years ago, with the necessary dose of humour, a very serious physicist and technologist, who also wrote some classics of science fiction under the name of Arthur Clarke, took up this sport. Below are some of his predictions, formulated around 1960, together with an indication on the current effective 'state of the art':

Foreseen for 1970:

Space laboratories: The first, Spacelab, may be in orbit by 1982.

Moon landing: This happened a year earlier than predicted.

Translating machines: Not fully operational: existing ones are still rudimentary.

Efficient electrical accumulators: These exist, but are still rather expensive.

Language of sea mammals: As far as we know investigation has gone no further than the first results of Lilly on dolphins. Their intelligence is comparable to that of dogs, and they have their own form of language that appears quite evolved, but which I don't believe has yet been deciphered.

Foreseen for 1980:

Planetary landing: This has not happened yet, and does not seem to be about to happen, but long-distance exploration is producing some surprising results.

Personal radio: I don't know what Clarke was thinking of: I believe this would be easily realizable, but perhaps it is better to leave it where it is.

Exobiology: This is the biology of extraterrestrial life forms. For the moment we know nothing about them. Exploration of the surface of Mars was disappointing; on the other hand, large organic molecules, possible precursors of life, have been found in space.

Gravity waves: This is being studied, with controversial results.

As a curious footnote, I remember Clarke predicting energy production by nuclear fusion for around 1990. The world desperately needs this prediction to come true.

In *Tuttolibri, La Stampa*, 3 January 1982

42   Our First Ancestors were Not Animals

War of Fire, by J. Rosny, is an adventure novel set in prehistoric times, when man knew how to keep fire but not yet how to make it. This French book was published in 1911; I liked it very much as a boy, and I still rather like it. It is almost a fable, and makes no claims to be educational: it is naive, an agreeable read and skilfully written. Its characters, especially the three who set out to conquer fire, are resourceful and brave, as faithful to their tribe as Homeric heroes, although they are perhaps a little too monogamous, too polite and clean for the time they live in.

The film made from the book, which I rushed to see, sins in the opposite direction. It is not naive in the slightest. Clearly it is difficult to remain naive when several million pounds are at stake, but it could have been agreeable, and the progenitors of this film have hardly been so at all. As for the characters, they appear surprisingly stupid and dirty. These ancestors of ours could hardly have been gentlemen and they certainly did not wash a great deal, but once they had learnt to wear the skins of animals they had killed, it is barely credible that they did not also invent a way of tying them around their body: not so much out of modesty (which must in any case have been invented fairly early on) but to protect themselves against the cold.

Garments such as the ones we see in the film serve no purpose whatever, unless it is to lead the spectator to the redundant notion that these savages were indeed savage. In my view it is likely they had a certain bodily nobility, precisely because they were animal-like. But here they are nasty, ridiculous orcs, moving with a clumsiness that seems out of keeping with the business of hunting. They hardly ever run, and when they do they are slow and awkward. But perhaps this is the fault of the actors, compelled by scientific consultants to go barefoot over all kinds of terrain without being given adequate training.

A couple of words about the consultants. Anthony Burgess, who already has *A Clockwork Orange* on his conscience, was not ashamed to have his name attached to the dialogue. But here there is no dialogue; there are only yells, grunts, and something approaching words, out of which just one word emerges clearly articulated, *atra*, evidently their word for fire. Burgess did not go to a great deal of trouble, but maybe this was just a jobbing contract for him. Neither was Desmond Morris ashamed to be cited as consultant for the gestures and movement. Morris had already appeared somewhat ambiguous in his famous book *The Naked Ape*, (in other words, man) and here he reinforces this impression of ambiguity.

Let us be clear. Pornography is an art belonging to all times and all countries, and this leads us to think that it answers a human need. Trying to repress it is a vain and silly waste of time; we should give the green light to pornographic films, and pornographic books too, but both should clearly label themselves as such, for those who enjoy and understand such things. Healthy commercial practice, as well as sound old common sense, forbids us to sell vinegar with an oil label on the bottle, or vice versa. Morris did just that, and so disappointed those who take a passionate interest in one or other of these approaches, the anthropological and the pornographic.

When we think about it, there are very few notable gestures in the film. The only entertaining movement sequence is perhaps the one when the protagonist returns from his victorious expedition, and 'recounts' his adventures beside the fire that he has himself conquered. He has come across mammoths, and he mimes their curved tusks, holding under his chin the skull of a billy goat with its crooked horns; with his hand and arm he imitates the movements of the trunk. His listeners understand, and they laugh. But in line with his vocation that we mentioned before, Morris has introduced another thematic gesture. There is a woman, a little less prehistoric than the other characters, who teaches the stranger the 'correct' position for coupling: these strangers, apparently, had never thought of it. He is a quick learner, and having learnt this he becomes civilized.

What a wasted opportunity! With a little taste and imagination it would have been possible to tell, or at least give some idea, how hard a journey it was to discover fire, reached only after centuries of near misses; trial and error, yes, but most certainly intelligent trial and error. There is nothing to prove that these beasts of Vico were more stupid than we are. Cinematically, too, it would have made a fine story. But all we get from this film is the idea that the vital trick for making fire with the system of a rotating stick is to spit on your hands first: the girl shows the stranger. And lo and behold, the fire is lit.

We could say the same, or worse, about the non-aggression pact with the mammoths. The producers could have chosen between the Kipling-like fable of the book and a seriously educational tone, but in the second case it would have been vital to give the viewer an impression of the passage of time in this fundamental stage of humanity, the taming of animals. In the film we see neither one nor the other: the whole episode is over and done with in just a few seconds, the elephants decked out as mammoths collaborate reluctantly, stumbling over the enormous prostheses in the shape of tusks which stick out of their mouths.

We know how risky it is to turn a book into a film, that the film is always completely different from the book, and generally worse. It is a pity though: all we have here is a tale about *les âges farouches*, as in the original subtitle of the book. There is barely a trace here of the future *homo sapiens*; these ancestors of ours were nothing more than poor naked apes.

La Stampa, 14 March 1982

43   Collectors of Torments

I have never seen an exhibition as clumsy and as pointless as the one currently cluttering up the Società Promotrice delle Belle Arti in Turin, extended goodness knows why and for how long, and baldly called 'Dreadful machines of torture throughout history'. It certainly delivers what it promises; the machines are there, authentic or reconstructed, and they are as dreadful as anyone could wish, but everything around them is pretentious and false.

The tone of the captions is false, or rather falsetto. Luckily they are placed in the wrong position, and the reflection from the lights makes many of them illegible. The tone swings between lazy self-satisfaction and a forced wittiness which in these surroundings sets one's teeth on edge. Some of these machines created for the express purpose of causing pain are praised for their 'success in causing agony'; the cat-o'-nine-tails is held up for its 'notable virtues'; and another type of whip or scourge is described as 'amusing'.

Here, I think, we glimpse the origin of this travelling exhibition. It came about through the joint efforts of a certain number of collectors in the field, both Italians and foreigners. I must confess a certain distrust of collectors, unless they are motivated by a specific cultural passion, or have overt speculative designs, or are under fourteen years of age (or whose mental age is such).

Unless at least one of these is the case, a collector is essentially someone who does not know what to do with his time, and if this is the case not too much harm is done. But if his curiosity turns towards arms, weapons, or worse, the 'dreadful' and so on, my distrust deepens. A collector of this kind cannot but have an *esprit mal tourné*; if he cultivates his mania as a private citizen within his own four walls, it is entirely his affair, or perhaps that of his analyst. But if he gets together with others of his kind and spills his passion amongst the rest of us, then it is everybody's business.

The cultural gloss the exhibition garbs itself in is false. I do not believe in the culture of someone who writes *strinto* for *stretto* [translator's note: *strinto* is erroneously given as the past participle of the verb *stringere*, meaning to tighten or to clasp], who speaks to me of *guerriglieri catalogni* [translator's note: from *Catalogna*, Catalonia. *Catalogni* is here mistaken for the adjective *catalani*, meaning Catalan], who confuses *informatica* (information science) with *informazione* (information), and cannot use the subjunctive correctly. Nor can I believe in this culture when he pretends to have a philological rigour which he does not in fact possess, and which would anyway be out of place when we are talking about a subject as obscene as torture.

Equally out of place is the pseudofeminist tirade about the maschilism of the torturers, and the revulsion expressed at past and present use of these contraptions seems fake and unconvincing. Anybody who is sincerely outraged by them does not collect them, and certainly does not put them on display. Rather, he thinks about the matter, tries to reconstruct an age in which the real or presumed crime was to be met by fitting punishment, and the condemned man was therefore deemed worthy of the torments of hell; a time in which these machines, rhetorical, excessive and even decorative as many of them are, served to highlight the theatrical aspect of punishment, and to strengthen faith and obedience to the earthy or divine order by reducing the transgressor from a human being to 'nothing'.

And this is the point. The supposed motivation is false and hypocritical: while claiming to be a crusade against torture, this circus act does more harm than good. The reappearance of torture in our century, in the wake of Hitler's and Stalin's regimes, has little to do with these machines.

These days, torture, which, appallingly enough, is present more or less everywhere (maybe a little less in Italy than elsewhere), has an exclusively formal relationship to these torture devices. It is no longer theatrical but secret; its goal is not theological or cosmic, but political. It is, unfortunately, 'rational', and it should be fought with the weapons of reason. It is the worst of evils, worse even than the death penalty; it destroys the body of the tortured victim and the soul of the torturer. But how will this gross exhibition of another kind of barbarism help free us of it? We can be sure that not one single potential torturer came out of this a changed man; indeed, this display will have kindled the sadistic streak which lies concealed in many of us.

La Stampa, 28 December 1983

44   Brute Force

. . . Al gener nostro il fato
non donò che il morire. Omai disprezza
te, la natura, il brutto
poter che, ascoso, a comun danno impera,
e l'infinita vanità del tutto.

Fate only gave our kind
The leave to die. Henceforward you can scorn
Yourself and nature, brutal
And hidden force that rules our common doom
And the vast vanity of everything.

Giacomo Leopardi, *Canti*, selected and introduced by Franco Fortini, and translated by Paul Lawton, Dublin, UCD Foundation for Italian Studies, 1996, p. 133

This is how the thirty-five-year-old Giacomo Leopardi addressed his weary heart, in this most desperate of his Cantos. Not everybody shares this despair, and those who do share it, do not share it all the time. The infinite vanity of the world, which few can refute, weighs down on us only in our moments of clearest vision, and in a normal life there are not many of these. Besides, if we have the sensation (whether true or false) that our actions are not pointless, and that they might serve for example to lighten a burden, or provide a moment of joy, this does not normally make us unhappy. Furthermore, to our great good fortune, or to our *ameno inganno*, our 'sweet deceit', there still exist on this earth dawns, forests, starlit skies, friendly faces and precious encounters that seem to us removed from brute force.

Yet this power appears unchallenged and clear (not *ascoso* or hidden, in other words) to anyone who has found himself fighting the old human battle against matter. Everybody who has done so has been able to see with his own eyes that, if not the universe, then at least this planet, is maintained by a perverse, not quite invincible force that prefers disorder to order, mixture to purity, confusion to parallelism, rust to iron, the heap to the wall and stupidity to reason. We need to defend ourselves against this power, which we have all felt, and which works inside of us, too. Our strongest fortress is the brain, which we should therefore keep in good condition, but we also possess smaller strongholds, destined for simpler services, which we share with lesser animals and maybe even with plants. We do not need the brain in order to sweat when it is hot, or to make our pupils contract in bright light; indeed, these are actions that the brain is incapable of carrying out.

When all of these mechanisms, cerebral and otherwise, are in proper working order, they allow us to maintain the status quo, which is no problem on the scale of days and weeks, but more of a problem on a scale of years and decades, in that we grow old and die. This capacity for self-preservation against the brute force of degradation and death is a property of living matter and its more or less sophisticated imitations, and is called homeostasis. Homeostasis allows us to resist the thousand internal and external variations that threaten to upset our equilibrium with the environment.

It has never been shown, of course, nor could it be shown, that distancing ourselves from our own identity is necessarily a bad thing. Whether it is or not depends on the initial quality of this identity, and how it is subjectively perceived. There are individuals who spend their whole lives in a sad earnest desire to change their skin, because (perhaps wrongly) they are unsatisfied with the skin they live in, and which they cannot themselves change because of an excess of homeostasis, but this is rare. In general, over the long term, homeostasis does not hold, and 'life' sees to it that you become another person: cowardly, non-responsive, mean, corrupt, a hypochondriac, because it nibbles away at your defences until it destroys them. Furthermore, 'life' changes us for the worse, and so homeostasis, although it is essentially conservative, is a good thing. Of course things like progress, reform, innovation and invention are all good things, but it is not given to everybody to put these things into action, while preservation of the self is a minimal requirement of all living things.

Not only living things. It is important to note that the devices used for maintaining one or more variables in a constant process came into being together with industrial civilization, with engines, to be precise. By 1787 Watt had already added a centrifugal regulator in order to impose a constant speed on his early steam machines. This consisted of a small vertical mast connected to the engine by a pair of conical cogs. From this mast hung two rigid and opposite pendulums, and connected to the pendulums was a system of levers controlling the steam emission valve. The higher the speed of rotation, the more the pendulums were raised by centrifugal force, and the tighter the valve was closed. Equilibrium could thus be reached, in other words a constant speed even with variable loads. In this way, long before the concept of homeostasis was theorized, Watt had developed what two centuries later would be called the 'feed-back loop', a cycle of retroaction: it is a 'cycle' because it acts on the feeding of the system. A notable example of retroaction is water heaters. These have a thermometer that not only measures the temperature of the water, but compares it with a value selected by the user, and interrupts the feed current if the first temperature is higher than the second. This mechanism achieves a somewhat crude 'all or nothing' regulation. The inertia of the system means that, rather than remaining constant, the temperature oscillates within a range of four or five degrees, which is fine for bath water (which will anyway be mixed with cold water for the desired temperature) but would not do in many other cases where shifts of temperature of even one degree, or even one hundredth of a degree, are unacceptable, such as when we wish to measure a physical or chemical property that depends heavily on temperature.

In these cases we turn to refinements closely resembling what happens in living organisms and which empirical practice has suggested to man since time immemorial. Regulation can be modulated, in other words the correction can be proportional to the observed shift; indeed, the water heater thermostat can be compared to a helmsman who can hold the rudder only in the two extreme positions, either completely to the left or completely to the right. A good helmsman will not work like this, but consciously or otherwise he will correct the rudder in proportionate measure to the shift of route shown him by the compass. The first will follow a wavy line, while the second will follow an almost straight line.

Other more subtle methods are also adopted. The correction can be triggered not by reaching the prescribed value but by the speed with which this value is being approached; in the case of the thermostat, by the speed at which the temperature falls or rises: *principiis obsta*, it opposes beginnings; the machine has been taught how to foresee and provide 'like a good father'. If the temperature rises rapidly, the instrument 'predicts' that the maximum value will soon be exceeded, and interrupts the feed before this happens.

In other cases the maximum or minimum value of the parameter to be regulated depends on its permanence through time. A sick man, for example, can tolerate a fever of 41°C for a few minutes, of 40° for a few hours, of 39° for a few days. Similar situations, where time finishes what heat started, are common in chemistry, and also in cooking, which is a more complex and less clear kind of chemistry. Thus there are regulators that take account of passing time and how much has gone before. Indeed, the most sophisticated instruments can be set to work in the 'all or nothing' manner, in the modulated manner, reacting to the speed of variation or its accumulation in time, or with varied combinations of all four. Even more astonishing perhaps is that those supervising the control, simple workmen, learn to operate the instruments in the manner most fitted to the operation under way, even if they do not have the faintest idea how the instruments themselves work, in the same way that we can learn to ride a bicycle without knowing the theory of the gyroscope.

Politicians down the ages have dreamt of mechanisms of homeostasis which would keep the regime they believe in healthy, or at least alive, but human societies are so complex, the parameters in question so numerous, that this dream will never be realized. Fifty years ago it used to be said that too much freedom leads to tyranny, and a tyranny that is over-severe leads back to freedom. If this statement could be applied generally, we would be able to make out an oscillation around an equilibrium, in other words a crude kind of regulation, however cruel, costly in terms of human life and unbearably slow. Unfortunately everything happening in the world around us today leads us to believe this statement to be false. The tyrannies of today tend to preserve themselves indefinitely in a sort of sclerosis, giving way only if they are toppled by military action or if they are subsumed in another tyranny. Excess of freedom, or licence, does not generate tyrannies, but stretches out into a cancer. This is where the sense of unease weighing us down these days comes from. We see no powers of recall, homeostasis or retroaction. The world seems to be heading towards some kind of ruin and all we can do is hope that the advance will be slow.

In *Notiziario Banca Popolare di Sondrio*, no. 33, December 1983

45   Note to Franz Kafka's *The Trial*

To read *The Trial*, a book saturated with poetry and despair, is to come away changed, sadder and wiser than before. So this is it, this is human destiny: we can be persecuted and punished for a crime which has not even been committed, which is obscure and which will never be revealed to us by the 'court'. And yet we can feel shame for this crime, up to and perhaps even beyond the moment of our death.

Now, the act of translation is more than the act of reading. I emerged from this translation as from an illness. To translate is to follow the tissue of the book under the microscope, to penetrate into it and remain caught up, ensnared within it. We are absorbed into this upside-down world where all logical expectations are disappointed. We travel with Josef K. through dark meanderings, through tortuous paths which never lead where you might expect.

We are hurled into the nightmare of the unknowable from the very first sentence, and on each page we come up against obsessive traits. K. is followed and pursued by external presences, by importunate busybodies who spy on him from both near and afar and make him feel naked. There is a constant impression of physical constriction: the ceilings are low, the rooms stuffed with furniture put in any old how, the air is always thick, muggy, dirty, dark and, paradoxically but tellingly, the sky is clear only during the merciless final execution scene. K. is afflicted by gratuitous and irritating contacts with other bodies, by avalanches of confused words that should clarify his destiny to him but instead further bewilder him, by stupid gestures, all against a background of desperate squalor. His dignity as a man is compromised right from the start, and then wilfully and determinedly demolished day by day. Only women can, or could, offer some salvation, for they are maternal and affectionate, but they are always inaccessible.

Only Leni lets him come close, but K. despises her and wants to be refused: he is not looking for salvation. He fears being punished and at the same time he desires it.

I don't think I have a great affinity with Kafka. Often during the process of translation I had the sensation of a collision, a conflict, the immodest temptation to comb out the knots in the text in my own way: to correct, in other words, and to modify lexical choices, to impose my own way of writing on to Kafka's. I tried not to give in to this temptation. Since I know that there is no such thing as the 'right way' to translate, I trusted my instinct more than my reason and held to a line, as honestly as possible, of interpretive correctness, even if this was not always coherent from page to page, because not all pages posed the same problems. I had in front of me Alberto Spaini's 1933 translation, which seemed to me at points to show an all too reasonable tendency to make smooth what was rough, understandable what was incomprehensible. The most recent translation by Giorgio Zampa (1973) takes the opposite line. Philologically it is utterly rigorous, respectful to an inordinate degree, even in the punctuation: it is a parallel, interlinear text. It is a translation, and it presents itself as such, not trying to disguise itself or pass itself off as an original text. It does not help the reader, does not ease his path and bravely maintains the syntactic density of the original German.

I tried to strike a middle path between these two. For example, while I'm fully aware of the obsessive and perhaps deliberate effect produced by the speech of the lawyer, Huld, which goes on doggedly for ten pages without a single paragraph break, I took pity on the Italian reader and introduced a few breaks. To conserve the leanness of the prose, I eliminated some limitative adverbs (almost, very, a little, around, maybe, and so on) which German can bear better than Italian. On the other hand I made no attempt to prune the accumulation of terms of the type 'to seem': likely, probable, to glimpse, to notice, as if, apparently, similar, and so on, for these seemed to me both typical and indeed indispensable in this story which indefatigably unravels events in which nothing is at it seems. And apart from that, I made every effort to balance faithfulness to the text with a fluidity of language. Where there were contradictions and repetitions in this notoriously tormented and controversial text, I have left them there.

(1983)

Note to the translation of *The Trial* by Franz Kafka, Einaudi, Turin, 1983, pp. III–V

46   Asymmetry and Life

When I was a student, around 1940, chemists had clear opinions about molecules, too clear perhaps. The molecule, 'the smallest part of matter to preserve the properties of the substance', was tangible and concrete, a tiny model. Physicists already knew a good deal about wave functions, the vibrations of atoms, about rotations and degrees of freedom of the global molecule and its parts, about the nature of valency, but organic chemists were reluctant to follow them onto this ground. They were still fascinated by the relatively recent discovery of stereochemistry, the branch of chemistry that studies, precisely, the property of the molecule as an object, endowed with mass, thickness, dents and protrusions: in other words, with form.

The path to this point had been a long one. The concept of molecular weight had been defined with precision since the middle of the previous century: the molecule had a weight that was the sum of the weight of all its atoms, and could be determined using a simple method, within the capability of most laboratories. Also firmly established was analysis of the elements, which made it possible to find out how many, and which, atoms made up the molecule, but nobody dared represent its structure: it was imagined as a packet, a formless cluster. Yet chemists already knew about pairs of compounds, such as acetone and propionic aldehyde, or ethyl ether and butanol, which had the same composition but totally different chemical and physical properties. The phenomenon had been given a fine-sounding Greek name (isomerism) some time before the analytical methods of the day came up with any explanation; chemists realized that it must be a matter of permutation, but their ideas about the spatial order of atoms in molecules were still somewhat vague.

Then even more remarkable pairs (or even trios) were observed. Their members were identical not only in composition but also in all their properties, bar two: one rotated the plane of polarized light to the right, the other to the left, and the third (at times) did not rotate it at all. A right-handed and left-handed lactic acid had been observed in nature, for example, or in fermentation products, while the acid produced in the laboratory was always inactive. Furthermore, the crystals of the right-left pairs often exhibited a curious asymmetry: the one could not be superimposed on the other but was its mirror image, just as the right hand is the mirror image of the left.

This phenomenon attracted the vigorous attention of the young Pasteur and indeed this extraordinary man, who was to revolutionize pathology, was more of a chemist than a doctor. It was understandable that products of synthesis were inactive on polarized light, given that optic activity was related to an asymmetry, and that the product of symmetrical reagents in the laboratory could themselves only be symmetrical. But how could the asymmetry of natural products be explained? It must be the result of a preceding asymmetry, this much was clear, but where was this primordial asymmetry?

Pasteur, together with his peers, understood that this taxing problem was far from purely academic. Not all asymmetrical substances, in the sense described above, belong to the living world (quartz crystals, for example, are asymmetrical); but major players in the living world, such as proteins, cellulose, sugars and DNA, are all asymmetrical. Right–left asymmetry is intrinsic to life, and indeed it coincides with life. It is invariably present in all organisms, from viruses to lichen to oak trees, fish and man. This fact is neither obvious nor insignificant; indeed, it has challenged the curiosity of three generations of chemists, and given birth to two great questions.

The first question is, as Aristotle puts it, that of the final cause, or in modern terms, the adaptive utility of asymmetry. Let's stick for the moment to proteins, the living structures in which the phenomenon manifests itself in its most clear and extensive form. As we know, the long protein molecule is linear: it is a filament, a rosary of hundreds and thousands of grains, and the grains are not all the same. They are made up of around twenty relatively simple compounds, largely the same for all living things, which are called amino acids. These are comparable to the letters of the alphabet, with which enormously long words can be made up, of a hundred or even a thousand letters. Each protein is one of these words: the sequence of amino acids is rigorously specific for each protein, determining its properties and determining also the form in which the filament can furl itself. Now, all the amino acids (except one) have an asymmetrical molecule, but all can be represented by one of the diagrams below, and the only difference between them is the nature of group R.

They are all 'left-handed', as if they had come out of the same mould, or as if someone had removed and destroyed their mirror image, their right-handed twins. But each protein has to have a rigid identity in every one of its grains; if just one of these was to change

$$
\begin{array}{cc}
R & R \\
| & | \\
\diagup C \diagdown & \diagup C \diagdown \\
H \diagup \;\; NH_2 & H \diagup \;\; COOH \\
\diagdown COOH \diagup & \diagdown NH_2 \diagup
\end{array}
$$

its configuration, the whole protein cluster would change its form. There is therefore a notable advantage in the fact that only one of these two mirror-image forms of each amino acid is available in the biosphere: if just one of the thousands of grains in a protein chain were to be substituted by its mirror image, many of the most subtle properties of the protein would change radically; above all, its immunizing behaviour.

But this asymmetry, so jealously transmitted by the living cell, is difficult to obtain and easy to lose. Whenever a chemist attempts the synthesis of an asymmetrical compound, he gets a mix of the two mirror images in exactly equal quantities which is therefore inactive on polarized light. Separation of the antipodes is possible, but only with tools or substances that are themselves asymmetrical. The conceptually simpler method goes back to Pasteur: the crystals of certain right-handed compounds are visibly distinguishable from their left analogues in the same way that a reasonably practised eye can distinguish a right-threaded screw from a left, and they can be separated manually. But again, the human eye, and everything behind it, is asymmetrical. A second method developed by chemists consists in combining the mirror images with another asymmetrical compound. For example, the mix of lactic acids D and S with the natural alkaloid D (even alkaloids with asymmetrical molecules are generally to be found in nature in just one of the two forms). Clearly the D-lactate of D-cinconica is the antipode of the S-lactate of S-cinconica, and not of the S-lactate of D-cinconica. In other words, a compound DD is the mirror image of the compound SS, and thus the two will have identical physical properties, but the compound SD will have different properties and it will be easy to separate it from DD, by fractional crystallization, for example. Furthermore, it is frequently the case that an acid D can be combined with base D but not with base S, in the same way that a right-threaded screw cannot be inserted into a left-threaded nut.

The opposite operation, that of cancelling the asymmetry desired by nature instead of imitating it, is infinitely easier. It 'goes downhill' with great energy. Outside living organisms, asymmetry is fragile and it takes nothing more than lengthy heating or contact with particular substances with catalytic properties to destroy it. More or less rapidly, half of the asymmetric compound transforms itself into its antipode: the order of asymmetry is mutated into the disorder of symmetry (or of compensated asymmetry), as when we shuffle a pack of cards ordered by suit or colour. With extreme slowness (we are talking about millennia here) this process also occurs spontaneously and at normal temperature, so that it is used to date finds which were once part of living organisms, such as bones, horns, wood, fibres and the like: the further advanced the destruction of asymmetry, the older the object.

In the light of life's maniacal preference for asymmetrical molecules, it seems to me that Miller's famous experiment loses something of its power to shock. In 1953 Miller subjected a mixture of water, methane, ammonia and hydrogen to electric discharges over several days, seeking to simulate the conditions of the primordial atmosphere slashed by lightning. He obtained a number of well-known amino acids, thus confirming that in order to synthesize them the elaborate and selective techniques followed to date by chemists were not indispensable. The fundamental building blocks of proteins 'want' to take form and take form almost spontaneously out of chaos as long as they are provided with energy, even in brutal form. Alongside them, astonishingly, some complex components of DNA were formed. But Miller, and his numerous followers, always obtained symmetrical products, in other words mixtures balanced by their respective antipodes. The fundamental building blocks of life want to take form, but not asymmetry.

Here we should take stock of a curious and disturbing fact. I do not know who the fool was who first stated that 'the exception proves the rule'. It does not prove it at all, but weakens it and casts doubt on it. Now, the rule by which all amino acids of living organisms are in optically active form (not mixtures of antipodes, that is) to date has no exception. But there is an exception to the rule which states that all these amino acids are of the left-handed series; here and there, in out of the way places, amino acids of the right-handed series have also been found: in the skin of some exotic batrachians, in the cuticle of some micro-organisms, possibly (and if it were so it would give us food for thought) in some cancerous cells. But the right-handed amino acids of the batrachians are not there by chance: they are part of substances with a high level of physiological activity, and if they are substituted with their regular mirror images, the left-handed ones, activity ceases. They therefore have a specific function, but the reason escapes us, as does the reason for finding them in these tissues and not elsewhere. Perhaps 'once' their presence was more conspicuous; perhaps these are the remnants of a different biochemical era? The exception does not prove the rule; it only stimulates doubt.

The asymmetry we are talking about is therefore fragile, but constantly present in living matter, where it is perhaps necessary from an evolutionary point of view in order to ensure that spatial 'errors' do not creep into the construction of proteins.

We have yet to discuss the second rather more mysterious question. We stay with Aristotle, and his notion of the efficient cause. Having admitted, or at least suspected, the usefulness of asymmetry (there are other asymmetries: the one in question has been called chirality; how easy it is to give Greek names to things we do not understand, to give us the illusion we understand them better!), the question becomes where it might have originated. From another asymmetry, clearly, but which one? Let us examine the various hypotheses that have been put forward, or that might be considered.

1   The earth spins round, and apparently the sun spins round the earth. In the northern hemisphere, and to the north of the tropics (and in analogous fashion to the south of the Tropic of Capricorn), asymmetry exists and is plain to see. If we are looking south, the sun rises on the left and sets on the right, a fact which certainly has an effect on the way vines curl and also, perhaps (and here I would ask experts to confirm or reject this) on the torsion shown by the trunks of many trees. It would be interesting to observe if the direction is the same, at least by and large, on all the trees of a certain type in the northern hemisphere, and the opposite in the trees of the same species in the southern hemisphere. Indeed the agency (the chirality, in other words) of all phenomena connected to the rotation of the earth is different in each hemisphere: the erosion of riverbanks, the preferred direction of the vortex, the direction of the trade winds. This presents a serious obstacle to our first hypothesis: it would have us admit that life, or at least vital asymmetry, however it comes into being, is born in just one of the two hemispheres, to spread later into the other when it is more established. This is not impossible, but it is not appealing. It brings to mind a phenomenon that is *una tantum*, a one-off, a possibility I shall return to, disliked intensely by many and liked equally intensely by very few.

2   In the laboratory it is easy to reproduce light polarized in circular fashion. It is less easy to explain in words what this light is: suffice it to say that it has the symmetry (or asymmetry) of the thread of a screw, in other words it is 'chiral', and can therefore be left- or right-handed. On appropriate wave lengths this light can be absorbed in differential measure by one of the two of a pair of antipodes, which can decompose it more swiftly than the other; or it can act on the reactive mix with which the chemist is attempting to synthesize an asymmetric compound. In both these cases experiments have led to effectively unbalanced mixtures which are therefore optically active, albeit in small measure. Now, in certain natural conditions, light reflected through water is polarized in circular fashion, but indeed, depending on the angles and the time of day, it is equally likely to be right- or left-handed. We come up against a difficulty similar to the one of the first hypothesis: is it feasible that life exists thanks to a single specific event? In other words that light was caught up, reflected in a particular moment in a particular pool of water?

3   As I indicated before, the asymmetry that interests us exists in nature in some inorganic crystalline structures: in common quartz, for example. There are right- and left-handed quartz crystals; in the laboratory syntheses of asymmetrical compounds have been achieved in the presence of quartz dust of homogeneous agency, and the product obtained was optically active. But again, left- and right-handed quartzes are equally common in nature. If truth be told some researchers have claimed that right-handed quartz is more abundant, while others have refuted this. Even in scientific research it is easy to come across those who mistake what is for what they would like to be.

4   The earth's magnetic field, which is currently very weak, possesses the required asymmetry, and possesses it in every point, without the inversions and intermittent quality which undermine the previous hypotheses. It might therefore have been able to pilot the same asymmetric synthesis over all the points of the earth's surface, in favour of one of the two antipodes. But here two further difficulties arise: in the first place, as far as I know (but I have never been in any way an expert in this field, and even less so now after a number of years away from chemistry; if there is someone who knows differently I will be glad to revise my opinions), there do not exist any organic reactions sensitive to a reasonable intensity of magnetic field, except perhaps those that involve iron,

nickel and cobalt atoms. In the second place, geologists are now sure that the orientation of the earth's magnetic field inverts at the rate of several tens of thousands of years. Is it conceivable that in far distant times this field was far more intense, and constant for a long enough period to incubate life?

5 The drama could have unfolded over several successive periods. First a 'primordial soup' such as the one Miller obtained in his test tube, composed in equal measure of right- and left-handed amino acids; then a coming together of these amino acids in filaments, most likely homogeneous, DDD and SSS; then coming into being, according to one of the many suggestions put forward, of life in 'binational' form, in which the two blocks were incapable of metabolizing themselves and were in competition between each other; then a very long journey, a silent struggle over millions of years between right-handed life and left-handed life, enemies to each other, incompatible; and at last, in the absence of any retro-action, the progressive dominance of left-handed life up to the current era, in which the enigmatic presence of right-handed amino acids in the skin of the tree frog could represent the minuscule survival of a fragment of an earlier age. It really is a shame that no trace has remained in fossils, except very recent ones, as indicated above; otherwise we might still entertain the hope of tracing the signs of this ancient struggle, which has something of Zarathustra about it. Or maybe the skeletons of sea urchins and diatoms exist in chiral forms? It would make an interesting degree thesis topic.

6 The hypothesis of the single event, of the *una tantum*, is not an attractive one and does not take us very far, but it cannot be ruled out. We have seen that it is presupposed by a number of the hypotheses outlined above. Perhaps a germ fell out of the sky (a DNA molecule, a spore, a protein fragment) containing within it the principles of asymmetry and of life. Indeed this suggestion has found much favour over the course of time and was recently dusted off by no less a figure than Francis Crick, discoverer of the genetic code. But it can only shift the problem into a space and time to which we have no access. There is still the scenario of the single earthly event, unique, spontaneous and a matter of chance: not impossible, but extremely improbable. Science cannot be constructed on single events; discussion is closed off, with nothing more than a simple act of faith (or rejection). This scenario, however, has been made less problematic by a phenomenon

studied by Giulio Natta (Nobel prize winner in 1963) and set out by him in his fine book, *Stereochemistry, Molecules in 3D* (Mondadori, 1978). If we construct long chains of molecules, polymers that is, without any particular contrivances, we obviously obtain symmetrical and inactive products. If, however, the polymerization is carried out in the presence of small quantities of inert but strongly asymmetrical substances, then the polymer obtained is also asymmetrical along its whole length. The inert substance behaves, then, like a mould; from one asymmetrical mould we can obtain virtually unlimited quantities of asymmetrical pieces. Let us use another simile. If we press dough onto a pierced dish we get a very long, rectilinear string of spaghetti. But if the hole in the dish is crooked, we get a string of spaghetti just as long but curled up, in other words asymmetrical, left- or right-handed according to the shape of the hole. There is therefore, or we can imagine, a multiplying mechanism which might have enlarged a local asymmetry produced in one of the ways described above or by an infinitesimal fluctuation, and led it to conquer the entire world. Besides, has the recent discovery of isotrope and fossil radiation not forced the majority of scientists to swallow the bitter philosophy of the single event together with the Big Bang?

7 Chirality might have universal roots. I will seek no fictions here, I will not pretend to explain what I do not myself understand and which cannot be understood in the ordinary sense of the word, in other words by taking refuge in visual models. Chirality might reside in the subatomic domain, where no language is valid any more except mathematics, where intuition has no place and all metaphors fail. One of the forces that tie particles to each other, weak interaction, is not symmetrical; the electrons emitted in some radioactive disintegrations are irremediably left-handed, without compensation. All matter, therefore, even when it is beyond the sensitivity of any of our measuring instruments, is optically active. The antipodes are never true antipodes: one of them, always the same one, the left one, is just a little more stable than its brother. The inactive mixtures obtained by the chemist are never exactly fifty–fifty: there is always an imbalance, of the order of one in a billion billion, but always there. It is small, but so is the key to a safe that contains a ton weight of diamonds. If this is how things are (and we are talking of very recent ideas, hot off the press), the entire universe appears to be pervaded by a tenuous chirality, and the compensations would be merely apparent: the

'real' antipode of right-handed lactic acid, or of my right hand, would no longer be earthy left-handed acid or my left hand, but the left-handed ones in the distant realm of anti-matter. And over the aeons the magnifying mechanisms we have spoken of here might have acted upon this infinitesimal penchant, this tendentious whim. All right? For the moment we will have to be satisfied with this answer.

Perhaps I should apologize: it is difficult to be clear about things that are not clear to ourselves, to make oneself comprehensible to non-specialists without boring or scandalizing specialists. Besides, I know I have been guilty of invading a field which is not (any longer) mine, but on which I once wrote my degree thesis. I have revisited it with reverence, with a little regret and with the fear of error: years of inactivity exact a price.

I have tried to give the latest views on a problem which is still open, despite the subversive hypothesis I described last, with the respect of the profane man who stops at the gates of the temple. It is perhaps a 'useless' problem, although perhaps not always. If pharmacologists had paid more attention to the question of optical isomerism, for example, the thalidomide tragedy would never have occurred. This product has an asymmetrical molecular structure, but was put on the market as a 'race mate', as a balanced measure of the two antipodes, as had been obtained in synthesis. Later research, like that of Blaschke and others (*Arzneimittel-Forschung*, 1979) on rats showed that only the left-handed antipode was teratogeneous, while the right one had a normal tranquillizing action. If the two antipodes had been separated and examined separately, nothing would have happened.

In any case it is a rich and fertile problem. Unlike philosophical problems, I do not think it will remain unsolved for ever. Some facts, however modest, might help. Are the amino acids which have apparently been found in meteorites optically active? Has anybody sought to carry out the synthesis of an asymmetrical molecule containing iron under a magnetic field? The discovery of the chirality of the universe, or at least of our galaxy, seemed to me a huge one, both dramatic and enigmatic. Does it have any meaning? And if so, what is it? How far will it take us? Is it not a 'game of dice', the same which Einstein refused to attribute to God?

In *Promoteo*, II, no. 7, September 1984

47 Preface to *Jews in Turin*

To celebrate the centenary of the inauguration of our Synagogue, which took place on 16 February 1884, we Jews in Turin resolved just for once to emerge from our double traditional dual reserve. First there is the well-known Piedmontese reserve, connected to geographical and historical roots, which leads some to see us as the least Italian of Italians. This is superimposed on the age-old reserve of the Diaspora Jew, forever accustomed to living in silence and suspicion, listening a great deal and saying little, not drawing attention to himself, because 'you never know'.

There have never been many of us: barely four thousand in the 1930s, and that was the highest figure we ever reached; today, there are just over one thousand. And yet we don't feel we are overstating the case if we say that we have counted for something, and we still count for something, in the life of this city. Paradoxically, our history as a mild and peaceful people is connected with the history of the greatest monument in Turin, which is certainly not mild, nor does it conform to our character. As is told at length in the essay by Alberto Racheli in this book [*Jews in Turin*], we ran the serious risk of sharing with Alessandro Antonelli the responsibility for the presence, right in the heart of the city, of that absurd exclamation point that is the Mole. We too, of course, like everybody from Turin, harbour a certain affection for the Mole, but our love for it is ironic and polemical, and we do not allow it to blind us. We love it as we love the walls of our homes, but we know it is ugly, presumptuous and of little use, that it has been a colossal waste of public money and that after the storms of 1953 and restoration in 1961, it is still standing thanks only to a metal prosthesis. In short, it is some time since it merited a place in the Guinness Book of Records; it is no longer, as they taught us at school, the 'tallest brick-built construction in Europe'. And so we are grateful, posthumously, to the municipal councillor, Malvano, our co-religionist, who in 1875 was smart enough to sell back to the local authority the building which had been commissioned but was not finished, and which was gobbling up money. If the operation had not succeeded, we would today be faced with a melancholy spectacle: the few hundred Jews who go to the Temple on solemn feast days, and the few dozen who go for daily services, would be almost invisible in the enormous space enclosed by Antonelli's dome.

Nonetheless, as I was saying, if we had not been there the city would have been different, and this exhibition sets out to demonstrate this point. When our ancestors (who for the most part were not from Turin but lived largely in the smaller towns of Piedmont) moved to the city, towards the end of the nineteenth century, they brought with them the great, perhaps the only, specific gift made by history to the Jews: literacy, culture, both lay and religious, felt as a duty, a right, a necessity and joy of life: and this at a time when the vast majority of the Italian population was still illiterate. And so emancipation did not catch them unprepared; and as is shown in the histories of many families outlined in the exhibition's panels, within one or two generations of leaving the ghetto Jews passed easily from being craftsmen and small businessmen to the emerging industries, administration, public offices, the armed forces and the universities. Indeed, particularly in the academic world Turin's Jews have left illustrious traces out of all proportion to their actual number, and their presence is still conspicuous in both quantity and quality. The rise of the Jews, which was paralleled by the rise of a large section of the Christian middle class, was also favoured by the fundamental tolerance of the population. It has been said that every country has the Jews they deserve. Post-Risorgimento Italy, a country of ancient civilization, ethnically homogeneous and immune from serious xenophobic tensions, turned its Jews into a class of good citizens who respected the law, who were loyal to the State and far removed from corruption and violence.

From this point of view, the integration of Italian Jewry is very unusual; more unusual still, perhaps, is the equilibrium of Turinese-Piedmontese Jewry, which integrated easily yet without losing its own identity. Except for a few rare and marginal cases, such as the Yemen and the Caucasus, all Jewish communities in the world bore (and continue to bear) the signs of the tormented history of the people of Israel, shot through with massacres, expulsions, humiliating separations, excessive and arbitrary taxation, forced conversions and migrations. Jews expelled from one country (from England in 1290, from France throughout the fourteenth century, from the Rhineland at the time of the Crusades, from Spain in 1492, up to the recent migrations to the Americas) sought refuge elsewhere, superimposing themselves on existing communities or else founding new ones. They were doubly strangers, for their religion and for their provenance. And so the majority of communities are stratified and internally structured, with occasional tensions and fractures. Israel

Zangwill gave a lively picture of this in his famous story *The King of the Schnorrers*. Set in London at the beginning of the nineteenth century, it narrates the meeting, or rather confrontation, between a 'Spanish' Jew, a learned and arrogant beggar, and an integrated 'German' Jew who is rich and careless. In Amsterdam the local Jews, of German origin, had welcomed Jews expelled from the Iberian peninsula, without the two layers merging to any great degree. In Venice there are still five synagogues, originally established for Jews from different lands with different rituals. There is a similar situation now in Paris, where Jews of ancient French origin live together with Algerian, Egyptian, Polish, Russian and German Jews and others. The most complex case, and the one with the greatest historical weight, is of course that of Israel, where the presence of Jews belonging to all the branches of the Diaspora together still constitutes an intricate problem of internal politics. And the most recent example is in Milan, where a huge influx of refugees from Arab states and from Iran is causing unease and unrest, together with an unexpected growth in numbers.

In comparison to this the Jews of Turin, whose distant origins are in France, Provence and Spain, have never undergone substantial encroachment from other regions. Infiltrations, yes, in various periods, as attested by some names of demonstrably German origin (Ottolenghi, Diena, Luzzati, Morpurgo, and, obviously, Tedeschi) and the solitary dialect and liturgical term *ij ursài*, for the anniversary of a death, which is a corruption of the Yiddish *yorzeit*, time of the year. But these infiltrations were rapidly absorbed into a social fabric which remained ethnically stable right up to the forty-year period (1880–1920) to which this exhibition is dedicated – indeed, right up to the present day, in strident contrast with what has happened in the city of Turin, which at the time of the economic boom swallowed up five or six hundred thousand immigrants in the space of two or three years, causing profound changes in all of the city's structures and superstructures.

This was a small group of people fully aware of their own identity, and endowed with a consolidated physiognomy, a village almost, inserted into the capital of Savoy; this much is demonstrated by its prevalent endogamy which rarely went beyond the borders of the region, and by the curious Judeo-Piedmontese language which is now an object of study for linguists and sociologists but had already been described by Alberto Virgilio, acute observer of all things Piedmontese. A profound integration with the majority population was vital in order for this linguistic hybrid to survive, as well as a reasonable memory of liturgical language (the only channel through which Hebrew and Aramaic have followed the currents of the Diaspora) and a climate devoid of real tension between the majority and the minority. Hybrid languages do not come into being where these tensions exist: there has never been, for example, a Jewish–Polish dialect, or Italian–German hybrids in the Alto Adige, while Italian emigrants to the United States, despite the minimal phonetic compatibility, developed right from the start their own specific way of speaking, which Pascoli adroitly drew on in a famous poem.

Our fathers, and especially our mothers, used this Judeo-Piedmontese language on a daily basis and completely naturally: it was the language of the family and of the home. They were nonetheless aware of its intrinsic comic force, which sprang from the contrast between the layer of language that was rustic and laconic Piedmontese dialect, and the Hebrew interpolations which derived from the language of the Patriarchs, remote but revived each day by public and private prayer, the reading of the Texts, worn smooth by the millennia as the river bed by the glacier. But this contrast mirrored another, the essential contrast of Judaism dispersed amongst the peoples, the Gentiles, stretched taut between divine vocation and the wretchedness of their everyday lives; it mirrored another contrast also, on a much larger scale, one intrinsic to the human condition, since man is bipartite, a dough made of divine breath and earthly dust. After the Diaspora the Jewish people lived this conflict painfully, and from it, along with its wisdom, has acquired its laughter, which is not to be found in the Bible and the prophets.

It is to these ancestors of ours, honest, hard working and sharp-witted, not heroes, not saints or martyrs, not too far off in space and time, that this exhibition is dedicated. We are aware of its limits, which have been deliberately drawn. There would be other, very different things to say about the history of the Jews in Turin over the following decades: their early anti-Fascist commitment, paid for with long years of imprisonment and exile, and which sprang from the thirst for freedom and justice which runs right through Jewish history; the exemplary lives of men such as Umberto Terracini, Leone Ginzburg, Emanuele and Ennio Artom, Giuseppe, Mario and Alberto Levi, the fallen partisans Sergio, Paolo and Franco Diena; the Jewish participation in the Resistance, once again higher than their mere numbers would suggest; and the 800 deportees, of whom nothing more remains than a tombstone in our cemetery. But on this occasion we did not wish to speak of victories, defeats, struggles and massacres. Here we want to remember, to invite others to remember, to introduce ourselves, before it is too late. For every human group there exists a critical mass below which stability is threatened, leading to an ever more rapid dilution and to a silent and painless dissolution. Unless the unforeseen occurs, our community seems set on this path. With this exhibition we wished to perform an act of filial piety and to show our friends in Turin, and our children, who we are and where we have come from.

From *Ebrei a Torino. Ricerche per il Centenario della Sinagoga* (1884–1984), Turin 1984

48   Itinerary of a Jewish Writer

In Italy and abroad, my readers and critics now think of me as a 'Jewish writer'. I have accepted this label cheerfully, but not without some initial resistance. Indeed, I fully accepted it only relatively late on in my life and in my itinerary as a writer. I adapted to the position of Jew only as an effect of the racial laws passed in Italy in 1938, when I was nineteen years old, and following my deportation to Auschwitz, which happened in 1944. I adapted to the position of writer even later, when I was more than forty-five years old, when I had already published two books and when the work of writing (which I have nonetheless never considered to be work) began to take precedence over my 'official' job as a chemist. In both cases it was more a question of an intervention of fate than of a deliberate and conscious choice. Whatever the case, I will here consider my works as a 'Jewish writer', focusing in particular on my books which have the flavour of autobiography or memoir, or which are in other ways pertinent to the theme of this conference. I will follow the actual order of events rather than the order in which they appeared reflected in my writing; the order I follow will thus be biographical rather than bibliographical.

Like the majority of Jews of ancient Italian descent, my parents and grandparents belonged to the middle classes and were profoundly integrated into the life of the country in terms of language, customs and moral values. Religion counted for little in my family, and I think this can be explained by the fact that equal civil rights were won by non-Catholic Italians only towards the middle of the nineteenth century, as a result of the predominantly lay nature of the Italian Risorgimento. Participation in the struggles of the Risorgimento meant that while not obliged to do so, people were strongly encouraged to think in lay terms. Despite this, awareness of our Jewishness had not completely disappeared, either in my family or amongst the general population of Jews. It manifested itself in the preservation of a few familiar rituals (especially the feasts of Rosh-Hashanà, Pesach and Purim), in the importance placed on study and education and in a modest but interesting linguistic differentiation. In analogous manner to the well-known hybrid structure of Yiddish, Jewish families throughout the various regions of Italy had developed curious dialectal variations, with Hebrew phrases more or less distorted to local phonetic patterns. From my early childhood I was curious about, and somehow touched by, this pathetic survival of biblical language in family and dialect speech. Many years after the beginning of my career as a writer, this became the subject matter for the first chapter in my book, *The Periodic Table*.

At first sight, this book is the story of the most important moments of my life as a chemist. Indeed, with the end of my professional life, I had felt the need to express how much I owed my trade, which was frequently tiring and dirty, and at times even dangerous; it seemed to me only right that the man of letters, as it were, should give due thanks to the chemist who had opened the door for him. But a deeper critical reading has seen in the book the more ample breath of pure autobiography. It contains the history of a generation; in many of its pages we see the traumatic experience of segregation of the Jews in Fascist and Nazi Europe, the blind rush towards war and massacre, and also the renewed sense of pride that accompanies every separation and every discrimination. The book is articulated in twenty-one 'moments', each of which draws its substance and title from one of the chemical elements. The chapters entitled Argon, Zinc and Gold are of particular relevance to this conference, since they refer to situations and events preceding my deportation, and reflect my position as a Jew in Mussolini's Italy, integrated and assimilated but not a Fascist. Argon is a gas that does not react with other gases, and is present in tiny quantities in the air we breathe. In the chapter of this title I suggested a playful analogy between this 'rare' and 'noble' gas and the ancestors of our small, rural Jewish communities in Piedmont. These communities were small, isolated groups, sometimes just single families, very much on their own. They still remembered distant persecutions. Neither loved nor hated, they were treated sometimes with contempt, sometimes with indifference. The only remaining trace of these remote and bizarre characters are a few lively anecdotes, a few 'sayings' handed down almost in parody of the famous rabbinical 'sayings' collected in the Talmud. With a sense of ironical and benevolent affection I tried in this book to bring back to life, for example, the story of a legendary uncle who in Chieri, near Turin, had fallen in love with his Christian servant. Since his parents opposed the marriage, this uncle took to his bed and stayed there for twenty-two years, until his parents died and he could marry the girl. In relating these strange and comical family stories I also tried to document the hybrid language I was speaking of before, a minor and Mediterranean Yiddish, more local and less illustrious, in which nonetheless I recognized my domestic roots:

> Its historical interest is meagre, since it was never spoken by more than a few thousand people; but its human interest is great, as are all languages on the frontier and in transition. In fact it contains an admirable comic force, which springs from the contrast between the texture of the discourse, which is the rugged, sober, and laconic Piedmontese dialect, never written except on a bet, and the Hebrew inlay, snatched from the language of the fathers, sacred and solemn, geologic, polished smooth by the millennia like the bed of a glacier. But this contrast reflects another, the essential conflict of the Judaism of the Diaspora, scattered among the Gentiles. That is, the *goyim*. Torn between their divine vocation and the daily misery of existence; and still another. Even more general, which is inherent in the human condition, since man is a centaur, a tangle of flesh and mind, divine inspiration and dust. The Jewish people, after the dispersion, have lived this conflict for a long time and dolourously, and have drawn from it, side by side with its wisdom, also its laughter, which in fact is missing in the Bible and the Prophets. It pervades Yiddish, and, within its modest limits, it also pervades the bizarre speech of our father of this earth, which I want to set down here before it disappears; a skeptical, good-natured speech, which only on careless examination could appear blasphemous, whereas it is rich with an affectionate and dignified intimacy with God [. . .] (Translated by Raymond Rosenthal, *The Periodic Table*)

In the chapter called 'Zinc' the chemical analogy, though still to some extent ironic, has shifted. We are in 1938; the racial laws have not yet been passed in Italy but they are in the air: papers and magazines, orchestrated by the totalitarian regime, persistently state that Jews are different, potential (or actual) enemies of Fascism, harmful 'impurities' in the pure body of the Italian people. They cite the Nuremberg laws as an example to be imitated, for example, and they pick up on the fanatical propaganda of Dr Goebbels: the Jew, reproduced in cartoons with traditional Semitic features, is simultaneously the capitalist who starves the 'Aryan' peoples and the bloodthirsty Bolshevik who sets out to destroy Western civilization. We should say first off that zinc is capable of reacting with acids only if particular impurities are present: if it is pure, it does not react. The younger self I describe here is proud, in a confused manner, of being an 'impurity': 'In order for the wheel to turn, for life to be lived, impurities are needed [. . .] Dissension, diversity, the grain of salt and mustard are needed: Fascism does not want them, forbids them, and that's why you're not a Fascist; it wants everybody to be the same, and you're not.'

And just a little further on:

> I am the impurity that makes the zinc react, I am the grain of salt or mustard. Impurity, certainly, since just during those months the publication of the magazine *Defense of the Race* had begun, and there was much talk about purity, and I had begun to be proud of being impure. In truth, until precisely those months it had not meant much to me that I was a Jew: within myself, and in my contacts with my Christian friends, I had always considered my origin as an almost negligible but curious fact, a small amusing anomaly, like having a crooked nose or freckles; a Jew is somebody who at Christmas does not have a tree, who should not eat salami but eats it all the same, who has learned a bit of Hebrew at thirteen and then has forgotten it. According to the above-mentioned magazine, a Jew is stingy and cunning; but I was not particularly stingy or cunning, nor had my father been.

This last passage that I have just quoted seems to me to encapsulate the state of mind and the condition of most Italian Jews on the eve of the racial laws.

In the chapter 'Gold', time has moved on. The Second World War is raging: in 1943 the Allies landed in Italy, Fascism has fallen, German forces have invaded Italy from the north. Although I was uninformed in either a political or military sense, I felt that the only decent choice was to join up with the anti-German Resistance. Many of my friends, both Jews and Christians, had done likewise, and in fact the participation of Jews in the Italian Resistance was notable, whether in terms of numbers or in leading the effort. But my partisan militancy was destined to be short-lived. Following a tip-off I was arrested by the Fascists on 13 December 1943, in the mountains of the Val d'Aosta. During the interrogation I was subjected to, I admitted being a Jew: partly out of exhaustion, but partly also out of a surge of the pride I was speaking of before, a pride which is the fruit of persecution; and the intensity of this pride is in proportion to the harshness of the persecution itself.

In February 1945 the Fascists handed me over to the Germans, who deported me to Auschwitz. The convoy which took us to the camp consisted of 650 people. Out of these 525 were murdered immediately, while 29 women were interned at Birkenau. Ninety-six men, myself amongst them, were sent to Monowitz-Auschwitz, a 'Nebenlager' belonging to the IG Farbenindustrie. Only about twenty of these men and women went back to their homes. I survived imprisonment because of a series of lucky chances: because I did not get sick, because an Italian bricklayer helped me, because for two months I was able to work as a chemist in the IG Farbenindustrie laboratory. I was liberated thanks to the rapid advance of the Russian Army in January 1945.

Even during my imprisonment, despite the cold and hunger, the beatings, the hard labour, the death of one companion after another, the overwhelming nature of each and every hour, I had felt an intense need to write of what I was living through. I knew that my hopes of salvation were minimal, but I also knew that, were I to survive, I would *have* to tell my story, that I would not be able to do otherwise. Not only this, but telling this story, bearing witness, was a reason for staying alive. Not to live *and* tell, but to live *in order to* tell. Even in Auschwitz I realized I was living the fundamental experience of my life.

Indeed, as soon as I returned to Italy, in October 1945, I began to write. I had no plan, nor did I worry about style. I gave precedence to the episodes freshest in my mind, or those which seemed to me important in themselves, or laden with symbolic value. I did not realize I was writing a book, for such was not my intention; it seemed to me I was fulfilling a duty, paying a debt to my dead companions, and at the same time satisfying a need of my own. I should make it clear that neither in this book nor in successive ones did I have to deal with problems of language: my background and education was exclusively Italian, Italian is the only language I know well and it would never have occurred to me to use any other.

My friends who read these pages pointed out to me that I was writing a book. They advised me to put them in order and finish them, and so *If This is a Man* was born, and published in 1947. It proved its vitality over the years to come: it has been translated into nine languages, adapted in various countries for radio and theatre; extracts from it appear in numerous anthologies, it is constantly being reprinted and it is still read today by young people, as evidenced by the many letters I receive about it.

It is not a book of pure witness. Rereading it all these years later, I recognize many connecting themes: the effort to understand 'how it could have happened', the almost scientific study of human behaviour (of others and of myself) in those extreme conditions, the painful daily contact with free life and the resurfacing (sometimes deliberate, sometimes unconscious and spontaneous) of literary memories of Dante's *Inferno*. But I would like to draw out one of these themes which is the reference to the Bible.

For the first time in my life, from the Italian transit camp at Fossoli onwards, I found myself segregated from the 'normal' world and forcibly immersed into an exclusively Jewish environment. It was a brutal confirmation of my status as a Jew, a condemnation, a fall, a reliving of the biblical stories of exile and migration. However, it was a tragic fall in which despair was tempered with the surprise and pride of a rediscovered identity. The following passage refers to the evening of the departure from Fossoli for Auschwitz.

> In hut 6A old Gattegno lived with his wife and numerous children and grandchildren and his sons- and daughters-in-law. All the men were carpenters; they had come from Tripoli after many long journeys, and had always carried with them the tools of their trade, their kitchen utensils and their accordions and violins to play and dance to after the day's work. They were happy and pious folk. Their women were the first to silently and rapidly finish the preparations for the journey in order to have time for mourning. When all was ready, the food cooked, the bundles tied together, they unloosened their hair, took off their shoes, placed the Yahrzeit candles on the ground and lit them according to the customs of their fathers, and sat on the bare soil in a circle for the lamentations, praying and weeping all the night. We collected in a group in front of their door, and we experienced within ourselves a grief that was new for us, the ancient grief of the people that has no land, the grief without hope of the exodus which is renewed every century. (Translated by Stuart Woolf, *Survival in Auschwitz*)

As the months of imprisonment go by, the biblical theme and tone recur frequently. Sometimes what comes to the fore is the intuition of man's destiny being decided over his head by an incomprehensible god:

> On the march to work, limping in our large wooden shoes on the icy snow, we exchanged a few words, and I found out that Resnyk is Polish; he lived

twenty years at Paris but speaks an extraordinary French. He is thirty, but like all of us, could be taken for seventeen or fifty. He told me his story, and today I have forgotten it, but it was certainly a sorrowful, cruel and moving story; because so are all our stories, hundreds of thousands of stories, all different and all full of a tragic, disturbing necessity. We tell them to each other in the evening, and they take place in Norway, Italy, Algeria, the Ukraine, and are simple and incomprehensible like the stories in the Bible. But are they not themselves stories of a new Bible?

The theme of linguistic confusion as punishment for man's insolence crops up insistently. But here the emphasis of the myth has been shifted; the insolence is that of Hitler's Germany which forces its slaves of a hundred tongues to construct its foolish towers, and for this it will be punished:

> The Carbide Tower, which rises in the middle of Buna and whose top is rarely visible in the fog, was built by us. Its bricks were called *Ziegel, briques, tegula, cegli, kamenny, mattoni, téglak*, and they were cemented by hate: hate and discord, like the Tower of Babel, and it is this that we call it: *Babelturm, Bobelturm*: and in it we hate the insane dream of grandeur of our masters, their contempt for God and men, for us men.

And finally, even at the moment of liberation the memory of biblical salvation is still present, if in ambivalent form:

> The Germans were no longer there. The towers were empty. Today I think that if for no other reason than that an Auschwitz existed, no one in our age should speak of Providence. But without doubt in that hour the memory of biblical salvations in times of extreme adversity passed through all our minds.

After writing *If This is a Man* and seeing it in published form I felt at peace with myself, as someone who has done his duty. I had borne witness, and those who wanted to could read it. Readers were few, though, because the book was only accepted by a small publisher and only 2,500 copies were printed. It had received good reviews, and every now and then I received a letter of solidarity or of praise for the book, or I met someone who had read it. But there was no talk of reprinting, or of translations, and after a couple of years the book was forgotten. I had dedicated myself seriously to my work as a chemist, I had married, I had been catalogued amongst the writers *unius libri*. I barely gave this solitary little book any further thought, even if now and then I dared to believe that the descent into the depths had given me, as Coleridge's Ancient Mariner, a 'strange power of speech'.

I started thinking about it again almost ten years later, when there was an exhibition on the deportations held in Turin which had been welcomed with extraordinary interest by the public, and especially by young people. I had contributed by giving a talk at the exhibition, and young people (but I was still quite young myself) crowded around me, asking questions, quoting the book almost by heart, asking me if I had no other stories to tell. I sent the book to the publisher Einaudi, they republished it in 1958 and from then on it has never been out of print.

Certainly I had other stories to tell. My liberation was not followed by a swift repatriation. Together with tens of thousands of other ex-prisoners held by the Germans, whether military or civilian, Christians or Jews, French, English, American, Greek and so on, instead of being sent back home via the shortest route I was sent into the heart of the Soviet Union where I spent the whole summer of 1945. We were not treated badly, but the whole thing seemed suspect to us and the justification given by the Soviet authorities (that there were no trains or that the war with Japan was not yet over) was not convincing. We were terrorized by the thought of being imprisoned again, in the dark as to the fate of those we loved and tormented by homesickness.

Encouraged by the success of my first book in its new edition, in 1961 I began writing the memoirs of my return, working in the evenings, on Sundays, during breaks at my work as a specialist in paints. The time was favourable in two ways: the hard post-war years in Italy were followed by a wave of optimism and relative well-being, while in the international sphere the Cold War had been somewhat mitigated by a slight thaw between the USA and the USSR. It had become a little easier to speak of the USSR in objective terms without being accused either of anti-Communism or of servility to the Italian Communist Party. In my second book, *The Truce*, I tried to depict the Soviets as I had seen them, 'from below', living amongst them, especially amongst the soldiers of the Red Army who were weary of war, drunk with victory and completely ignorant of the Western world.

This voyage home was not a pleasurable one but it had offered an excellent vantage point for viewing worlds normally barred to Italians. Amongst these I have to mention the direct contact with Ashkenazi Jews. In the camp I had only very sketchy and distorted ideas about them, but then everything in the camp was distorted: there were millions of Jews in Russia and Poland and the Nazis had sent them to the camps and exterminated them. Over the course of the long journey forced on us by the Russians, this picture gradually acquired detail and shading. The countries I passed through were very different from Italy; they were desolate and savage, primitive and violent. Hostility towards the Jews long preceded the German invasion; it was endemic and constant; for years the Jews had lived in separation, linguistic as well as material. In our wanderings across the Ukraine and then in White Russia we met Jewish soldiers in the Red Army, young people who had fought with the partisans, families who had fled the *Einsatzcommandos* and sought shelter in far-off regions and who were now returning to their towns and villages as best they could, tiny villages in the midst of forests which had held flourishing Yeshivas, now destroyed. Tattered remains of a Jewish world exploded, wounded to the quick and in search of a new equilibrium. A few years later I wrote the following brief poem about this:

> Our fathers of this earth,
> Merchants of many talents,
> Wise and shrewd and with all your children
> Whom God has scattered around the world
> As mad Ulysses salt in the furrows:
> I found you again in every place
> Many as the sands of the sea,
> You people with your proud heads,
> Tenacious, poor, human seed.

> [Padri nostri di questa terra,
> Mercanti di molteplice ingegno,
> Savi arguti dalla molta prole
> Che Dio seminò per il mondo
> Come nei solchi Ulisse folle il sale:
> Vi ho ritrovati per ogni dove,
> Molti come la rena del mare,
> Voi popolo di altera cervice,
> Tenace povero seme umano]

I will not give much space here to the two volumes of short stories, *Storie naturali* and *Vizio di forma* [translator's note: both translated and collected in a single volume in English, entitled *The Sixth Day*]; they are not well known abroad, they are less engaged politically, and the Jewish theme appears only intermittently. In fact, the short stories vary considerably in subject matter, some of them bordering on science fiction, and they were written at various times and for various reasons. Nonetheless some of them reconnect, perhaps unconsciously, to the Midrashic tradition of the moral tale. 'Angelic Butterfly', for example, posits a Nazi scientist who has discovered that man is nothing more than the larval state of a different animal, as the caterpillar is to the butterfly, but he never reaches the point of change because he dies too soon. Perhaps this change would transform him into an angel, or a superman? The scientist administers drugs designed to speed up the transformation to a group of prisoners in a concentration camp, but instead of becoming angels, they are transformed into monstrous, ugly birds who are unable to fly, and are then devoured by starving citizens during the days of the battle for Berlin. 'The Servant', an ironic reworking of the legend of Golem, imagines that the Rabbi Löw of Prague knew the secrets of genetics and computer science, and thus Golem, his own creature, was nothing more than a robot. Another story supposes that on the sixth day of creation a committee of technicians discusses in strictly business terms 'Project Man'; they decide to create a bird-man but God the Father rejects this with the full weight of his authority, deprives them of their position and in an instant creates a vaguely ape-like, mammal-man, using one of his ribs to then create a woman.

I have already mentioned the pages of *The Periodic Table* that refer to Jewish matters. The next book, *The Wrench*, is the only one of my books in which the Jewish theme is completely absent. The central idea of the novel is the dignity of work, especially the work of the craftsman as modern analogue of the search for adventure and creativity. This is a theme I believe to be valid for all times, all places and all social structures. Nonetheless, as I wrote it, the many allusions to the nobility and necessity of work, found scattered throughout the Talmud, were not far from my mind.

The volume *Lilìt* consists of 36 short stories, almost all of them previously published in newspapers or magazines. Of these, the first twelve, the ones to have received the most critical attention, make up (as I say in one of the stories) 'the Paralipomena of my first two books'. Thirty years on, it seemed to me that the patrimony of memories from the concentration camps was not entirely spent, and that it was worthwhile going over it once more. My perspective had changed, of course. I no longer needed inner liberation, nor did I feel an urgent need to bear witness. I believed I had said everything I could about the sociology of the camps, about its essential horror, its aspect as distorting mirror of the modern world, its rules. Instead I felt the desire to take another calm, close look at some of the characters from those times, victims, survivors and oppressors, who had remained clearly etched in my memory against the grey, collective, impersonal background of the 'drowned', whom I had described thus in *If This is a Man*:

> Their life is short, but their number is endless; they, the *Musselmanner*, the drowned, form the backbone of the camp, an anonymous mass, continually renewed and always identical, of non-men who march and labour in silence, the divine spark dead within them, already too empty to really suffer. One hesitates to call them living: one hesitates to call their death death, in the face of which they have no fear, as they are too tired to understand.
>
> They crowd my memory with their faceless presences, and if I could enclose all the evil of our time in one image, I would choose this image which is familiar to me: an emaciated man, with head dropped and shoulders curved, on whose face and in whose eyes not a trace of thought is to be seen.

Amongst these characters I have 'revisited', there is a mild and honest prison companion in whom I had tried very hard to instil the need to steal from the Germans in order to survive; another companion, an observant Jew, who had refused to eat his soup on the eve of Yom Kippur; and a third, who tells me the troubling legend of Lilith, Adam's wife and God's concubine. One of these stories, the most important to my mind, sketches in a few pages the story of Chaim Rumkowski, president of the *Judenrat* in the Lodz ghetto. As is well enough known, this man compromised himself in every possible way in order to hang on to the miserable power his German appointment had conferred upon him. Without hesitation, and without the slightest sense of the ridiculous, he adopted all the external, 'regal' trappings of power, which he bravely defended against the Germans themselves. According to a rumour then rife in Poland, when the ghetto was broken up and he himself was condemned to the concentration camp like everyone else, he sought and obtained permission to make his final journey in a special railway carriage. In the Shakespearean flavour of this grotesque and tragic story, I had glimpsed a metaphor for our civilization: above all, the imbalance in which we live, and to which we have become accustomed, between the enormous quantity of time and energy we spend in order to attain power and prestige and the essential futility of such aims. We tend to forget 'that we are all in the ghetto, that the ghetto is enclosed, that outside the enclosure are the masters of death, and that just a little distance away the train is waiting'.

It is just left for me to speak of my last book, *If Not Now, When?*, published just last April. It is a novel whose origins are far back in time. The book developed largely from two seeds of an idea. The most distant is a memory engraved on my mind, an episode of our adventure-filled return from deportation. In October 1945, on the Italian border, we noticed that the enormously long goods train taking us back to our homeland no longer had 60 carriages, but 61. I had described this in *The Truce* like this:

> A new truck was travelling with us towards Italy at the end of our train, crammed with young Jews, boys and girls, coming from all the countries of Eastern Europe. None of them seemed more than twenty years old, but they were extremely self-confident and resolute people; they were young Zionists on their way to Israel, travelling where they were able to, and finding a path where they could. A ship was waiting for them at Bari; they had purchased their truck, and it had proved the simplest thing in the world to attach it to our train: they had not asked anybody's permission, but had hooked it on, and that was that. I was amazed, but they laughed at my amazement: 'Hitler's dead, isn't he?' replied their leader, with his intense hawk-like glance. They felt immensely free and strong, lords of the world and of their destinies.

The other source is a story told to me by a friend in 1971. In the summer of 1945 this man, who had previously sought refuge in Switzerland, had volunteered his services to help foreign Jews pouring into Italy in all directions from central Europe. They were wretched, traumatized people who had lost family, home, money, country, health: everything, except the hope of building a future for themselves somewhere else. Mixed in among them were a few other small groups of refugees who arrived in Milan. These were men and women who refused the status of 'displaced persons', claiming instead the name of 'Partisans', and they told him how for years they had been carrying out acts of guerrilla warfare and sabotage against the German troops.

These two seeds lay dormant for a long time, but were awoken by the inter-generational polemic which blew up a few years ago, in Israel amongst other countries, over the behaviour of the Jews in the face of Nazi massacre. Did they really let themselves be led to slaughter without resisting? If so, why? If not, how many, when, where had they resisted? To my mind this was a deeply anti-historic debate, polluted by prejudice: as an ex-partisan and ex-deportee I know very well that there are political and psychological conditions in which it is possible to resist, and others in which it is not. It was not therefore my intention to enter into the debate, but I felt I had sufficient narrative energy to let these two seeds germinate into a story worth reading. The book presented itself as a historical novel; perhaps it was also, in a more subtle way, a *roman à thèse*; but fundamentally it was an action novel on a large scale. Besides this, I wanted to pay homage to all Jews, however few or many, who in their desperation had found the strength to oppose the Nazis, and who had rediscovered their dignity and liberty in this unequal combat.

This was a congenial theme to me. My concentration camp stint, my reading of authors of Yiddish origin, other trips made to the Soviet Union in the course of my work, had all left me with a lively curiosity for Eastern Jewish culture, fabulously rich and vital yet destined to be uprooted or to become extinct. But it was not my culture. My own experience and knowledge were not enough, and a period of study was indispensable. Before beginning writing, I dedicated almost a year to collecting and reading documents and books; I wanted to write a novel, but I had no desire to find myself contradicting historical facts and thus distancing myself from reality. I consulted documentation in Allied Soviet and Italian archives, even a history of the Jewish partisan war (*Di milchome fun di Yiddishe Partisaner in Mizrach-Europe*) written by the partisan leader Mosché Kaganovič, and published in Yiddish in Buenos Aires in 1956. I studied a little Yiddish grammar and vocabulary, because it is difficult to reproduce a social environment and make characters speak when you do not know their language. Since Yiddish, like all patriarchal and pre-industrial civilizations, is impregnated with popular wisdom and proverbs, I did not neglect collections of sayings and proverbs, including the collection of 'Yiddishe Witze'. It is no accident that the very title of the book is taken from a famous line of the *Maxims of the Fathers* (*Pirké Avoth*).

This is perhaps the only time I have found myself confronted with a real (but unusual) linguistic problem: I had to give the reader the impression that the dialogues between my characters, which were obviously in standard Italian, were translated from Yiddish, a language which I know badly and which the Italian reader does not know at all. I do not know whether I succeeded in this or not: it is for my readers who know enough Yiddish to make that judgement.

I did not, then, set out to write a true story, but to reconstruct the imaginary yet plausible itinerary of one of the bands of people described in the texts I had read, and which revealed that within the broad weave of European resistance, the Jewish presence was more significant than is commonly believed.

The thirty or so characters of *If Not Now, When?*, both men and women, are Russian and Polish Jews: put to flight by the Red Army, survivors of the ghettoes and the massacres of the *Einsatzkommandos*, at first they do not have a definite political or ideological framework.

Only one of them, a woman, states that she is simultaneously a Communist, a Zionist and a feminist; the others are motivated principally by the need to defend themselves, and by a vague desire for revenge, rehabilitation and freedom. They meet up and join together 'like drops of mercury', either individually or in groups, in the forests of White Russia and the swamps of Polessia, sometimes accepted and sometimes rejected by the Soviet partisan groups:

> Each of them, man or woman, had a different story behind them, but searing and heavy as molten lead; if the war and three terrible winters had left them the time and breath, each should have mourned a hundred dead. They were tired, poor, and dirty, but not defeated: children of merchants, tailors, rabbis and cantors; they had armed themselves with weapons taken from the Germans, they had earned the right to wear those tattered uniforms, without chevrons, and they had tasted several times the bitter food of killing [. . .] in the *partisanka* adventure, different every day, in the frozen steppe, in snow and mud, they had found a new freedom, unknown to their fathers and grandfathers, a contact with friends and enemies, with nature and with action, which intoxicated them like the wine of Purim, when it's the custom to abandon usual sobriety and drink until you can't tell a blessing from a curse. They were light-hearted and fierce, like animals whose cage has been opened, like slaves who have risen up in vengeance [. . .] many amongst them had never tasted the flavour of freedom, and they learned to know it here, in the forest, together with adventure and brotherhood. (Translated by William Weaver)

Following an order from Moscow, they move west in order to remain behind the German lines, but they stay together because they no longer have country, home or family. They hope to begin life again in the Land of Israel, of which they have an age-old, mythical image in their minds. The harshness of the life they have been forced into, with its interminable marches, skirmishes, searches, flights and discomfort, has made them primitive and wild, but they have not lost those characteristics which differentiate them from other partisans they meet: creative fantasy, the old Jewish self-irony which immunizes them from rhetoric, a taste for dialectical debate, the conflict between traditional mildness and the need to kill. Temporarily welcomed by a Soviet partisan formation, they participate in actions to divert German parachute drops, they block and destroy a train, they help Polish peasants with the harvest, they kill the guards of a small German concentration camp and free the surviving prisoners. Overtaken by the front, they are interned by the Russians but flee in a stolen armoured car; at the end of the war, in Germany, one of the women is killed by an Austrian sniper, and the band avenge her in a bloody reprisal. Finally they cross the Italian border in a truck bought on the black market, they reach the Centre for Refugee Assistance in Milan and here one of the women in the band gives birth to a child: it is 7 August 1945, the day of Hiroshima. The story closes on this double, deliberately ambiguous sign.

This book is meeting with enormous success with the Italian public and critics. It has been one of the most read books of the summer season and has won two of the most coveted Italian literary awards, the Viareggio and the Campiello. It is now being translated into French. The chance coincidence of its publication with the war in Lebanon has increased the book's publishing fortune, while at the same time twisting its meaning for some critics and readers, who have mistaken it for an 'instant book'. And proof that in certain circumstances even Jews know how to fight seems, these days, to be superfluous.

Turin, 12 September 1982

Text presented to the 'Conference on Jewish Literature', supported by the Rockefeller Foundation and held at Bellagio 29 November–3 December 1982. In *La Rassegna Mensile di Israel*, vol.1, May–August 1984, pp. 376–90

49   With the Key of Science

Whilst we cannot choose our relatives, we can choose our friends, our companions on our journey through life. Italo Calvino and I were linked by a tie both subtle and profound. We were almost the same age, we had both emerged from the formative experience of the Resistance, we had been promoted to the status of writers in the same (memorable, for us) review by Arrigo Cajumi, who in these very pages discussed together Calvino's *Path to the Spiders' Nest* and my *If This is a Man*. Both of us were reserved by temperament, and we never spoke for any length of time – there was no need. It took very little – an allusion, a rapid hint on our respective 'works in progress' and our mutual comprehension was immediate.

Not only comprehension; I owe Italo a great deal. When he was editor at Einaudi, in Turin, it was natural for me to turn to him. I felt him to be a brother, or rather, an older brother, although he was four years younger than me. Unlike me, he belonged to this trade; it was in his blood. He was the spiritual son of Pavese, from whom he had inherited editorial wisdom, severity and swiftness of judgement. His corrections, his advice, were never either generic or gratuitous.

There were other links between us. Italo was the son of scientists, and almost uniquely on the Italian literary scene, he was hungry for science. He cultivated it, he nurtured himself on it as a cultured and critical dilettante, and with it nourished his most mature books. Nature and science were for him one and the same thing: science as a lens with which to see more clearly, a key that allowed him to penetrate more deeply, a code for understanding nature. Nothing in his nature tends towards the lyric or the idyll, and yet he was a great poet of nature, even in the negative, such as when he described its absence in the cities. Only half ironically, he claimed to envy my decades of front-line work as a chemist, in laboratories and factories. We talked about working together on vague, grandiose programmes for a literature that would mediate between the 'two cultures', while drawing on both. As far as this went he came much closer to it than I did; not only was he equipped with a vast, broad culture, he was also familiar with many of the greatest intellectuals of our times. He was an admirer and pupil of Raymond Queneau in Paris, and recently invited me to look over some difficult points in the translation of *Cosmogonie Portative*, and this was for me a spiritual feast. I was fascinated by his sharpness as a philologist, to which my modest experience as technologist had little to add.

His untimely disappearance leaves a painful emptiness. He was at the height of his powers and still had so many things to construct, things that were his and his alone, which nobody else will ever be able to say in his own inimitable way, cutting and light at the same time, never repetitive, never gratuitous; often playful, never facile, never content with the mere surface of things.

La Stampa, 20 September 1985

50   Preface to *The Jews of Eastern Europe*

This volume contains the proceedings of a conference, held in Turin in January 1984, on the itinerary of Jews in Eastern Europe 'from utopia to revolt'. It holds a number of surprises for the Italian reader, Christian and Jew alike. We have read a good deal about the final steps of this itinerary, about the bloody, desperate revolts in the ghettoes and in the camps, and in many different forms, ranging from historically serious and thoughtful works to epic transfigurations and popular novels. Even the cinema has taken up the theme, here too with varying results in terms of artistic dignity and philological rigour. About everything that came before, on the other hand, about the intricate social and historical events leading to revolt, and from which revolt drew its exemplary force, either we knew next to nothing or the little that we knew was partial and distorted.

In the West, and especially in Italy (where the Jewish presence has always been numerically tiny, and where even during the terrible years when Hitler's barbarism washed over Europe there were comparatively few Jewish refugees in search of safety), people had a vague, poetic notion of Eastern Judaism, imported through the channels of literature. Joseph Roth and the Singer brothers had made a huge, overwhelming mark on literature with their books of transfiguring power; here the reader gains a fundamental notion of a Jew torn out of the world, confined, whether voluntarily or otherwise, in his *shtetl*, which is simultaneously prison and nest: this Jew is a stranger, ignorant of the world, untouched by the political convulsions that changed the face and the borders of European countries over the course of the nineteenth and early twentieth centuries; *luftmensch*, 'men of air', nourished by ingenuous faith, family affections, picturesque and fantastic legends; mild, shabby, erratic and neurotic. Another, more negative, image superimposed itself on this one, the fruit of Fascist propaganda or the residue of ancient prejudice: Judaism, which on the surface is scattered amongst the nations (the *goyim*), is in fact a unitary block, an astute and perverse power embarked on the economic conquest of the world, consolidated by secret links that bypass all frontiers.

The picture which leaps out from these writings, on the other hand, whether personal testimonies or historical reconstructions, is radically different. Not only is it more fully articulated, it is more concrete and credible, and more suited to the purpose of making us understand the reality of past and present. In the second half of the nineteenth century the picturesque, daydreaming civilization of the *shtetl* still survives, but is marginal: in the Jewish world, as in the rest of Europe, an intense process of urbanization is under way. Small rural Polish, Russian and Lithuanian communities are becoming deserted as factories in the big cities attract artisans and the commercial middle class, who feel themselves more protected here from the murderous peasant pogroms. An urban Jewish proletarian is born, both similar and different to the proletariat majority. Similar in the merciless exploitation to which he is subject; different, and more restless and divided, because to exploitation is added the hostility which he feels all around him. The Jewish member of the proletariat lends an attentive ear to Socialism and Marxism, but does not forget his identity: he is split between two loyalties, to his class and to his origins. This tension gives rise to an astonishing variety of solutions held out before him, but towards the end of the century two main paths are taking shape, incompatible in themselves, and both laden with Messianic promise.

The Dreyfus affair prompts the birth (or rebirth) of Zionist prophecy. Here in Europe, and even in America, you are a stranger and you will always be a stranger: if you forget you are a Jew there will be 'others' to remind you. You have a land, the land of your fathers; it is far away, little better now than a desert, but if you cultivate it, it will flourish, milk and honey will flow. If you redeem the land, the land will redeem you; no longer will you be either stranger or slave. It seems like a dream, but if you wish, it will become reality. Paradoxically this invitation awakens the benevolent attention of the Tsarist authorities. Why not indeed? If they want to go, why put obstacles in their way? The Zionist leaders even have discussions with the functionaries of the Tsar's police in a smart and broad-thinking move which scandalizes Jewish Socialist Internationalism.

Out of the various tendencies in competition with each other in this arena a Social Democratic movement soon emerges, which in 1897 forms itself into a union party, first clandestine and later official. This is the General Union of Jewish Workers in Lithuania, Poland and Russia, the Bund. Here we are far removed from any stereotypes. The members of the Bund are workers and intellectuals, and they are neither humble nor resigned. Their dual loyalty has transformed itself into a dual pride: the pride of the proletariat, and the pride of the Diaspora. *Alijah*, the return to the land of the Zionists, is a desertion, a flight: why uproot themselves and go to Palestine just to reconstruct over there a hated bourgeois society? This is our country, where we were born and where our flesh-and-blood ancestors were born, not the Patriarchs of the Torah. We are here, and here we want to stay, in Poland and in Russia, workers amidst all the workers of the world, because our struggle is their struggle. But we are not like them. We have, and we wish to retain, our cultural autonomy, which means our language above all. Not Hebrew, the language of the Rabbis, language of a religion that we reject as we reject all religions, but Yiddish, *mame-loshn*, our mother tongue, which has been spoken in our homes for centuries. The centre of gravity of Jewishness is us, it is here, *do* in Yiddish; our patriotism is the *doikeyt*. 'The Messianism of the Bund, absorbed during our childhood and youth from parents, grandparents and teachers, even when it was rejected at a conscious level, nurtured in an entirely natural manner the Messianic eschatology of the Socialist conception of the world' (Frankel).

Around the turn of the century, the Bund is the most important Jewish workers' party in the Tsarist Empire. It is flanked by numerous smaller parties with which it is in permanent disagreement, and like every Socialist party it is riven by internal conflicts, but unlike other Socialist parties it has no propensity for compromise. Indeed, by means of strikes, congresses, demonstrations, it seeks to keep its followers at a permanent pitch of tempestuous rage. In 1905 it reaches the high point of its revolutionary endeavour; it has at its disposal a well-trained paramilitary organization and is one of the great revolutionary parties of European Russia. In June of that year, when the sailors of the battleship Potëmkin mutiny, it is a young woman of the Bund, Anna Lipsic, who holds a rally attended by tens of thousands of people and with Cossack and police rifles pointed at her. But the Bund emerged weakened from the failed revolution of 1905. It was hounded out by the Bolsheviks in 1919 alongside other parties of the Left. It survived in Poland up until the Nazi massacres, but neither in Russia nor in Poland did it die a natural death.

With the wisdom of hindsight, the utopian thrust of the Bund might appear foolhardy, but at the time nobody could have foreseen the measure, or rather the absence of measure, of Hitler's or Stalin's regimes. The history which followed showed that the detested Zionists, 'anti-Semites who spoke Yiddish' according to one of the Bund's slogans, were right: for the Jews of Eastern Europe the only path to salvation was emigration. But the ideological and moral vigour of the Bund was displayed in tragic splendour during the crucial years of Nazi terror, for without the Bund's experience of insurrection the uprising in the Warsaw ghetto and other heroic revolts in ghettoes or in the death camps would not have happened, or would have been reduced to improvised and localized spasms devoid of idealistic content. Only in the ghettoes besieged by hunger, by daily massacre and by epidemics, only in the single European resistance which held to the last without the light of hope, did the enemy fraternities of the Bund, the Zionists and the Communists, find concord in the unity of action.

Thanks to the pages gathered here, it seems to me that the fighters of the ghetto acquire a new physiognomy for the Italian or generally Western reader, a physiognomy that is historically credible and above all modern, far removed from the simplified heroes and the stainless paladins dear to folklore down the ages, closer to us and to our still controversial choices, to our perennial Jewish search for identity. And their precursors, the indomitable activists of the Bund, of early Zionism and all the other countless tendencies and factions (reflected in the plethora of political parties which still complicate the political life of Israel) were, like us, blind in the face of the future, but they had understood early on, as their history shows us, that inertia and servility do not pay.

From *Gli ebrei dell'Europa orientale dall'utopia alla rivolta*, eds. M. Brunazzi and A. M. Fubini, Edizioni di Comunità, Milan 1985, pp. ix–xiii

51   What was it that Burned Up in Space?

What can we say? This is not the moment for any exalted rhetoric of heroism. News of the failure of the Shuttle mission, which spread around the greater part of the whole world in real time, or as close as possible to it, cannot be compared to an unfortunate accident at work. Not only have seven young lives been lost, but with them a high level of skill invested in experience. All of the astronauts, aside from the unfortunate lady schoolteacher, had garnered a precious capital of knowledge which vanished in an instant, in an apocalyptic flame.

Is this a useful or useless sacrifice? It would be cynical to make any kind of calculation, but one thing is certain. The shuttle was less safe than had been claimed. It is unlikely that the goal of a recoverable spaceship will be abandoned, but it will be achieved only by dint of an unspecifiable number of steps towards complete safety, as happened decades ago with air flight.

As well as the technological 'fallout', which right from the first has produced unexpected results in the most diverse of fields, we should now expect fallout specifically oriented towards the protection of life. Maybe it was wrong to go ahead with manned space flights so soon: probably the time was not right and the risks were greater than foreseen.

We have no way of knowing exactly what the aims of the Shuttle project were. Perhaps they were aims largely of prestige value: if we can do this, we can do other things that we can't and won't tell you about. It is probable, and it is very much to be hoped, that this failure will serve as a warning: the time has not yet come to think in the short term of the spaceship as the aeroplane of tomorrow.

Together with our sorrow for a collective and all too sudden death, together with the frustration that accompanies each failed enterprise, let us make a wish, that this tragedy might help prevent other and greater tragedies that would otherwise have occurred in the future. The almost simultaneous and remarkable circumnavigation of Voyager around Uranus has given us tangible proof that the exploration of space which so preoccupies us today can be carried out without risk to human life.

La Stampa, 30 January 1986

52   The Plague has No Frontiers

We had just begun to get over Sindona's poisoned coffee, then came the seismic shock of the methanol, followed by the collision in Libya between two forms of senseless arrogance: aircraft carriers and missiles were mobilized, together with a bunch of assassins and an avalanche of lies, in a fight for infantile prestige. Before we'd had time to swallow Libya, to trace the uncertain line between right and wrong, we find ourselves suddenly faced with the catastrophe of Chernobyl.

We cannot yet be sure of all the consequences, but we can begin to outline some thoughts. The American enterprise in Libya was a free gift for the Soviets, a way for them to embellish their own image; but now the Soviets have suffered a disastrous reversal of fortune, firstly because such a disaster has occurred at all, and secondly because of the way in which the news has come out. This has been – and still is – so vague and tight-lipped that even now nobody has any precise information, either about the number of victims or the extent of present or future damage. The veil of modesty drawn over internal mishaps, and the trumpeting of the mishaps of others, is an old sickness of centralizing regimes. Many will recall that during Fascism a party directive forbade publishing news of cases of suicide; as a result journalists, caught between the devil of prohibition and the deep blue sea of professional duty, had to make do with the oft-repeated episode of the unfortunate citizen who, running through the house or along the street with a loaded pistol (it was never explained why) in his hand, fell and was struck by an accidental bullet.

The sheer size of the Soviet Union, and the length of time it has been in existence, means that its history is encrusted with incredible censorships, impossible denials and absurd silences. Famous examples are the delay in informing the people of the Nazi invasion, and the censorship of information on the camps and the extermination of the kulaks. In the current case, given the scarcity of official news, the people will have to trust themselves to hearsay and will panic all the more. This obsessive secrecy signifies an undeserved contempt on the part of the Soviet government for its citizens, who are neither immature nor mentally impaired.

But the conduct of the Western press has not been beyond reproach, either. It can barely contain its malign joy, as if similar disasters could never happen 'over here'. Yet we Italians know that of our nuclear power stations 'only' the one in Latina does not have a sealed dome of reinforced concrete: but, we are reassured, it's a very small power station. This means that were there to be an accident, it would 'only' be necessary to evacuate Rome. The two dead announced by the Soviets is doubtless an underestimate, but the two thousand or more announced by America are (we hope) too many. On our side information is guilty of the opposite sin: instead of being slow and skeletal, it is hasty and sensationalist. They are pathologically avaricious, we are muddled and prodigious.

Unfortunately, technology and nuclear biology are intrinsically difficult, and for the profane it is difficult to draw up a risk–benefit balance. Now, we are all profane: the few who are not are deeply involved and not always immune from any *parti pris*. As one of the profane I dare to foresee, or at least hope, that Chernobyl will be a turning point in energy choices, in the style of information and perhaps in the political relationship between the two great power blocs. We can learn much even from misfortune, and a pessimist would say especially from misfortune.

The most important thing is this: nuclear pollution is subtle and insensitive, and there are no sure defences against it. It mocks our frontiers, it rides the wind and the waves, it infiltrates the food chain; radioactive iodine can fall from the sky thousands of kilometres from its source, rooting itself in our thyroid, becoming a thousand times more concentrated and threatening our well-being. The radiation from products of fission can alter the genetic heritage of men, animals and plants over the entire planet, damaging their future reproduction. A nuclear accident spreads in all directions like the plague and is not an internal matter of exclusive concern to the country where it happens. The waters of Dnepr lap around Chernobyl but wash into the Black Sea and onto the Turkish coast where there are no nuclear plants: why should they pay for the mistakes of others?

Gorbachev was wrong to keep silent and right to ask for help. Let us Italians, too, give it to him (as long as the help is competent and not mere propaganda) but afterwards, when we hope this matter will come to a swift conclusion, he should agree to come to the negotiating table. If he really is a new man, let him speak the language of people willing to take responsibility.

La Stampa, 3 May 1986

53   The Community of Venice and its Ancient Cemetery

The impression given by the Jewish cemetery of San Nicolò di Lido to the visitor unfamiliar with the intricate and glorious history of Judaism in Venice, is a contradictory one, of age-old care and equally age-old neglect, of piousness and more worldly concerns, of fidelity to ritual and traditional rigour and a simultaneous consensus with the tastes and fashion of the moment. This does not normally happen in village cemeteries, where the dominant sensation is one of homogeneity and continuity. The reasons for this singularity are several and closely linked to each other.

As this volume affirms, the cemetery is ancient and profoundly stratified in time. It houses graves from times of both abundance and poverty, of cohabitation and of separation. On a synchronic scale, too, it cuts across class boundaries. Indeed, it reflects the intensely composite character of the Venetian community, made up of an only partially integrated mix of Jews of Ashkenazi and Sephardi origin, originating from Germany, Poland, the Iberian peninsula, from the East and from the rest of Italy, as well as the more ancient nucleus whose origins are lost in time.

The impression, or at least the predominant impression, is not one of mourning. Mourning is the recent and painful grief of those who have lost a family member, a person dear to them and whose appearance, habits and voice are still fresh in their minds. Here, mourning is remote, swept aside by the centuries, and a sensation of peace prevails, the eternal peace promised by all rituals to the dead. On closer inspection a different feeling emerges alongside this, whereby the intrinsic melancholy of the place is shot through with a trace of worldly pride, which here takes on a sadly ironic hue. The proudest and most showy of these sepulchres watch over the remains, or more often just the memory, of Jews, men and women, who enjoyed fame, riches and success: bankers, armourers, women of letters and of the 'intellect of love', merchants, doctors, pious and lay wise men. And now, as in Spoon River, they all lie here, levelled in death, in the shadow of the headstones desired by the dead themselves or by their families, and which are at times ingenuous, at times pretentious and at times curiously profane. Over all of them spreads the green cloak of climbing plants, image of rude life, with no other thoughts, which submerges memory.

A more careful study of the inscriptions and the monuments reveals a characteristic trait of Venetian Jewry, which makes it perhaps unique in the world. It is the fruit of a meeting between two singularities, between two historical and anthropological exceptions. It was unlikely, a challenge to history, that a middle-eastern people of modest political and military strength, unable to tolerate first Greek and then Roman domination, tormented by violent internal conflicts and then defeated, massacred, deported, dispersed and persecuted for centuries, would survive the millennia, jealously preserving its religion and its traditions, preserving, what's more, its feeling of substantial unity. It was equally improbable that a community of refugees, swept along like so much flotsam and jetsam by the advance of the invaders, would find permanent shelter on a minuscule archipelago of marshy islets, and that there over the centuries, with ant-like effort, a city of stunning beauty would be built; that this city would come to control a vast and fertile hinterland; that the new Republic would prosper, throughout brief periods of peace and long wars, until it became the merchant capital of the eastern Mediterranean, a political power of the first order, a state of exemplary laws and an artistic centre whose originality was never imitated, or only with ridiculous results. For several centuries, this was the most powerful and the most respected of the Italian states.

Venetian Jewry is the fruit of the marriage between these two impossible civilizations and calls to mind a frequently quoted statement of Thomas Mann: that everything valid produced by humanity has been produced 'in spite of', in spite of adversity, turning adversity to one's own will, and drawing vigour from pain and intelligence from hard work.

Every cemetery is a mirror. The one on the Lido is the mirror of an ancient cohabitation of two substantially different civilizations brought together by their cosmopolitan outlook and their mercantile vocation. Just as there were Jewish settlements in all the ports around the Mediterranean, so there were also, at least for short periods of time, Venetian outposts, garrisons and settlements in Crete, Cyprus, Dalmatia, Albania, Syria, on the Black Sea. Often one group coincided with another. As this book documents, cohabitation has not always been easy: in the stormy history of Venice, measured out by bitter wars on land and sea, periods of tolerance and intolerance have followed each other, but rarely has this reached the point of violence against the

Jewish minority. Normally good sense has prevailed, mutual understanding, or at least compromise. While numerically it has always been slight, the Jewish presence has not been negligible from an economic point of view: from simple merchants and brokers, they become bankers and armourers; towards the end of the seventeenth century between 5 and 10 per cent of maritime transport in the Mediterranean was in the hands of Venetian Jews.

The monuments in the cemetery permit an indirect, stratified reading of this symbiosis. It is of course an unreliable, partial sample, which leaves out of count the great mass of the disinherited, whose presence and whose manner of living are attested by the very high, squalid buildings still visible today at the entrance to the Ghetto. But despite this, one cannot read without emotion and reverence the memorial stones, whose text is printed here, of Elia Levita, grammarian, of Leone Modena, doctor, teacher and preacher (but also gambler), of Sara Sullam Copio, a cultured and beautiful woman, poet in both Hebrew and Italian. We learn of her long, moving, epistolary idyll with the Genoese nobleman who fell in love with her intelligence and tried in vain to convert her to Christianity. No, the story of the Venetian Jews is not one of a culturally segregated and stifled minority, but of an energetic and versatile component of local society, active not only in financial but also in intellectual terms.

The members of these great families, whom we can follow down numerous generations through the mute testimony of the tombstones, seem to us to be urged on by an articulated and modern social motivation. They wanted to be Jews, in other words different: almost without exception, the inscriptions we read are in the Hebrew alphabet and language. But they also wanted to compete: it was not assimilation they sought, for this amounts to dissolution; they wanted to be considered as equals. Hence the most curious feature of these tombs: sometimes they are of refugees from Spain or Portugal who, in times of tolerance, had effectively received titles of nobility; but even when a title was not conferred from on high, many families fashion themselves *motu proprio* a heraldic sign. This is a custom of the *goyim*, and, worse still, transgressive of the Biblical injunction, 'thou shalt not worship images' (you have to move with the times, though, and social standing matters); but in between the patterns and swirls of the heraldic emblems there are Jewish symbols: the bunch of grapes, the hands of Kohanim in blessing, the pitcher of the Levites, the stylus of the scribes: or else figures drawn from the Hebrew name of the deceased: the lion, the stag, the eagle, the dove. In this one place, in a few handfuls of stone corroded by time, we see faithfulness to a tradition conjoined to consensus to life. And besides, in the Holy Language, the cemetery is Bet-Hayyim, the House of Life.

November 1985. In *La comunità ebraica di Venezia e il suo antico cimitero*, ed. Aldo Luzzatto, Milan 2000, vol. I

54   The Philosopher-Engineer and his Forbidden Dreams

It is natural, and largely appropriate, that the science fiction writer evolves from a different, more specialized kind of *humus* than that of the writer *tout court*. If this is not the case, he needs to research in the way that every serious writer does, or should do. On this point, Asimov's brief preface to his collection *Twelve Times Tomorrow*, which has recently come out in Italian, seems to me exemplary, and exemplary in the opposite sense to the obvious inadequacy of Dürrenmatt's *Physicists*, clearly the result of inadequate research. But Roberto Vacca does not need to do this kind of research; given who he is, he seems to be roaming a literary landscape that is his alone, the only one to offer him all the freedom of expression that he requires.

A front-line engineer, a university lecturer, polyglot by nature and by family tradition, energetic and full of life, Roman to his bones but as much at home in America as he is everywhere else, a good mathematician and physicist as well as humanist, Vacca is integrated in the best sense of the word. The modern world flows around him in all its variety, invoking in him not hostility, diffidence or anguish but rather offering him a hand of friendship, full of ideas and full of temptation. His science fiction dreams are never nightmares, not even when he wishes them to be. The still-read *Il robot e il minotauro* ('The Robot and the Minotaur', 1963), the Perengane Chronicles, and these latest, *Esempi di avvenire* ('Examples of the Future', Rizzoli), are his portrait and his autobiography.

These books portray (unusually, in our literary world) a man at the height of his powers, curious, highly intelligent, often ingenuous, never neurotic, never abstract, engaged in honest and open polemic with the marvels and the monsters of technical civilization. The 'heathen cynicism' in which he glories can scandalize nobody: even where he sets out to demonstrate that man is a highly complex sequential machine, despite himself his writing exhales a joyful strength, a youthful love of the world, which to date no machine has been able to display.

The deep knowledge Vacca demonstrates of cybernetics and neuro-logy are at one and the same time the value and the limitation of these stories. Not all of them are accessible to everyone: the most serious of them, the most conceptual, and above all the essays, leave the average reader puzzled and therefore cold, when Vacca expects him to find his way through alphanumerical codes and memories of a 'pushdown' nature. The excessive use of technical terms, and at other points the use of calques of slang or colloquial American, does not always seem to me to work, and reveals a certain level of innocent exhibitionism. The same can be said of the frequent satisfaction he finds in accumu-lating details of time and place, in open contravention of the 'prohibi-tion of useless dicourse' that nonetheless lies behind one of the most entertaining sketches.

Elsewhere, on the other hand, Vacca adheres to this prohibition with fervent zeal: it is a real shame that so many splendid ideas appear here as flashes, just as they were conceived, still at the stage of thumb-nail sketches, of 'short-cut tales', as if someone other than the author might tell the whole story as it should be told. For example: the State of Israel demands from the entire Christian world copyright (past as well as present) on all the editions, translations and adaptations of the Bible ('Proprietà letteraria riservata' ['Reserved Literary Property']); the suggestion of using bank deposits during closing hours ('L'estensione creditizia' ['Extension of Credit']); the metaphysical 'querelle' between red and white blood cells ('Noi sentiamo di avere il libero arbitrio, e voi?' ['We Believe we have Free Will, What about You?']) which is crim-inally rushed through in half a page, as if similar inventions were to be found at every turn.

To conclude, Vacca appears at times to struggle to find a balance between prolixity and shorthand but, when he finds it, his privi-leged status as *doctus utriusque juris*, of scientist who doubles as philologist, in other words of a modern minotaur, allows him to produce high quality pages that are both airy and believable, and this is the highest of praise for those who cultivate this literary genre. Stories like 'I sensi trascurati' ['The Neglected Senses'], 'Due in una carne sola' ['Two in Just One Flesh'], and the exemplary 'Incomunicabilità I' ['Incommunicability I'], which descends in spirals, like a vulture, towards its unexpected and chilling conclusion, spark off our imagination and make us think. They constitute a pleasure accessible to everyone, albeit a pleasure of a high level.

Il Giorno, 5 January 1966

55   Guest of Captain Nemo

There is a strange ship sailing in the Sicilian Channel, halfway between Cape Bon and Mazara del Vallo. It is called *Beaver Six* because it is the fruit of a rapid, Darwinian-like evolution that began with *Beaver One* about ten years ago. This beaver dynasty belongs to Saipem, a company within the Eni consortium, and consists of ships whose purpose is to lay pipes along the sea floor. The *Beaver Six* set sail from Tunisia on 13 December last year, and is placing on the bottom of the Mediterranean a pipe that will bring methane from the oil wells of the Algerian desert into Italy and Europe (and will meet 7 per cent of Italy's energy requirement). This pipe does not run in a straight line: the planners have chosen the cheapest route, not necessarily the shortest one, but the one which avoids the roughest or most uneven underwater terrain. Nonetheless it was impossible to avoid the 600 metre deep chasm cutting across the Sicilian Channel, and for the moment the *Beaver Six* is the only ship in the world capable of laying a pipe at such a depth.

There is no other ship like it. A ship by definition, in that it is a floating construction built by man and able to move by itself, it is certainly not a ship in appearance. It consists of a platform, 50 by 150 metres, supported by ten enormous pillars that rest in their turn on two underwater hulls. On the platform there is a forest of cranes, radar antennae, capstans, winches, sections of piping, the whole dominated at the stern end by the towering workstation (called the 'Cathedral') from which the pipe descends, piece by piece, into the sea. The roof of this workstation is the heliport for the helicopter that maintains close contact with land.

The workstation itself, the command bridge, the ramp down which the pipe descends and the two hulls, are full of wonders. I had the good fortune to be shown round these mechanical viscera by the ship's captain and Eni technicians, and I felt as though I were reliving the famous 'guided tour' given by Captain Nemo to Professor Aronnax around the equally portentous innards of the *Nautilus* in *Twenty Thousand Leagues Under the Sea*.

The extraordinary thing about the *Beaver Six*, and the factor that determines its strange shape, is its ability to stay still in the water despite the wind, currents or the rocking of the waves, and to move with precisely controlled speed. The pipe laid down is rigid and heavy. It is made up of sections twelve metres long and fifty centimetres in diameter, two centimetres thick and covered in polyethylene and cement; each section weighs between three and four tons. The *Beaver* is continuously supplied with these sections by two service ships shuttling between platform and shore, and the sections are then welded together with fairly sophisticated techniques (seven layers of welding are needed), the joints are checked by X-ray and ultrasound, protected by molten pitch, and the pipe is then 'launched' into the sea at a distance corresponding to that of the section, in other words twelve metres exactly.

The moment of the launch, which if everything goes smoothly is repeated every twelve minutes or so, is an unforgettable sight: at the command of the electronic brain overseeing all the ship's operations, the forty thousand ton weight of the *Beaver* shifts immediately and weightily twelve metres towards the Sicilian shore. The movement is so smooth that no one on board even notices it, just as they are not aware of the waves, even when the sea is rough. All they see is the pipe moving down the ramp, and it is as if the pipe, rather than the ship itself, is moving, and the ship is standing still. It is a concrete illustration of Galileo's relativity, and Dante's Garisenda comes to mind, seeming to lean towards earth when the clouds are pulled along by the wind behind.

The pipe, which when finished will be more than 160 kilometres long, has bends, but is monolithic and rigid. Nonetheless, as it is being laid it bends down from the launch ramp to the seabed as if it were a flexible cord, following a curve like a chain that joins it to the contour of the seabed, and which must at no point be pushed out of shape by sudden movements of the ship. Precise control of position and speed are essential, and has been achieved by a system that seems, to the profane such as myself, surprising. The *Beaver* is endowed with four powerful propellers that can change position, and these, too, obey the automatic control system. Thanks to them the ship can move, or counteract tidal flow, but as a norm they are inert, functioning only in cases of emergency or when the ship is being moved. When everything is going normally, position and speed are determined by the mooring system alone.

Around the *Beaver* is a spider web of twelve huge anchors that bite into the seabed with their 20 to 25 ton weight. They are placed far off from the ship so that the traction of the cables is virtually horizontal, and the ship itself 'walks', dragged by the anchor cables, step by step. When the ship comes too close to the anchors on the Sicilian side, they are hauled up and put back down further on, while the anchors on the Tunisian side are brought closer in to the ship. Rather than sailing, the ship is towed along.

Times, angles, and distances of the repositioning of the anchors are continually dictated by the on-board computer, and the operation is carried out by tugboats that follow and surround the *Beaver* like servants at the ready. Everything is on a gigantic scale: the mooring cables are $7\frac{1}{2}$ cm thick and 2700 metres long; the buoys indicating the positions of the anchors, the tug boats, the supply boats shuttling between the ship and land and bringing pipes, fuel, food and so on, spread over several square kilometres of sea.

As well as all of this, there are also four pocket submarines, each with two crewmen on board and equipped with cameras, video, lights and external grippers. These control the laying down of the pipe sections, and their mechanical hands are capable of placing special controllable supports under sections of pipe that on inspection appear to be lying awkwardly.

The 'mind that controls the mass' is an electronic brain, but this is in turn controlled by human minds. The crew of the *Beaver* are a new kind of marine engineer, most of them very young and genuinely enthusiastic about the adventure they are living through. The command bridge, their place of work, unleashes the imagination of the profane. It contains around forty television screens that communicate instantly, in the form of numbers or images, all the information necessary for this navigation of tiny, very precise steps: deviations of the piping from the prescribed location, the (minuscule) inclinations of the ship, the direction and distance of the anchors, the tension of the cables, pressure of the pipe, down to the temperature of the small round cushions on which the launch capstans and winches are mounted; other screens reproduce on the bridge everything that is happening in the welding stations.

On board there are radar and electronics experts, a meteorologist, two ultrasound experts, two radiologists who oversee the welding, crane operators, divers for the underwater inspections; but there are also the manual workers, the cooks and even bakers, because a crew that carries out such a delicate and important operation has the right to fresh bread at all hours of the day and night.

The men told me that while the work is repetitive and obsessively precise, it is never boring. An operation to lay a pipe at this depth has never been carried out before, and it therefore needs new ideas, new instruments and new men. It would be ingenuous to think that in such a complex system, operating in such unusual conditions, everything can be foreseen and all accidents avoided. There have, on the contrary, been several accidents, and one in particular shows the value, even in this computer age, of experience and the inventive imagination when a new problem has to be solved swiftly, with whatever tools happen to be at hand.

A generator is used for the radiographs checking the work. This is located inside a trolley that runs inside the pipe as it is being constructed, or to be more accurate it is always in the same position relative to the ship, and the pipe runs round it, and the trolley is held by a cable. In the course of the work, for some reason that has remained a mystery, the generator suddenly disappeared; the cable had snapped, the trolley had followed the angle of the pipe and the vastly expensive piece of equipment had slipped down the length of three hundred metres, down to the horizontal section that was already on the seabed.

The damage was serious. Aside from the enforced interruption of work (one minute of the *Beaver*'s work costs 280,000 lire!), the trolley was completely obstructing the pipe, and had therefore to be moved immediately and at whatever cost. A summit of technicians was convened, and came up with various suggestions, the most picturesque of which was to phone Tunisia to send a rubber bullet down the pipe and pump compressed air behind it: the bullet would reach the trolley on the bottom of the ocean floor and shoot it back out again.

Discussions were still going on when a young crew member came forward. He was a former fisherman, and it seemed obvious to him that the trolley had to be hooked out. His suggestion was simple, fast and would cost only a few thousand lire. The man was taken down to the workshop where a large hook was fashioned and attached to a heavy weight. He introduced hook and weight into the mouth of the pipe, and after a few minutes of patient and expert attempts, he managed to hook the generator and pull it out.

I did not meet the anonymous fisherman, but I recognized signs in the faces glimpsed on the *Beaver*, signs, which are difficult to find elsewhere. These are the signs to be found on the faces of those who know that their work is intelligent and useful; that even if it is the fruit of other people's talent, there is still room for talent in those who carry it out. Still today, in an age of work that is no longer physically demanding but is alienating, in the middle of the Sicilian Channel you can find the age-old pleasure of competence put to the test and of work done well.

La Stampa, 6 April 1980

Index of Names

Boston Public Library

Customer ID: ************9401**

Title: The black hole of Auschwitz /
ID: 39999052013677
Due: 05/01/12

Total items: 1
4/10/2012 5:19 PM

Thank you for using the
3M SelfCheck™ System.